Labor and the
Legal Process

Labor and the Legal Process

by

Harry H. Wellington

New Haven and London, Yale University Press, 1968

Library of Congress catalog card number: 68–27769

Designed by Marvin Howard Simmons,
set in Baskerville type,
and printed in the United States of America by
The Colonial Press Inc., Clinton, Mass.

Distributed in Great Britain, Europe, Asia, and
Africa by Yale University Press Ltd., London; in
Canada by McGill University Press, Montreal; and
in Latin America by Centro Interamericano de Libros
Académicos, Mexico City.

To Sheila

Preface

This book examines the national policy toward labor and explores the role of law and of legal institutions in the development and effectuation of that policy. In some ways it is an inquiry into the limitations of law and of legal institutions, for it should provide insights into the disutility as well as the utility of employing law to attain social goals.

The book does not attempt to cover the field of labor law. However, it does contend with several of the important problems that policymakers in the field must face; and it offers the law student and the labor lawyer a framework for viewing—perhaps with fresh vision—their professional problems. It should, moreover, cast light upon the concerns of the student of industrial relations and upon the problems of those whose work it is to speculate about the American legal system. The book can also acquaint the interested layman with the outlines of our labor policy and give him a sense of the legal institutions that figure so importantly in the success of that policy.

I am happy to record my thanks to two former research assistants, Ruben A. Hasson and Martin E. Lowy, whose work helped me fashion this book.

Alexander M. Bickel, Boris I. Bittker, Barbara A. Black, Charles L. Black, Jr., Henry W. Broude, Ralph S. Brown, Jr., Guido Calabresi, Jan G. Deutsch, Ronald M. Dworkin, Abraham S. Goldstein, Stanley Lebergott, Leon S. Lipson, Clyde W. Summers, and Ralph K. Winter, Jr., each read some or all of one or another draft of the book. From each I received helpful suggestions; to each I am, indeed, grateful.

I am grateful also to the Ford Foundation and to the John Simon Guggenheim Memorial Foundation for buying my time and giving it back to me; to Dean Louis H. Pollak, of the Yale Law School, for cooperation above and beyond the call of his office; and to Professor G. S. A. Wheatcroft and the Law Faculty of The London School of Economics and Political Science for the hospitality they extended me when I was in London and working on the book.

My thanks are due as well to Mrs. Elizabeth B. Manley and Mrs. Dorothy C. Egan who typed the manuscript; and to members of the staff of the Yale Law School library, who went to great lengths on my behalf.

Finally, my thanks to the editors of the *New York University Law Review,* the *University of Pennsylvania Law Review,* the *Supreme Court Review,* and the *Yale Law Journal.* Each has permitted me to rework for inclusion here a portion of an article that earlier I published there.

H.H.W.

New Haven, Connecticut
January 1968

Contents

Introduction

In the first spring of his presidency, Lyndon Johnson temporarily rescued collective bargaining in the railroad industry from a slow, gangrenous demise. Faced in April 1964 with the collapse of negotiations and the prospect of a nationwide strike, he invited industry and union panjandrums to the White House; forced them to talk for what must have seemed endless hours; and then, with a virtuoso display of political finesse, moved them from intransigence to agreement. "I have," said Mr. Johnson, "great faith in the capacity of true collective bargaining." So has said every president since Franklin Roosevelt.

Until recently the stated faith of presidents has been widely shared by the public. Most people have been impatient with collective bargaining when inconvenienced by strikes; some have shared the worry of economists over possibly inflationary wage settlements. Students of labor-management relations have called for reform of collective bargaining; and some businessmen, for its containment. But there had been remarkably little advocacy in favor of abandoning the experiment. And, of course, government support of collective bargaining is only an experiment. Until the fourth decade of this century, American workers often fought government as well as employers in their efforts to unionize. While there were earlier beginnings, it was in the 1930s that government changed sides and began to foster collective bargaining as a method for solving such problems as low wages, poor working conditions, industrial strife, and the psychological frustration of the modern

worker. Since the thirties, collective bargaining has come
to occupy a position at the center of national labor policy.

Now it again may be in danger. In July 1967, Congress
halted a nationwide strike on the railroads. In the summer of 1966, it was quite ready to enact legislation ending
an airlines strike that shut down many, but far from all,
carriers. Some years earlier, it had determined that a nationwide railroad dispute could be resolved only by compulsory arbitration. In all of these adventures Congress
had the backing of the press and, as best one can tell, the
public. The nation has become very tired, indeed, of major
work stoppages. Moreover, the concern in the administration and the newspapers of the land with the hurtful effects of collective bargaining settlements on national economic policy has reached an intensity which may well
shatter existing institutions unless accommodations are
forthcoming.

I am concerned in this book, first, to examine the role
of the legal process in moving collective bargaining to its
present position at the center of national labor policy. In
this enterprise, I do not take as my task tracing the law
which for many years restrained collective bargaining and
then evolved into an instrument of support. That is an
often told and interesting tale, but it reveals too little. My
task rather is to search for theories which explain the relationship between the legal process and the political, economic, and social forces that combined ultimately to ele-
vate collective bargaining to its present position.

Second, I propose to examine in some detail a variety of
problems created for government by collective bargaining.
Two of these problems, the major strike and the terms of
settlement, threaten the survival of existing labor-management institutions. The other three, union participation
and management prerogatives in the negotiation and administration of the collective agreement, the individual in
the collective structure, and unions in the political process,

do not pose such a threat, in my judgment. They are, nevertheless, problems of major importance to the nation at this time. My inquiry throughout is directed toward the proper role of law in the solution of these five problems and their numerous parts.

It is nothing short of extraordinary that these contemporary problems, with which the bulk of the book is concerned, are the problems (transmuted though they may be) initially foreseen by the judges in the early nineteenth century when law first touched labor with its heavy hand. This is reason enough to begin at the beginning of American labor law, but I have an additional purpose. It is at the beginning that one can best commence to develop a legal theory of collective bargaining.

Part I

The Origins and Structure
of National Labor Policy

Chapter 1

Legal Theory and
Collective Bargaining

Labor collided with the law at the beginning of the nineteenth century when the structure of markets, and hence of industries, in the United States was undergoing fundamental change. Whereas previously most finished products had been made to order or occasionally made for inventory and sold on the premises of a master craftsman, in the evolving system large orders for delivery not only outside the shop but often in distant regions became commonplace. The changes were facilitated by better communications, a frontier advancing too fast to remain self-sufficient in the production of goods requiring special skills, and a supply of trained labor constantly enlarging on the coast. As the frontier markets grew and transport improved, the established cities of the eastern seaboard vied for the new trade. The widened competition intensified attempts to cut costs of production by increasing the number of apprentices in each shop, and substituting machinery and less skilled labor for skilled workmen. And rising immigration helped the process along. These changes threatened the means and prospects of the journeyman: it became steadily less feasible for him to set up his own shop if his master failed to pay enough. More and more the rising cost of entry hampered individuals in striking out on their own successfully.

To meet the new situation journeymen began to band together, collectively resisting the downward pressures on their earnings. The shoemaking industry provides an early example of how the workers attempted to increase their bargaining power. Forming societies in the major manufacturing centers they demanded higher wages. But merely demanding higher wages was not enough, for not all journeymen were willing to join the societies. There were always some journeymen who would not endure the hardships of a strike, others who received special consideration from the masters, and some from other areas who would come in to fill the needs created by a society walkout. The organized journeymen's hope of forcing the masters to agree to terms lay in preventing potentially dissident journeymen from working during a strike. To this end the organized instituted the "scab system," refusing to work in a shop with anyone who had worked for a master during a strike. And after striking they set as a condition of returning to work the dismissal of all who had scabbed. In essence this was an attempt to institute a union shop.[1]

It was during strikes of journeymen in these early days of the nation that the law first was called upon to intervene, not with the later and hated procedure of the labor injunction or an action for damages, but with the morally unequivocal instrument of the criminal law. The striking employees were indicted for, and in several cases convicted of, criminal conspiracy. It should be added that criminal conspiracy cases turn up after the Civil War as well as in this early period; indeed, the doctrine found favor with the courts in the 1880s.[2]

The substantive law of criminal conspiracy is of marginal interest today in labor relations, for it is no longer with us. Moreover, it is not clear precisely what collective actions the courts found punishable. Few cases were appealed and, perhaps because the juries in the earlier cases were, after guidance from the bench, arbiters of law as well as fact, the lower court decisions are not carefully drawn. While the indictments in a number of cases had a count alleging simply that the workers had combined to raise wages, it seems that the scab system was the heart of the illegality. The celebrated decision of Lemuel Shaw in the

1842 case of *Commonwealth v. Hunt* is remarkable because it found legal a strike to cause the discharge of a scab.[3]

It is the courts' rhetoric, however, that remains important. First, the fears expressed by the judges that workers would band together reveal values that are implicated in many contemporary labor problems. Second, the expressed fears encountered a compensating rhetoric reflecting a compensating set of values that pressed for recognition. And third, it has been the province of the legal system and its several branches to mediate among these underlying values, values shaped by history and presented by economic and political power.

The target of judicial rhetoric in the conspiracy cases was employee group action. If the societies of workers were to have their way, what would happen to the employer's right to manage his business, the dissenting employee's freedom to dissent, the locus of political power in the community, and the economic well-being of the people? By and large, the judges could see only disaster.

A Connecticut court pictured an official of a workers' society lecturing an employer in the following improbable way:

> It is true we have no interest in your business, we have no capital invested therein, we are in no wise responsible for its losses or failures, we are not directly benefitted by its success, and we do not participate in its profits; yet we have a right to control its management and compel you to submit to our dictation.[4]

A Philadelphia court expressed a similar fear of illegitimate control:

> Is there any man who can calculate . . . at what price he may safely contract to deliver articles, . . . if he is to be regulated by the journeymen in an arbitrary jump from one price to another?[5]

A deprivation of employee rights was perceived in the pressure which forced unwilling journeymen to join the societies and strike with them. The same court continued: "If the purpose of the association is well understood, it will be found that they leave no individual at liberty to join the society or reject it." [6] Was it not an interference with both freedom and property to prevent a man from selling his own labor? Why should private societies have the right to decide who should work and at what wages? Perhaps the dissenting worker had greater skill and could profitably make goods at a lower price than the members of the society. Should he not be permitted to do so? The policies of the society destroyed the advantages of good craftsmen and forced the masters to treat all alike.

The courts were clear, too, that the societies were a danger to the body politic, for they were a faction which might destroy the republic by gaining control of it. And workers' societies would have power over large numbers of people through their ability to deny work. One judge reasoned:

> If such a system was tolerated, the constitutional control over our affairs would pass away from the people at large, and become vested in the hands of conspirators. We should have a new system of government, and our rights be placed at the disposal of a voluntary and self-constituted association. [7]

Moreover, the economy of the nation, moving in its natural and proper course, would be disrupted. In the first case at Philadelphia in 1806, the defendants introduced a passage from Adam Smith to support their contention that unless workers organized, the employers would always force them to work for subsistence. But the prosecution urged, and the court seems to have agreed, "[t]hese things will find their level like water . . . if there be no improper combination to force journeymen out of the employer's shop." [8] Such monopolies as the journeymen attempted to establish served only to "have a capital left unemployed." Any locale which permitted the societies to take root would inevitably suffer a decline in trade and importance because the higher prices and uncertainties of strikes would make competition with other areas impossible. "It exposes [commerce] to inconveniences, if not to ruin," said the court in Philadelphia, "therefore, it is against the public welfare." [9]

Not only did the courts profess a belief in the natural workings of the market, they also asserted a concern for the individual members of the public. After all, it was reasoned, the employers would have to pass on to the consumer the increased costs of production.[10]

The rhetoric of the courts in the conspiracy cases is intriguing because the problems rehearsed are so plainly the ancestors of our own. Reviewing them is rather like passing through a gallery in a great English house where one sees in the portraits on the wall the face and figure in different dress of the man selling souvenirs by the door. The linkage between the nineteenth-century labor problems and those today is in the underlying values appealed to by the courts; values not easily put aside, although surely no longer held in their pristine form.

The courts' concern for the employer appeals for its acceptance to the value society places on private property and to its received understanding of the control that comes with ownership. To diminish control is to dilute ownership, and on the desire for and responsibility of ownership we premise a great many of our notions about man and his community. Freedom of contract is a necessary part of the social mechanism of ownership, and when a society of workers can dictate who may be hired and at what price, the employer's freedom of contract, his freedom to use the traditional power of his property, is impaired.

The courts' stated regard for the dissenting worker looks for its acceptance to a related complex of values (and this, of course, is true no matter what one thinks of the judges' motives). The worker's property is his ability to be productive and his right to sell his skills. Freedom of contract is necessary for him, too, because unless he can sell his work freely he loses control of his property and his destiny. These attributes of property, combined with political rights to speak and vote, add up to a good portion of the individualism which we value today, and deeply so.

The courts' rhetoric addressed to the political and economic consequences of worker groups also invites acceptance by an appeal to traditional values which have persisted. The power of privately assembled groups of men ever has been feared as a threat to governmental stability and the personal security it affords. In the tenth *Federalist* Madison regarded factions as perhaps necessary evils, but nonetheless evils to be kept under control; and today we remain anxious about the impact on politics and representative government of group power. Finally, the economic well-being of the nation is a necessary condition for the happiness of its people, and whether or not happiness here means more than the pursuit of property, it too is found prominently displayed in the atlas of national values.

What most of us would reject out of hand today, however, is the solution to the problems of group action offered by the conspiracy courts. While rarely interdicting all collective activity, the courts made it a crime for employees jointly to pursue their own self-interest in anything like effective fashion. What the courts did, and said they were doing, was to put to one side the interests and aspirations of the employees who desired to act as a group. To these interests and aspirations, society today attaches a very high value indeed.

It is not fair to criticize early nineteenth-century judges for ignoring mid-twentieth-century values. These values are conditioned by the subsequent growth of American capitalism (with its dehumanizing methods of production and its dependence on the ever larger corporate complex), by the vast political power that the business community began to exercise after the Civil War, and by the workers' reaction to this: their drive to escape poverty and achieve dignity through the use of collective economic and political action. But the courts in the conspiracy cases may be criticized on grounds that are not anachronistic. This criticism will develop a theory of judicial abstention which may be thought of as one aspect of a legal theory in support of collective bargaining.

COLLECTIVE BARGAINING AND A THEORY
OF JUDICIAL ABSTENTION

One of the large questions in early nineteenth-century America was what the appropriate role should be for English common law in domestic jurisprudence. It precipitated a major political controversy between Jeffersonian Republicans, who were strongly opposed to any transference, and Federalists, who vigorously supported the adoption of the mother country's corpus juris. This issue was an integral part of the postpartum turbulence that beset the nation: hatred and suspicion of law—any law—on the one hand, the quest for order and stability, on the other. Debate over the role of English common law figured importantly in what Perry Miller has called "the basic challenge of the law to an explosive, dynamic democracy." The "lawyers' real controversy with their society," he has said, "was that they stood for the Head against the Heart." [11] Wherever one comes down on these issues, the ultimate domestication of English common law must be admired as a truly great achievement of the American Bar.

Reliance upon the precedents of the common law of England, however, to justify convictions in the early con-

spiracy cases is far from edifying. First, despite extensive
scholarly inquiry into the English precedents, the conclusion of Richard B. Morris seems wholly valid: "Whether
or not English common law provides historical justification for these convictions of American labor combinations
must remain a debatable issue." [12] Second, historical justification hardly would be enough. The two countries were
vastly different, and the common law itself, if properly understood, would not permit of its American domestication
by an easy transference of precedent. "It is one of the great
merits and advantages of the common law," said Lemuel
Shaw in 1854,

> that, instead of a series of detailed practical rules, es-
> tablished by positive provisions, and adapted to the
> precise circumstances of particular cases, which would
> become obsolete and fail, when the practice and course
> of business, to which they apply, should cease or
> change, the common law consists of a few broad and
> comprehensive principles founded on reason, natural
> justice, and enlightened public policy modified and
> adapted to the circumstances of all the particular cases
> which fall within it.[13]

It is only this understanding of the common law that
should have been relevant for the new nation. Yet, in the
conspiracy cases, English decisions of doubtful validity
were appealed to as binding precedent. A search for Shaw's
"broad and comprehensive principles" will begin to disclose the mischief in such a use of prior decisional law.

The energy of English law was expended in hedging
about the authority of the monarch. Without a monarch
and with a Bill of Rights, America might expect law to
play a larger "part in activating the energies of the community." It was no less central a figure than Joseph Story
who envisioned law as the "great elastic power which pervades and embraces every human relation . . . ; it is the

'bond' or 'cement' of society; or, most frequently, it is the 'ligament.' " [14] But this groping toward a dynamic and purposeful conception of law encountered the growing fear of what lawyers called " 'faction,' 'party,' a 'spirit of insubordination,' 'mobocracy,' or most succinctly 'anarchy' "; those forces inescapable in a democracy, that Madison believed would be checked and balanced by the governmental structure of the new Republic.[15] This fear pushed the legal profession back toward a more restrictive conception of law and away from Story's liberating vision.

Perry Miller urges us to consider the conspiracy cases in light of this tension in American legal thought between law as "ligament" and law as restriction upon the forces of "anarchy." From this tension emerged a "broad and comprehensive" principle which Shaw himself was able to employ in *Commonwealth v. Hunt*. To quote Mr. Miller:

> Beginning with the Philadelphia Shoemakers' Case in 1806, down to Lemuel Shaw's ruling of 1842 in *Commonwealth v. Hunt*, the judges had regularly found unions an incipient form of democratic conspiracy against the stability of society, and condemned them as uproar and confusion. These convictions have acquired infamy with posterity, and have generally been denounced as politically inspired. Because in the Massachusetts case the journeymen shoemakers were defended by Robert Rantoul, an enthusiastic Jacksonian, and the charges delivered against them by Judge Peter O. Thacher in 1832, 1837, and 1840 were patently Whig expressions, historians have found it easy to identify the cause of labor with the Jacksonian party. . . . Actually both Thacher and Shaw, before whom the case ultimately arrived, were Whigs, and so, to the extent the term applies in America, were "conservatives." But to the charge of criminal conspiracy, Shaw declared that the journeymen committed no crime in

banding together: "Such a purpose is not unlawful."
The difference between them points up the confusion
in legal thinking as to just how and where the principle of restriction should be applied so that it might
somehow also be a constructive principle. The operations of society, said Thacher, cannot proceed unless
the law, "which like the air, is over every thing, and
pervades every thing, and is the life of every thing,
protect, in full extent, the principle of equal and fair
competition." Hence he concluded that when individuals combined together to gain an advantage over
others, they violated this principle. But Shaw discovered that the purpose of the journeymen's combinations was not pernicious; on the premise that the law
pervaded all society, adjudicating peaceful disputes
by incessant pressure, he found it not criminal "for
men to agree together to exercise their own acknowledged rights, in such a manner as best to subserve their
own interests." Shaw's opinon had, as hardly need be
remarked, immense effect on the subsequent history of
labor relations, but he himself was unconscious of
what he wrought. He was simply adhering to the one
rule which the philosophy of American law left to
him, that the ligament of society is a neutral umpire
within the machine. "It is through competition," he
said, "that the best interests of trade and industry are
promoted." He was willing that a union compete with
a corporation. We pervert the logic of the period
when we read too glibly into juridical differences con-
notations which arose only after decades of industrialization.[16]

As helpful as these insights are, they are only a beginning. For while the "broad and comprehensive" principle
forced upon Shaw by the philosophy of American law was
"that the ligament of society is a neutral umpire within the

machine," and while context may seem to turn this to support for competition—for what Holmes some fifty years later was to call the "free struggle for life" [17]—context also might be thought to require further refinement. Violence by the journeymen in the pursuit of economic self-interest could not be condoned. Nor can one blink the values appealed to by lesser judges than Shaw in the rhetoric we have considered. That Shaw is right, I have no doubt, but the difficulties in moving from broad and comprehensive principles to standards of decision may explain, in part at least, why *Commonwealth v. Hunt* did not, as Mr. Miller tells us it did, have "immense effect on the subsequent history of labor relations." Conspiracy convictions followed the Shaw opinion;[18] and when they yielded it was not to the power of neutral principle, but to the effectiveness of the labor injunction.

Our task must be to bring Shaw's principle to bear, to elaborate it in the context of the judicial process. Perhaps the place to begin is with the purpose of courts. They exist first and foremost to adjudicate disputes. The dispute is usually over the legality of someone's conduct, and it is expected that the legality of the conduct will be judged as of the time it took place. It is also expected that the judging will be fair; and here, fair, at a minimum, would seem to mean in accordance with reasonably knowable, preexisting standards. Within these limits, and without bothering about qualification, the actor should himself have been able to judge, if not the legality of his conduct, at least whether it was considered improper by the community. He should not suffer now if, at the time he acted, he could not have been expected to know that his conduct, in this sense, was wrong.

One would hardly think it fair, therefore, for a judge to fashion a standard from his private stock of values, and

this would have been so even in the conspiracy cases where the jury, as trier of law, legitimately could have rejected the judge's standard; for it would have been difficult, indeed, for the jury not to have been influenced strongly by a learned and officially disinterested judge. Suppose, however, that the judge did not turn to his private stock of values, but to values widely shared by the community? This might seem fair for it would reduce the element of surprise. The actor would have been able himself better to judge the propriety of his conduct. Of course, it depends a good deal on how widely and deeply the particular values are held. But in the criminal as well as the civil law one does not want to overstate the evil in a little surprise, or, to put it the other way, the importance of very great certainty. Even when the standard to be employed in adjudication is prior and closely analogous decisional, or for that matter enacted, law, some surprise must sometimes be expected. Law is just not that certain.

There is, however, another aspect to the fair decision question—one unrelated to the issue of surprise—that must be considered for its bearing upon the problems of the conspiracy cases. In a democracy, a decision drawing heavily on the personal values of the judge is objectionable. Law should not be made in this way by one wise man. And the judge does make law as well as resolve the dispute before him, for once he fashions a standard it is an important source of decision in all subsequent, analogous cases. This objection, of course, also loses force if a decisional standard is shaped by resort to values widely shared and deeply held in the community.[19] But here, perhaps more than with the issue of surprise, one must inquire into how deeply and widely the particular values are held before one can say how much those values should count; and for this purpose, the political environment may be an important judicial guide.

The values appealed to in the rhetoric of the conspiracy

cases were not personal to the judges. But the mistake of the majority of judges was that they failed to be guided by political considerations in deciding how to count these values. My claim is not that decisions should have been politically inspired in the sense that Perry Miller suggests they were not; quite the contrary. I claim rather that the political environment is a legitimate aid for the judge in his difficult judicial task of deciding how to count particular values.

At the time of the early conspiracy cases, the nation was deeply divided politically over issues that the prosecution of journeymen seemed to objectify. Writing of the 1806 *Philadelphia Cordwainers* case, Walter Nelles describes the "legal controversy, both out of court and in, [as] part of the major political controversy of the time—then still usually expressed as between 'aristocracy' and 'republicanism' (which meant Jeffersonian democracy)." [20] Mr. Nelles sees only purity and goodness in Jeffersonian democracy; only self-interest and evil in Hamiltonian "aristocracy." But while this badly flaws his work, he does show clearly that political attention was focused on the Philadelphia case, and that views indeed were polarized.[21]

That the case should have had a symbolic quality is not difficult to understand. Hamiltonian "aristocracy" was committed to fostering governmental support of manufacturing. The Jeffersonians were against this. They were not, to be sure, especially concerned with the urban worker and his problems. Their central trust was in the farmer; on his future did the republic's depend. But they feared the mob less than the Federalists did, and if they were not all true lovers of democracy and the forces and factions it stimulated, they often spoke as if they were.[22]

These differences were both a cause and effect of differing visions—"philosophies" would suggest too much—of the appropriate role of government in the new republic. Hamilton's vision was expansive and he had to some extent harnessed governmental energy in support of domestic industry. Richard Hofstadter describes the Jeffersonian countervision (a vision that did not always conform to its owner's actions).

Jefferson and his followers had seen the unhappy effects of British governmental interference in American economic affairs, and they regarded Hamilton's system of state economic activity ("the contracted, English, half-lettered ideas of Hamilton") as merely a continuation at home of English economic ideas. Hamilton had set the government to helping the capitalists at the expense of the agrarians. The Jeffersonian response was not to call for a government that would help the agrarians at the expense of the capitalists, but simply for one that would let things alone. Where modern liberals have looked to government interference as a means of helping the poor, Jefferson, in common with other eighteenth-century liberals, thought of it chiefly as an unfair means of helping the rich through interest-bearing debts, taxation, tariffs, banks, privileges, and bounties. He concluded that the only necessary remedy under republican government would be to deprive the rich of these devices and restore freedom and equality through "natural" economic forces. Because he did not usually think of economic relationships as having an inherent taint of exploitation in them, he saw no necessity to call upon the state to counteract them. It was not the task of government to alter the economic order: the rich were not entitled to it and the poor would not find it necessary.[23]

How should this political environment have informed the courts in the early conspiracy cases? I suggest that it should have been taken by the judges as a warning, a warning that it was inappropriate for judges to appeal to the

values which in fact their rhetoric did appeal to as a justification for imposing governmental restraints on the journeymen. Those values did not count that much in the community. They were undercut or neutralized by the support for Jeffersonian laissez-faire thinking, which, of course, also could not count as a standard for decision.

But if this is so, what was a court to do? Mr. Nelles in his article proposes as follows:

> A safe and sensible position for a court of 1806 might have been this: The question is of American public policy and cannot be deemed controlled by English authorities. Society is divided with respect to it; there is no such approach to unanimity as might justify a court in feeling that it had a mandate from society to decide it, and no such indifference as to make a decision either way preferable to none at all. Such a question of policy is more appropriate for legislative than for judicial consideration; and so long as the legislature has not spoken, society may be presumed to will that the subject shall remain unregulated by law.[24]

This is a troublesome suggestion that many students of the legal process would have difficulty accepting. How, except in lawless fashion, can a court having jurisdiction refuse to decide a case that properly comes before it for decision? The court's principal purpose is to resolve the dispute between the employer and the workers, and this is so even though in form this is a criminal and not a civil case. Of what interest or relevance is it to these parties that, in some abstract sense, the underlying issues of public policy would be resolved better by a legislature? The legislature speaks to the future, if it speaks at all. The claims put to the court relate to the past.

Perhaps what Mr. Nelles means, however, and surely what he ought to have meant, is not that the court should have refused, as such, to decide. Rather, the court should have given judgment for the defendants on the ground that no preexisting standard made defendants' conduct improper. Mr. Nelles may be employing no more than an illuminating shorthand when he says the question was "more appropriate for legislative than judicial consideration." The point is that no judgment against the defendants could have been fair, because there was no legitimate standard available to the court for judging the defendants' conduct illegal.

A decision on such ground (and the ground itself) may be called "institutional." First, for convenience: to distinguish it from other types of decisions to be discussed. Second, to signal that the decision rests upon an explicit determination of the appropriate limits of judicial lawmaking.

One surely is entitled to ask how an institutional decision would differ from a decision for the defendants upon what might be called Jeffersonian ground; that is, upon a determination that laissez-faire (government ought to stay out) values command the necessary community acceptance to be employed as a judicial standard for decision (or for that matter, the position ultimately embodied in the Wagner Act, that the aspirations of the journeymen are paramount)? The answer must be that the reasons advanced for the holding in the two situations are altogether different. Of course the employer and workers factually are in the same position one way or the other. But that proves little, for here the same would be true if the decision were to deny jurisdiction; yet a jurisdictional decision is different from one on the merits. The implications of any holding on the merits may vary enormously with the ground of decision.

The institutional ground is different from the Jeffersonian ground in two respects: First, in an institutional decision, fiat alone is not the basis of judicial authority as ultimately it must be seen to be if the Jeffersonian ground is used. The political environment shows that the "government ought to stay out" position does not command sufficient community acceptance to be employed as the decisional standard in adjudication. And I doubt that many of us would think that it is appropriate in a democracy for judicial decisions to rest on fiat alone. Second, the consequences of the decision to the ultimate formation of community opinion may be very different. A decision on Jeffersonian ground is not neutral to a general acceptance of the Jeffersonian position. It rather is a positive force leading to such an acceptance. An institutional decision, on the other hand, specifically attempts to avoid any such effect. It is in this respect that it is closely related to a jurisdictional decision.

What the courts should have done then in the early conspiracy cases was to have held for the defendants on the institutional ground that decisional standards were insufficient to resolve the dispute in conventional terms; that no fair decision could be entered against the defendants because there were no general enough preexisting standards prohibiting them from acting in the way they had; "that the ligament of society is [indeed] a neutral umpire within the machine."

The conspiracy cases were the law's first response to what was to become a great social movement—the growth of unions and of collective bargaining—and it has been characteristic of America that law works on social change initially through its courts rather than through its legislatures. Perhaps this is less true today, but it has been important to the development and impact of ideas and institutions. Courts are functionally very different from legislatures. Their nature sometimes makes them seem conservative, sometimes liberal; and the opinions that accompany their judgments help to fit change into the exist-

ing social order and, at the same time, to change that
order.

When courts make theoretical mistakes, as they did in
the conspiracy cases, the mistakes may be perpetuated by
the nature of the judicial process. While the criminal conspiracy doctrine fell into disuse and was replaced by civil
litigation and the labor injunction, the judge-made substantive law remained much the same. New law was fashioned as new problems with new difficulties came to the
courts for decision, but Edwin E. Witte was able to observe
in 1926 that: "The decisions of the courts today upon what
conduct in the furtherance of the objects of labor unions is
lawful, are not one whit more liberal than the doctrines
announced in the earliest [conspiracy] cases." [25] At least
part of the reason for this can be explained by the simple
fact that prior judicial decisions are an important source
of subsequent decisional law. Even wrongly decided cases
sometimes should be followed because of the disruptive
consequences of striking out in new directions. There may
be disruption for the parties who arrange their affairs in
accordance with law, and for the judicial process itself,
which cannot afford to reexamine every issue afresh. But
wrongly decided cases often should not be followed; and
some judges found it appropriate to reject the substantive
doctrines of the conspiracy cases. Considerations emerged,
with experience, to support their position; and here much
can be learned from Holmes.

Following the era of criminal conspiracy, the courts were
asked by employers to enjoin union activities aimed at establishing collective bargaining and at achieving various
bargaining goals. Holmes suggested that the question for
a court should be whether the union was privileged to
harm the employer through the use of economic pressure
—strikes, picketing, boycotts. He found such privilege in
the pursuit of self-interest—the "free struggle for life"—
and he refused generally to draw nice distinctions as to

the means used, so long as they were peaceful, or as to the purposes sought, whether bargaining rights, higher wages, or a closed shop.[26]

The views of the great jurist, however, did not prevail. Most courts found it congenial to distinguish among objects and among peaceful means: enjoining some, permitting others.[27] While dazzled by these nice refinements, one may wonder, as new issues presented themselves for decision, how the distinctions were made. Holmes suggests that: "The ground of decision really comes down to a proposition of policy of rather a delicate nature concerning the merit of the particular benefit to themselves intended by the defendants, and suggests a doubt whether judges with different economic sympathies might not decide such a case differently when brought face to face with the issue." [28]

The judges, whose sympathies perhaps brought them to restrain unions, employed a rhetoric with which we are familiar and appealed to values we have seen evoked. They, too, counted these values in an inappropriate way, and in part for the same reasons that the judges in the conspiracy cases had. The issues brought to the courts for decision were important political questions about which there was a monumental lack of agreement.[29] Nor could most of these issues be resolved by turning to precedent or legal analogy.

One found in that source of law distinctions that were based on no visible principles and that, accordingly, could not be rationally elaborated. It was simply unclear, for example, why peaceful picketing for a legal union shop was itself illegal, while peaceful picketing for higher wages was not.[30] Once again, therefore, holdings should have been for defendants on grounds related to the appropriate limits of judicial lawmaking, but were not. Once again, judicial restraint was required by legal theory but rejected by courts.

Moreover, the habits of mind and the errors of judgment displayed in the injunction cases worked mischief elsewhere. The Sherman Act was applied to unions and a body of irrational law evolved;[31] and statutes limiting hours of work or making yellow-dog contracts illegal were struck down by judges who counted the values appealed to in the conspiracy cases not merely as standards for decision but, indeed, as constitutional imperatives.[32]

The result is well-known history. The growth and development of unions and of collective bargaining was wrongly impeded, the courts were rightly viewed as instruments of the employer class; they were brought into disrepute, and their general effectiveness thereby was reduced.[33]

COLLECTIVE BARGAINING AND A THEORY
OF LEGISLATIVE ACTION

The burden of the argument thus far is that it was wrong for judge-made law to impede collective bargaining's development. It also would have been wrong for the courts actively to have participated in that development. An understanding of this position perhaps will be deepened by a rather different type of analysis, one which attempts to explain, in legal process terms, why it was appropriate for active support to have come, as ultimately it did, through legislation. This analysis constitutes the second aspect of a legal theory in support of collective bargaining.

The place to begin is again with rhetoric; this time not of the conspiracy cases, but of the labor movement and of the politicians and intellectuals who spoke for it. That rhetoric is almost as diverse as the history of ideas, but four claims have influenced and shaped contemporary legislation. The first is the desirability of industrial democracy, a concept which emerged in response to the changing nature of industrial life. The production line is emasculating, and thus the quest must be to restore manhood to man. It is dehumanizing, and thus the worker must again be made human. It is uncreative, and thus the man at his machine must be given a creative outlet. Participation in industrial government is a way to achieve these goals. Moreover, it is necessary for the continuation of political democracy. Without manhood, a democratic nation is not possible.[34]

Industrial democracy depends upon unions, for the employee by himself is disenfranchised. If there is to be industrial democracy, decisions must be made by the employer and the representative of his employees. And if industrial democracy is to be more than stage makeup, for long-range viewing only, the employee's voice must be heard in the councils of his union. Thus, industrial democracy requires union democracy.[35]

The second claim is that interest groups are desirable institutions in the life of a democracy. The individual in a complex society must be associated with various organizations if his voice is to be heard and his views to count. Labor unions are organizations which represent the individual in political, economic, and social matters. The existence of a multiplicity of interest groups results in the diffusion of political power. The conflict among groups, and the fact that the individual at any given time may owe fealty to a number of antagonistic groups, make it unlikely that any one could become powerful enough to capture a community's political processes.[36]

Claim number three is that the establishment and practice of collective bargaining will substantially reduce the economic strife bequeathed by industrialization. Instead of class battle, collective bargaining offers negotiation and the exploration of mutual interests and purposes.[37]

Finally, and most importantly, the rhetoric claims that collective bargaining is necessary because of inequality of bargaining power. Equality does not exist between the employer and the individual worker. The employer, it is argued, has the power unilaterally to set the wages, hours, and terms and conditions of employment. When workers organize and bargain collectively, they have the power that comes from numbers. It is a power which offsets or countervails that of the employer, often itself a collectivity of individual investors in the corporate form.[38] This claim, unsophisticated as it may sound in this form, is the most important for legal theory because on examination one finds that it directly challenges legal doctrine. It asks what relevance the underlying assumptions that support the law's commitment to freedom or liberty of contract have for the agreement between the individual worker and his employer.

Freedom of contract means many things. People should be free to make agreements, and government should not interfere. Government should accept, by inaction, what the parties agree to unless one of the parties calls upon it, through its courts, to implement the agreement by enforcement. Where such aid is requested, the agreement usually should be enforced according to its sense. Thus, where there is a dispute between two parties to a contract over rights under it, the contract itself provides the standard to be applied by a court in resolving the dispute. The task for the court, as traditionally put, is to ascertain the intention of the parties; but since this means intention objectively manifested, it may be less misleading to speak of the court's task as determining the sense of the parties' agreement. Its task is not to impose upon the parties other people's wiser agreement, or its own notion of what would have been an intelligent agreement, or the notions of some other government official on the matter. To be sure, where there is doubt about the parties' meaning, because of silence or ambiguity, they will be taken to have acted in conformity with general practice; but they can depart from the general and the sensible by being clear in their agreement. In someone's enduring phrase, "the parties are sovereign." [39]

Much can be said in support of freedom of contract. The parties generally are wiser about their own affairs than others, including government acting through its legal institutions, can hope to be. This surely is an operating assumption of all democratic societies. Second, the cost of substituting governmental for private decision-making is very great. Indeed, as a practical matter it cannot be done across-the-board. Friedrich Kessler suggests that "the law cannot possibly anticipate the content of an infinite number of atypical transactions into which members of the community may need to enter." [40] Moreover, to the extent that government tries, power to make a variety of different types of decisions shifts away from private parties and toward government. This is a shift to be avoided, if one believes that it is important for a democracy to have power spread about.

The desirability of freedom of contract, however, *may* be put in serious question if one party to the contract is in a position to set the terms of agreement without dickering with the other party.[41] While the market, through competition or some other form of coercion, usually is able adequately to restrain the party who sets the terms, if it fails to do so he is likely to exploit the situation to the great disadvantage of the other party. In a case where the extrinsic check of the market fails, governmental acceptance of the agreement through inaction, or implementation through enforcement of the sense of the agreement, is a dubious policy at best. It represents an example of misplaced governmental neutrality. After all, it is one thing for government through law to defer to the joint will of the parties to a contract; it is quite something else again for government to accept by inaction, or implement by enforcement, a virtually unilateral private decision that may be unfair to the weaker party.[42]

The question then that must be asked about inequality
of bargaining power in the area of labor is whether the
individual contract of employment, the terms of which
usually were fixed by the employer, was unfair; or, to put
it the other way, whether there were adequate extrinsic
checks on the employer. A worker is not likely to enter an
unfair contract if he has alternatives; and thus the existence of alternatives could be an important check on over-
reaching by the employer. Alternatives are one aspect of
the labor market's role—a powerful extrinsic force indeed
—in shaping the individual contract of employment.

The professional economic literature on the role of the
labor market is vast and agreement among economists hard
to come by, but most professionals probably would sub-
scribe to much of the following from Lloyd Reynolds'
standard work on labor economics:

> Elementary economic texts describe the operation of
> a competitive labor market and the results it might be
> expected to yield. The broad argument is that, given
> free and informed competition among workers and
> employers, each worker must be paid the value of his
> contribution to production. He cannot be paid more,
> because the employer could not continue to operate.
> He will not be paid less, because the employer would
> be making abnormal profits and some other alert busi-
> nessman would enter the industry and bid up the
> price of labor. There is thus little scope for contro-
> versy or bargaining over the price of labor. . . . This
> is of course a very simplified and idealized picture. It
> assumes many small employers competing for labor, no
> collusion among employers or workers, adequate
> channels of information, and a number of other
> things. It is no secret that actual labor markets depart
> considerably from this competitive ideal. Many em-
> ployers are large and the worker's choice is often re-

stricted to one or a few companies; employers often
get together on wage rates and on policies which make
it hard for workers to change employers; channels of
information are poor and there is no effective central
clearinghouse for labor; the exchange of a machinist's
labor for a "package" of wages and working conditions is a more complicated transaction than setting a
price on a loaf of bread; workers dislike changing
jobs, and when forced to do so, they hunt new jobs
in a haphazard and ill-informed way; during periods
of heavy unemployment the worker's bargaining
power—which depends basically on his power to
change jobs—is seriously reduced. . . . Despite these
numerous deficiencies, the labor market is a reasonably effective instrument both for determining relative wage rates and for raising the general wage level
as national output rises.[43]

Mr. Reynolds' conclusion while surely responsive to the
inequality of bargaining power argument, and a powerful
partial answer, does not (nor does he suggest it does) begin
fully to dispose of it. The numerous deficiencies in the
market mechanism (many of which come down to the inadequacy of information available to the worker) and the
worker's human tendency to disregard future contingen-
cies may lead to unfair or oppressive individual contracts
of employment.[44] This may be a short-run phenomenon—
all of a man's working life—and at any given time it may
be limited to particular regions of the country or segments
of the economy. In the long run, everything may work itself out happily in terms of aggregates; but that hardly does
justice! There remains substantial doubt, therefore, about
the wisdom of ubiquitous governmental neutrality, that is,
governmental reliance upon the individual employment
contract.

This doubt is powerfully reinforced by the fact that the

plainly economic terms of the employment contract represent only one important criterion in judging its fairness. The conditions under which a man works also must figure importantly; and before unions these conditions sometimes were physically frightful and administratively arbitrary. The foreman often was possessed of management power. There was little in the way of grievance procedure; there were few rules governing layoffs or promotions; administration was in the foreman's discretion. And since the foreman could discharge at will and hire by whim, he, as might be expected, frequently used his power for personal gain or private revenge. The stories are endless.[45]

In theory, of course, many aspects of working conditions probably can be translated into monetary terms. Perhaps the firm with bad working conditions in the long run must pay a higher wage for workers than the firm with better conditions. But, in judging the fairness of an agreement, few people, whether laymen, judges, or legislators, would be prepared to think in long-run economic terms and there end their inquiry. While the relationship between wages and working conditions is surely an element in the question of fairness, for most of us it does not by itself determine fairness. In part this may be because of a belief in the imperfection of the market. In part perhaps it is because at some point each of us may, after all, value what he takes to be a wise decision for someone else more than he values freedom of choice for that someone.

Haltingly, law has tended to reject freedom of contract in those classes of cases where experience suggests its retention too often will result in unfairness between the parties. A number of approaches can be observed. The courts, through interpretation or through the management of ancient doctrines, may strive to mitigate an unfair result which would follow from enforcing the sense of the agreement;[46] or a court, in a contract enforcement case, may be more candid. Thus, for example, provisions in new car sales contracts which attempt to limit automobile manufacturers' liability for harm resulting from defective, nonnegligently produced cars, have been struck down as unfair.[47]

Nor is candor a modern development. It was in 1873— a decade before the decline of the conspiracy doctrine— that the Supreme Court of the United States decided *Railroad Co. v. Lockwood*.[48] The railroad made a standard contract with shippers who traveled with livestock, placing on the shipper "all the risk of injury." The Court declined to give effect to this clause of the contract in a case where the shipper was injured as a result of the railroad's negligence. The Court said:

> The carrier and his customer do not stand on a footing of equality. The latter is only one individual of a million. He cannot afford to haggle or stand out and seek redress in the courts. His business will not admit such a course. He prefers, rather, to accept any bill of lading, or sign any paper the carrier presents; often, indeed, without knowing what the one or the other contains. In most cases, he has no alternative but to do this, or abandon his business.[49]

And the Court went on: "Contracts of common carriers, like those of persons occupying a fiduciary character, giving them a position in which they can take undue advantage of the persons with whom they contract, must rest upon their fairness and reasonableness." [50]

Observe that the *Lockwood* decision does not suffer from the theoretical mistakes found in the conspiracy cases. There, the courts fashioned new legal doctrine by overweighting particular values. In *Lockwood*, the Court was not creating new legal doctrine in the same sense at all.

Its task rather was to probe behind existing freedom of contract doctrine to the principles that support it, and to use those principles in the concrete situation posed by the particular controversy. That this is a lesser judicial task does not detract from the fact that the Court performed it with both considerable aplomb and admirable skill.

Of course, the case for a court insisting that a contract between a railroad and one of its customers must be fair and reasonable is more powerful than the case for such insistence where the contract is between an individual worker and his employer. The latter case, however, is surely no less powerful than that of the automobile manufacturer and the purchaser of a new car. And even in *Lockwood* it is a degree of difference; the cases are not different in kind. The market mechanism, perhaps to a lesser extent, also restrains the railroad in the exercise of its power unilaterally to fix the terms of contract. Moreover, the extent of its liability to customers is easily seen as reflected in the price the customer pays for service; so too, of course, in the automobile example.

The *Lockwood* approach, however, has little utility for the employment contract, and the conspiracy cases provide some insight as to why. In *Lockwood* the Court, after striking down the unfair contract, easily could fill the resulting gap. What would be fair? The established common-law negligence rule; the rule that would apply in the absence of a contract provision. Railroads owe their customers the duty of not injuring them negligently. It was this duty that the railroad unsuccessfully tried to eliminate by contract. And in the automobile case, the contract attempted to eliminate what in its absence the law calls an implied warranty of merchantability. When the contract was struck down, the underlying law provided the judicial standard of fairness between the parties. However, if the contract of employment in any of its terms is thought to be unfair— if it is thought that the market cannot be counted upon to produce a fair result—how is the court to fill the gap? How is it to write a fair term? There is no underlying body of law to supply the decisional standard, and if a court were to turn to community values, would it not be on even more shaky ground than were the courts in the conspiracy cases? What is a fair wage; a fair rule of seniority; a fair rule respecting discharge? Is it the same for the steel worker as for the shoemaker? To ask these questions is to expose how much easier it often is to decide that a result is unfair than to suggest a fair result. Nor could the courts administer a *Lockwood* approach in the employment contract field. How could they possibly deal with the endless number of contracts they would be called upon to review? In short, then, it was impossible for courts to fashion and apply the standards necessary to perform here the task that the *Lockwood* Court or, much later, the courts in the automobile cases were able to perform with respect to particular contractual provisions. And indeed, the courts were not asked to do so, perhaps because their institutional limitations in this regard are so apparent.

Since *Lockwood* has little utility for the employment contract, the search must be for other approaches. Consider the approach to the establishment of passenger fares or freight rates on the railroads or airlines—a tariff system created by statute. Henry M. Hart, Jr., and Albert M. Sacks are suggestive:

> The device of the tariff had as its central purpose, the establishment of an effectual mechanism for the prevention of discrimination among shippers. But, although this may not have been fully appreciated, it represented at the same time the invention of a new form of private law making of portentous significance. The railroads themselves wrote the tariffs, acting either separately or in groups through traffic bureaus or other agents. To the extent that the tariffs were per-

mitted to stand, law had been made by private law makers acting unilaterally without even the formality of concurrence by the shipper. But, of course, there was a check in the form of the Commission's power of review and revision, and a possibility of judicial review.[51]

Whatever one may think of the tariff system as it exists today in transportation—and there is little reason to believe that it has been successful—its approach, if applied to the employment contract, would not work well. It would require the establishment of an administrative agency to review the contracts that had been drafted unilaterally by employers or groups of employers. The problems for such an agency would be similar to at least some of the problems a court would confront under a *Lockwood* approach. The agency, of course, would have fact-finding advantages, and the advantages of specialization and perhaps of expertness. But this would not be enough to make promising the chances of success. The unilateral lawmaking would have to be tested by a standard of fairness or reasonableness. To give content to that standard in a national or even a statewide context with diverse industry and regional considerations would be a staggering task. Indeed, it probably could not be done in a meaningful way, and if the attempt were made the required bureaucracy would be truly enormous. The costs of such an approach, in terms of the previously adumbrated values underlying the freedom of contract doctrine—private parties generally are wiser about their own affairs than government; it is harmful for democracy to have a wholesale shift of power over important economic matters from private parties to government officials—count heavily against it.

Another approach, and one that has been extensively employed, moves from the proposition that it is easier to decide what is unfair than to suggest what would be fair.

Through the political process society may conclude that women and children should not work at hard labor, that no one should be required to work for more than a certain number of hours a day (or at least that such employment should be deterred by making it expensive), that coal mining may not proceed unless minimum safety precautions are taken, or that wages below a stipulated rate are unfair, and therefore illegal, irrespective of the type of work, the worker's skill or the state of the labor market.[52] This approach lacks flexibility, and while very important, is, therefore, of limited utility.[53] Moreover, if it is to be successful on a large scale, it requires either fairly substantial governmental administrative enforcement machinery,[54] or private policing by employee associations.

The drawbacks of these alternatives to contract (and there are other alternatives with powerful drawbacks, such as direct governmental wage setting) and the values which support the freedom of contract doctrine make the case for collective bargaining an appealing one.

If a union bargains for the worker, perhaps the contract between union and employer can be treated according to the usual freedom of contract dogma. The collective contract is negotiated. Its terms are not established by one party—restrained though he is by a less than perfect market—but by both parties, each of whom is restrained. The collective contract simply is less likely to be unfair to one of the parties than an individual contract, and it is more likely to reinforce important societal values than its alternatives. In this sense, then, the unequal bargaining power rhetoric of the labor movement makes an attractive legal brief against private ordering by individual contracts of employment and for private ordering by collective bargaining agreements.

However, two points should be made clear, for it may be easy to read more into what I have said than I meant it to contain. First, I am not suggesting that the legal relevance of this portion of the labor movement's rhetoric alone caused Congress to enact legislation supporting collective bargaining. All the rhetoric was influential. Nor do I entertain the notion that the rhetoric and its effectiveness can be disassociated from the political and economic power of the labor movement; or, for that matter, that the political and economic power of the movement can be disentangled from the force of its rhetoric. What I do insist upon is that the bargaining power argument makes a particularly weighty claim upon a system of law that points proudly to freedom of contract as one of its major doctrines.

Second, I am not suggesting that a contract which is fair as between the parties is necessarily fair to the public or good for the society. It may be morally, economically, or politically bad. I take this to be a discrete question, and one which has enormous importance when asked about collective bargaining agreements. It will not go unnoticed in these pages; but its consideration must be postponed until Chapter 9.

LEGAL THEORY AND THE CONTEMPORARY STATUTORY STRUCTURE

Responsive to both aspects of the legal theory that supports collective bargaining and its subsidiary institutions are today's federal statutes regulating labor. Four statutes are centrally implicated. The Railway Labor Act is the earliest of the four, dating from 1926.[55] It deals exclusively with collective bargaining on the railroads and airlines; and, while strikingly different in detail from its more general counterpart, R.L.A. is not sufficiently different in its goals or structure to warrant special attention here. A second statute, the Landrum-Griffin, or Labor-Management Reporting and Disclosure Act,[56] is principally concerned with the internal affairs of unions. L.M.R.D.A., which in its most important sections is responsive to the rhetoric of industrial democracy, plays a major role in Chapter 5, and its structure will be examined there. The statutes of present concern, then, are the Norris-La Guardia Act of 1932 and the Wagner, or National Labor Relations Act of 1935, amended most importantly by Taft-Hartley in 1947 and by Landrum-Griffin in 1959, and occupying center stage in these pages generally under the title of the Labor-Management Relations Act.[57]

Norris-La Guardia seeks to accomplish through enacted law much of what the abstentionist theory would have accomplished through judicial decision. The Act was a belated legislative answer to the massive and wrongheaded judicial intervention in labor-management relations, via the civil courts, which followed the fading away of criminal conspiracy. That intervention (which Congress earlier had made a halfhearted and totally unsuccessful effort to restrain in the Clayton Act of 1914[58]) began late in the nineteenth century and continued until stopped by Norris-La Guardia and similar state statutes in the 1930s.[59]

After the criminal sanction had been replaced by the injunction, the courts had continued to act far beyond their range of competency; adjudicating without standards, without principles, and without restraint. And the federal courts frequently had been involved in this abuse of power. The abuse, moreover, extended to the procedures the courts employed and the decrees they issued as well as to the substantive law they developed. Yet there were no institutional reasons for this. Standards of fair procedure and experience with equitable remedies existed, but were simply disregarded. Injunctions often were issued by trial courts, on the basis of affidavits, in *ex parte* proceedings. Indeed, in the 118 labor injunction cases reported in the federal courts from 1901 to 1928, "70 *ex parte* restraining orders were granted without notice to the defendants or opportunity to be heard." [60] And, because unions were weak, it was the trial court's *ex parte* injunction that usually disposed of a case. Decrees were extremely broad and sweeping in scope. The punishment for violation of a decree was fine or imprisonment for contempt; the trial summary and without benefit of jury.

The Norris-La Guardia Act, which removes jurisdiction from the federal courts to grant injunctions in peaceful labor disputes, was a clearcut political response to these abuses. It was a legislative endorsement of the theory of judicial abstention; and understanding of that theory provided some of the impetus for the statute's enactment.[61] Impetus for passage came too from the growing political acceptance of the claims made in the rhetoric of the labor movement: the need for industrial democracy, the importance of the roles performed by interest groups in a democracy, the inequality of bargaining power between the individual worker and his employer. Louis D. Brandeis, testifying before the Commission on Industrial Relations in 1915, sounded a call. The "end for which we must strive," he said, "is the attainment of rule by the people, and that involves industrial democracy as well as political democracy." [62] And the statute itself insists that,

> under prevailing economic conditions, developed with aid of governmental authority for owners of property to organize in the corporate and other forms of ownership association, the individual unorganized worker is commonly helpless to exercise actual liberty of contract and to protect his freedom of labor, and thereby to obtain acceptable terms and conditions of employment.[63]

The faith of Norris-La Guardia is collective bargaining; the method of its attainment is judicial abstention.

The key sections of the Act are 4, 7, and 13(c). Section 4 is a flat prohibition of the issuance by a federal court of an injunction restraining certain enumerated conduct "in any case involving or growing out of a labor dispute." The enumeration is lengthy and it covers the gamut of peaceful union activity—strikes, picketing, and boycotts.

Section 7 in terms applies to any other conduct growing out of a "labor dispute," and requires a federal court to follow civilized procedures and to find specific facts before it is empowered to issue "a temporary or permanent injunction." The required procedures are calculated to eliminate the abuses of the past; the finding of specific facts, to restrict injunctions to cases involving fraud, violence, or destruction of property. And section 13(c) defines "labor dispute" broadly to include "any controversy concerning terms or conditions of employment, or concerning the association or representation of persons in negotiating, fixing, maintaining, changing, or seeking to arrange terms or conditions of employment."

The Norris-La Guardia Act successfully achieved its goal of neutralizing the federal courts. However, it is difficult to know what would have happened to the development of the unions and collective bargaining in the United States if that statute long had continued to represent the government's principal approach to labor policy. Employers still retained many self-help weapons with which to fight the establishment of collective bargaining, if, as often was the case, they desired to do so. They were legally free to refuse to bargain; to fire workers who joined unions; to employ strikebreakers and labor spies; and to resort to most other peaceful means of resistance. Moreover, there had been many examples of employers using resistance methods that were far from peaceful, and many examples of unions engaging in violence too.[64]

The passivity of Norris-La Guardia, however, soon was joined to a policy of active governmental support for collective bargaining. The short-lived National Industrial Recovery Act was the first general (the R.L.A. was special), non-wartime move in this direction. The workers' right to organize and bargain collectively was recognized in the context of a governmentally sponsored program to promote business cartels.[65] N.I.R.A. was followed quickly by the Wagner Act of 1935. That statute, which in its amended form, is the principal source today of collective bargaining law, is a logical governmental response to the theory of legislative action. Impetus for its passage can be traced to the political acceptance of the claims made by the labor movement, most importantly those dealing with inequality of bargaining power and industrial peace. To quote the statute on the latter: "denial by employers of the right of employees to organize and the refusal by employers to accept the procedure of collective bargaining lead to strikes and other forms of industrial strife or unrest, which have the intent or the necessary effect of burdening or obstructing commerce." [66]

The central provision of the Wagner Act, and of today's Labor-Management Relations Act, is section 7. In its contemporary form it reads:

> Employees shall have the right to self-organization, to form, join, or assist labor organizations, to bargain collectively through representatives of their own choosing, and to engage in other concerted activities for the purpose of collective bargaining or other mutual aid or protection, and shall also have the right to refrain from any or all of such activities.

The statute in section 8(a) makes it an unfair labor practice for an employer, among other things, to "interfere with, restrain, or coerce employees in the exercise of the rights guaranteed in section 7"; to dominate a labor organization; to encourage or discourage union membership by job discrimination; and to refuse to bargain collectively with the representative of his employees.

To enforce these employee rights, the statute does not rely upon private suits in courts—understandably suspect in the 1930s—but establishes the National Labor Relations Board.[67] This administrative agency has a general counsel who functions as the statute's chief enforcement officer. He is in charge of the regional offices of the agency, to which private parties can bring complaints, and through which investigations are conducted, settlements arranged, and litigation initiated.[68] The litigation of alleged unfair labor practices is before a trial examiner—an independent and often highly skilled specialist—and the proceeding is similar to what one would find today in a federal trial court.[69] A panel of the Labor Board itself, or the full Board, composed of four members and a chairman, serves as a reviewing tribunal. Its judgments, in turn, are subject to review by the federal courts of appeal; and indeed, violation of a Board decree carries no sanction until enforced by a court.[70]

The 1947 and 1959 amendments designate certain union activities, found by Congress to be objectionable, unfair labor practices. Thus, for example, many secondary boycotts and some organizational picketing are today prohibited. Union unfair labor practices are handled in much the same fashion as are employer unfair practices; that is, initially by an administrative agency.[71] But amendments in 1947 did bring the courts back in a more active role. The statute today requires the agency in some situations to seek a court injunction against a union where there is reasonable cause to believe that the union has committed an unfair labor practice; and, the agency may request injunctive relief in other cases of union or employer unfair practices.[72] Moreover, section 301 now requires federal courts to entertain private suits to enforce the collective bargaining agreement.

In addition to its unfair labor practice jurisdiction, the National Labor Relations Board has another tremendously important function. Section 9 of the statute provides that: "Representatives designated or selected for the purposes of collective bargaining by the majority of the employees in a unit appropriate for such purposes, shall be the exclusive representatives of all the employees in such unit for the purposes of collective bargaining." One of the things this means is that there will be collective bargaining if a majority of employees want it, and one of the ways of determining majority will is through the Labor Board. The Board's tasks, in part, are to determine the "unit appropriate"; to umpire the preelection campaign between the union (or unions) seeking representation and the employer, who frequently strives to keep his establishment unorganized; and to conduct the election itself and determine its outcome. Often these are sensitive and difficult tasks.

The determination of the appropriate "election" unit, of course, may be decisive to the outcome of the election.[73] Moreover, if, as often is the case, this unit becomes the bargaining unit in fact as well as in theory, it may be important to the economic strength of union and employer in future collective bargaining. And finally, it is important to the fair representation of employees; for all employees in the unit are represented by the majority union.[74]

The Board has a number of criteria it employs in determining the appropriate unit. These include: the bargaining history of the parties; bargaining practices, where they exist, in similar establishments; the organizational arrangement of the employer's establishment; the community of interest of the employees and their physical proximity to one another; and the ability and willingness of the union to represent certain employees.[75]

The Board's role in umpiring the election campaign and in running the election requires a nice sense of balance. The goal of the statute is a free and informed choice by the employees. This means that the employer and the union cannot coerce or threaten; but the definition of coersion or threats is often complicated by the varying circumstances and diverse interests which may be at stake. Employer and union freedom of speech is one such interest. Employer control over his property is another.[76]

In the representation area, the Board is much closer, at least in the short run, to being absolute sovereign than in the unfair labor practice area. While there is judicial review of Board determinations, it is limited and often circuitous.[77]

As this sketch of the Labor-Management Relations Act surely makes clear, the statute is complicated. Moreover, the gloss that has been placed upon it through the process of "litigating elucidation" is often difficult to understand. We shall look at many examples in the following chapters, but several points now should be put in view.

First, L.M.R.A. is a federal statute that has displaced most state law,[78] decisional as well as enacted, in the area to which it applies. That area, however, does not include all that falls within the concept of interstate commerce. The statute empowers the Labor Board to limit its jurisdiction to some extent, and this the Board has done.[79] Nevertheless, in the private sector, most important collective bargaining in the United States, not covered by the Railway Labor Act, does fall within the jurisdiction of the National Labor Relations Board.

Second, the statute's most important goals are: to establish a climate within which employees can freely determine whether they wish to collectivize their employment relationship; to provide for free collective bargaining, which means freedom of contract between employer and union; and thereby, to promote industrial peace.

Third, L.M.R.A. does not eliminate the problems that disturbed the judges who decided the conspiracy cases so long ago. The statute rather converts these antique problems into pressing problems of contemporary law and modern life. Consider the problem of collective bargaining's interference with an employer managing as he thinks best. Far from resolving this problem, the statute presents it in wonderfully sophisticated form, involving questions of the subject matter of collective bargaining and the role of governmental decision-making. Consider the problem of the dissenting employee and collective bargaining. Surely this becomes of urgent concern under a statute that makes the union of the majority the representative of all. And finally, consider the problems of union political and economic power and the consequences of the exercise of that power. The Wagner Act put government behind the unions at least to the extent that it made collective bargaining legitimate. This was a great helping hand to union growth, and resulted in a vast increase in union political and economic power. How that power is to be exercised is a major problem for modern law.

It is the aim of this book in the following chapters to examine many of the ramifications of these modern problems of ancient lineage, and to inquire into the utility of law and of legal institutions in attempting to solve them.

Part II

Management Rights and Union Participation

Chapter 2

Collective Bargaining and Freedom of Contract

Collective bargaining law, while dedicated to the concept of private ordering, imposes numerous restrictions upon the freedom of the contracting parties in order to protect directly affected third parties. Thus, for example, out of concern for job applicants, the law prohibits closed shop agreements; to shield from injury employers who are not parties to the agreement, it makes it illegal for the parties to negotiate "hot cargo" contracts—contracts designed to further the interests of employees who are not in the bargaining unit.[1] In the commercial area similar restrictions exist: antitrust and antidiscrimination laws, among many others, cut back upon freedom of contract. But collective bargaining law does more.

The theoretical freedom to deal with whom he pleases is a freedom lost to the employer once workers organize. Negotiation must be with the union alone; alternatives generally are illegal.[2] Unionization, and the law that supports it, in this way restrict management's right to manage. The logic of the restriction, however, is compelling. If a recalcitrant employer were free to contract with whom he pleased, and strong enough to get away with it, he could subvert collective bargaining by playing worker off against worker, union against union. This would render nugatory the Labor-Management Relations Act's election procedures, and invite industrial conflict. It would return to the strong employer the power to dictate the contract of employment, and it would once again stir public concern with contractual fairness and with governmental reliance on freedom of contract. Results so plainly inconsistent with the goals of the statute cannot be tolerated.[3]

However, the fact that the employer (and the union too) is locked into a relationship does not mean that freedom of contract should be abandoned and something else substituted. The parties still generally are wiser about their own affairs than government, and the cost of substituting governmental for private decision-making remains very great.

If the Labor-Management Relations Act went no further than to aid workers to establish collective bargaining, there would be no important contemporary issue of management's right to manage. That right is reduced to the extent that the employer's freedom to deal with whom he pleases is interdicted, but such reduction is necessary. The statute, however, goes beyond. It places upon the employer the legal duty to bargain in good faith with the union over wages, hours, and other terms and conditions of employment; refusal to do so is an unfair labor practice.[4] Moreover, the statute makes the collective bargaining agreement a contract enforceable in the courts.[5]

For the employer this legal duty to bargain and the enforceability of the contract must raise several questions concerning his right to manage as he thinks best. First, what does good faith mean? As a practical matter does it require the employer to act toward the union in a fashion that some Washington bureaucrat (Labor Board official) thinks reasonable? If so, it may be impossible to include within a collective agreement those seemingly unreasonable views that the employer considers not only reasonable, but, indeed, vital to the economic health of his enterprise.

Second, what do terms and conditions of employment mean? Does that bureaucrat in Washington or a court in Oshkosh decide? Suppose the governmental decision-maker concludes—because of the relationship of wages to prices—that the employer must bargain in good faith with the union about the company's pricing policies. This surely would be an intrusion upon traditional management prerogatives, upon an employer's right to run his business as he thinks best. Moreover, it would be such an intrusion even if good faith did not require the employer to act reasonably. To force the employer to bargain about a subject at all is to limit his freedom of action. The scope of the duty to bargain may significantly shape the collective agreement and its substantive terms.

Finally, the judicial power to enforce collective bargaining agreements inevitably carries with it the power to construe contractual language. This is, of course, always the situation with contract enforcement, but because of the nature of collective agreements, their flexibility and ongoing character, the judicial role may prove particularly intrusive. That court in Oshkosh may make the employer act in a way its judge thinks reasonable even if the employer believes he agreed to something very different. In this way the court may play a part in the writing of contractual terms and thereby interfere with the employer's right to manage as he thinks best.

Observe that in each case the union could be substituted for the employer. The Labor-Management Relations Act places on the union the same duty to bargain that it places on the employer,[6] and a union too can become a defendant in a contract enforcement case. Thus, if the law were to be so interpreted, the union might find that it is precluded from taking bargaining positions which the Washington bureaucrat thinks unreasonable; that it has to bargain about its internal affairs because of their relationship to plant efficiency; that it is at the mercy of the judge in Oshkosh.

What this suggests, then, is that in one very real sense the old issue of the employer's right to manage has in contemporary law evolved into an issue of private versus public decision-making; public decision-making that in a given case may seem to a party to be "pro-union" or to be "pro-employer." This can be stated in another and per- haps more illuminating way: the real issue today is the extent of reliance that labor policy places upon freedom of contract—freedom, that is, of collective contract.

Since the national policy toward labor-management relations—its myth and its reality—does have as one of its important goals the maximization of freedom of col- lective contract (the goal is enshrined in legislation; and it is what is meant by "free collective bargaining," a con- cept to which labor, management, and government regu- larly proclaim fidelity), it is appropriate to ask why the statute created a duty to bargain and made the contract enforceable in the first place. For the existence of the duty and the enforceability of the contract may make it more difficult to achieve the desired freedom. It is also appro- priate to inquire whether the statutory duty to bargain and the right to sue have been elaborated by the Labor Board and courts in a way that is as consistent as possible with the goal of freedom of contract, given other goals of the statute, such as industrial peace.

THE DUTY TO BARGAIN IN GOOD FAITH

Once a majority of employees in an "appropriate" unit choose to collectivize their employment relationship, the employer has a duty to bargain with the union of his em- ployees' choice, and that union has a duty to bargain with the employer. The Labor-Management Relations Act in section 8(d) tells us something, but unhappily little, about this duty. It provides that:

> to bargain collectively is the performance of the mu- tual obligation of the employer and the representative of the employees to meet at reasonable times and con ter in good faith with respect to wages, hours, and

other terms and conditions of employment, or the negotiation of an agreement, or any question arising thereunder, and the execution of a written contract incorporating any agreement reached if requested by either party, but such obligation does not compel either party to agree to a proposal or require the making of a concession.

With "respect to wages, hours, and other terms and conditions of employment," the employer can no longer act unilaterally or bargain individually without violating the statute. He must meet with the appropriate union officials and attempt to hammer out a mutually acceptable collective agreement.[7] Bargaining demands and methods vary, but it is common for union officials to come forward with proposals—often written—concerning a range of subjects including wage rates, hours of work, provisions regarding seniority, holidays, union security, grievance procedures and arbitration, perhaps pension and welfare plans, merit wage increases, severance pay, supplementary unemployment benefits, and so forth. In the stock situation, meetings are arranged, proposals discussed, counterproposals made, positions clarified and often modified, some requests dropped, others perhaps added. And in the background is the ever present possibility that failure to reach agreement may lead to a strike on the one hand, or to the employer continuing his present practices on the other. The employer at some point may lock out; but this is rare. He may, if bargaining breaks down after good faith efforts on his part (that is, if a bargaining impasse is reached), unilaterally put into effect the terms he has offered the union. For the one thing that is clear from the language of the statute and its ambivalent legislative history is that the duty to bargain is not a duty to agree. Agreement is the hope of the statute, not its requirement, and the principal behavioral premise supporting this hope is simply that the parties will try to avoid the unpleasant economic consequences of failure.

Much less clear, however, are the reason or reasons for Congress having included in the statute a legal duty to bargain.[8] Why isn't the possibility of a strike or the use of other private economic sanctions enough of a guaranty that there will be collective bargaining, even as it seems to have been thought enough assurance that there would be agreement? Part of the answer to this question may be found in legislative history. A Senate report advised:

> It seems clear that a guarantee of the right of employees to bargain collectively through representatives of their own choosing is a mere delusion if it is not accompanied by the correlative duty on the part of the other party to recognize such representatives as have been designated . . . and to negotiate with them in a bona fide effort to arrive at a collective bargaining agreement. Furthermore, the procedure of holding governmentally supervised elections to determine the choice of representatives of employees becomes of little worth if after the election its results are for all practical purposes ignored. Experience has proved that neither obedience to the law nor respect for law is encouraged by holding forth a right unaccompanied by fulfillment. Such a course provokes constant strife, not peace.[9]

But surely one is entitled to ask why the logic of this position does not extend to placing on the employer a duty to agree? The answer comes in two parts. First, the potential loss of meaningful freedom of contract would be far greater if agreement as distinguished from good faith bargaining were a legal obligation. In order to make a duty to agree workable, the Labor Board would have to pass upon the reasonableness of proposals made and rejected, and in the absence of agreement would have to impose upon the parties its judgments of what would be fair. What other content could a duty to agree possibly have?

Second, the chance of agreement is itself often advanced by requiring good faith bargaining. Discussion is likely to disclose the parties' true positions, while the art of persuasion, when given a chance, may lead to an accommodation of seemingly irreconcilable views. In other words, the duty to bargain, as well as the economic consequences of a failure to agree, sustain the hope that the parties will reach agreement and reach it peacefully. In a 1902 report to Congress, the Industrial Commission expressed the faith this way:

> The chief advantage which comes from the practice of periodically determining the conditions of labor by collective bargaining directly between employers and employees is, that thereby each side obtains a better understanding of the actual state of the industry, of the conditions which confront the other side, and of the motives which influence it. Most strikes and lockouts would not occur if each party understood exactly the position of the other.[10]

This analysis of the absence of a statutory duty to agree suggests two reasons for a statutory duty to bargain. Both reasons find support in the purposes of the Labor-Management Relations Act. A legal duty to bargain may be seen as supportive of the statutory structure that assists employees wishing to collectivize their employment relationship. In the absence of a requirement of good faith negotiation, collective bargaining may never occur. The employer may unilaterally impose the terms and conditions of employment. The statutory scheme of protecting organization from unfair practices and of allowing employee choice between union and no union in such a situation would be frustrated.

The duty to bargain also may be seen as having an independent function. If a union and an employer are required to explain fully their respective positions, to listen carefully to reasoned arguments, and to pursue the quest for agreement with true sincerity, the chance for agreement without warfare may be enhanced.[11]

The extent to which a legal duty to bargain will tend to undercut the statute's freedom of contract goal depends upon whether the supportive or independent function of the duty is emphasized by the tribunals charged with its elaboration. The greater the emphasis on the independent function the greater will be the concern with industrial peace; and the greater the concern with industrial peace the greater will be the role of the government tribunal.

The quest for industrial peace reflected in the concept of an independent duty to bargain demands of the parties that their negotiations be conducted in a proper fashion. The Labor Board may insist that the parties explain their respective positions, listen to reasoned arguments, and pursue the search for agreement with sincerity and earnestness. And it may be quite difficult for the union or the employer that acts in a seemingly unreasonable manner or makes seemingly unreasonable demands to persuade the Board or a court that it has negotiated in this proper fashion. The pressure on the parties, therefore, is toward reasonable behavior; the tendency on the part of the Labor Board is to expect reasonable behavior. This could mean, as Russell Smith once suggested, that the duty to bargain would require "the making of objectively reasonable proposals," [12] and the employment of objectively reasonable negotiating procedures and practices. It would be the government that decided, through the Labor Board and the courts, what were and were not reasonable proposals, procedures, and practices.

A general requirement that bargaining conform to objectively reasonable criteria would make, of course, a substantial inroad on the statute's goal of freedom of contract. We have seen that the erosion of the common law doctrine of freedom of contract is justified—indeed required—when the doctrine, as applied to a class of contracts, cannot be counted upon to produce generally fair results between the parties. This is not an important problem here because of the supportive duty and the statutory provisions it supports. The claim is rather that the goal of industrial peace demands the subordination of freedom of contract. Apart from whether peace is worth the loss of freedom—both, after all, are statutory goals—the claim depends upon the validity of a simple insight concerning human relations and industrial peace. But it is questionable whether one can assert with assurance that substantial progress toward agreement without warfare will be made by requiring employers and labor organizations to behave toward one another in a fashion deemed reasonable by the government.

This is particularly true in the bargaining situation because of the difficulty of an outsider giving acceptable content to a requirement of reasonableness. The substantive problems the parties face, their habits, customs, and temperaments may resist the generalized solutions that a reasonableness standard necessarily imposes. And there is very little hope of any enduring peace if the requirements imposed upon the parties fail substantially to meet their particular needs.

This is not to say, however, that the insights into human behavior underlying the claims of an independent duty to bargain are without merit; their utility in shaping legal doctrine simply is limited. This has been realized, and probably has been a factor in the nature of decisional law that has given definition to the statutory duty to bargain.[13]

The decisional law has been concerned with the requirement that collective bargaining be conducted in "good faith." [14] "Good faith" could have easily become a requirement that the parties make "objectively reasonable proposals" and employ "objectively reasonable practices and procedures," [15] since a good faith state of mind, or the lack of it, must be inferred from the acts of the parties. That this has not happened in any substantial measure is traceable to generally wise judicial review, and particularly to the wisdom in decision and expression of the Supreme Court.

The expression has set a mood, a mood reflected perhaps in these quotations:

> The Act does not fix and does not authorize anyone to fix generally applicable standards for working conditions.[16]

> The Board may not, either directly or indirectly, compel concessions or otherwise sit in judgment upon the substantive terms of collective bargaining agreements.[17]

> It must be realized that collective bargaining, under a system where the Government does not attempt to control the results of negotiations, cannot be equated with an academic collective search for truth—or even with what might be thought to be the ideal of one. The parties—even granting the modification of views that may come from a realization of economic interdependence—still proceed from contrary and to an extent antagonistic viewpoints and concepts of self-interest. The system has not reached the ideal of the philosophic notion that perfect understanding among people would lead to perfect agreement among them on values.[18]

This mood supports what may well be the best statement of approach to the duty to bargain. The statute is violated, Judge Magruder tells us, when one of the parties bargains in a fashion that discloses "a desire not to reach an agreement." Of course,

> if the board is not to be blinded by empty talk and by the mere surface motions of collective bargaining, it must take some cognizance of the reasonableness of the positions taken . . . in the course of bargaining negotiations. . . . Thus if an employer can find nothing whatever to agree to in an ordinary current-day contract submitted to him, or in some of the union's related minor requests, and if the employer makes not a single serious proposal meeting the union at least part way, then certainly the Board must be able to conclude that this is at least some evidence of bad faith.[19]

Judge Magruder's formulations are an approach reflecting a mood rather than a definition, and represent a happy blending of the supportive and independent functions of a duty to bargain. That the reasonableness of proposals, practices, and procedures is not to be ignored by the Labor Board is patent. But the approach surely is gentle to freedom of contract. An employer or union can be unreasonable without violating the statute. By and large only the party bargaining with a desire not to reach agreement is guilty of an unfair practice. From time to time concern with freedom of contract allows even such a wrongdoer to escape without sanction.[20]

With Judge Magruder's approach as a touchstone, we may turn to one of the liveliest problems in this area of law: the application of the duty to union and employer bargaining practices. This is an excellent area for testing the wisdom of the enforcing tribunal in accommodating freedom of contract values and the claims of an independent duty, serving directly the goal of industrial peace.

Three aspects of the problem are of special interest. First, the technique of bargaining employed by one party or the other; second, the extent to which an employer must give information to a union in order to facilitate bargaining; and third, the relationship between economic pressure and the good faith obligation.

First: The General Electric Company, said the Labor Board, negotiated with the unions representing its employees in the following, perhaps unique, way:

> As the record in the case reflects, Respondent regards itself as a sort of administrative body which has the unilateral responsibility for determining wages and working conditions for employees, and it regards the union's role as merely that of a kind of advisor for an interested group—the employees. Thus, according to its professed philosophy of "bargaining," Respondent on the basis of its own research and evaluation of union demands, determines what is "right" for its employees, and then makes a "fair and firm offer" to the union without holding anything back for later trading or compromising. It professes a willingness to make prompt adjustments in its offer, but only if new information or a change in facts indicates that its initial offer is no longer "right." It believes that if its research has been done properly there will be no need to change its offer unless something entirely unforeseen has developed in the meantime.[21]

The *General Electric* case itself is enormously complex. There was considerable additional evidence in the record, relied on by the Board, to suggest a lack of good faith on G.E.'s part. On the other hand, it is less than clear that the Board in the portion of its opinion quoted above described accurately G.E.'s technique of bargaining. But if it is accurate, it seems fair to characterize G.E.'s practice of collective bargaining as the Board majority did. "Respondent's 'bargaining' position is akin to that of a party who enters into 'negotiations' with a predetermined resolve not to budge from an initial position." This should be a violation of the duty to bargain, for very little damage to freedom of contract is worked by incorporating into the statute that portion of the faith of an independent duty which insists that the art of persuasion, when given a chance, may lead to an accommodation of seemingly irreconcilable views.

Second: Certain information in the possession of an employer must be produced if requested by the union, for without that information collective bargaining would not be possible. Thus, a union hardly can bargain about wages if it has no information about existing wage structures.[22] In the *Truitt* case, where the employer claimed that he could not afford to grant more than a token wage increase, the Supreme Court affirmed a holding of the Labor Board: "It is settled law," said the Board, "that when an employer seeks to justify the refusal of a wage increase upon an economic basis, . . . good-faith bargaining under the Act requires that upon request the employer attempt to substantiate its economic position by reasonable proof." [23]

Bargaining about wages surely can proceed, and often does proceed, without the union having information concerning the financial position of the employer. The case, therefore, cannot be equated to one in which there is a demand for information about existing wage rates. Nor did the totality of evidence suggest employer bad faith. But the decision seems correct when tested by the purposes of a duty to bargain. By claiming poverty, the employer made his financial position a relevant issue. He did it, not the Labor Board. In such a case, the directions of an independent duty to bargain can be followed without eroding freedom of contract values.[24]

Third: During otherwise good faith contract negotiations between the Prudential Insurance Company and the

Insurance Agents' International Union, the union had its members participate "in a 'Work Without a Contract' program—which meant that they would engage in certain planned, concerted on-the-job activities designed to harass the company." For example, union members refused "for a time to solicit new business," "to comply with the company's reporting procedures," and to participate in a company business campaign. The agents reported late for work, distributed leaflets, and appealed to policyholders to support their cause. In short, union member-agents engaged in a partial strike, the equivalent of a slowdown or intermittent work stoppage in an industrial establishment. Prudential complained that this constituted a refusal to bargain, and the Labor Board sustained the company's position. In effect, the Board held that the union's work without a contract program was per se a violation of the union's statutory duty to bargain. The union's program, the Board asserted, was not consistent with reasonable bargaining practices or procedures. "Reliance upon harassing tactics during the course of negotiations for the avowed purpose of compelling the Company to capitulate to its terms," the Board contended, "is the antithesis of reasoned discussion . . . [required by the statute]." [25] Such tactics, the Board claimed, are not "traditional" or "normal." Indeed, they are subject to the public's moral condemnation.

The Supreme Court would have none of this.

> We think the Board's approach involves an intrusion into the substantive aspects of the bargaining process. . . . If the Board could regulate the choice of economic weapons that may be used as part of collective bargaining, it would be in a position to exercise considerable influence upon the substantive terms on which the parties contract. As the parties' own devices became more limited, the Government might have to enter even more directly into the negotiation of collec-

tive agreements. Our labor policy is not presently erected on a foundation of government control of the results of negotiations.[26]

The *Insurance Agents'* case and this statement are perhaps the high water mark for freedom of contract in modern labor-management relations.

THE SCOPE OF THE DUTY TO BARGAIN

The preceding section has been concerned to examine the content of the duty to bargain and to analyze the reasons for the tension with freedom of contract that the existence of a legal duty inescapably must produce. The scope of the duty to bargain, in terms of the subject matter to which it applies, invites a similar examination and analysis. Freedom of contract values are no less importantly at stake. Administrative and judicial sensitivity, however, will here be found blunted. The result is far from happy and is urgently in need of repair.

To understand the present state of law in this area, it is helpful to attend to a hypothetical situation drawn from several actual cases. Consider the situation where an employer and a union each approaches the bargaining table with a sincere desire to reach agreement. The parties negotiate in good faith about such things as wages, shift differentials, seniority, and holidays. They also negotiate in good faith about a clause proposed by the employer giving him unilateral control over the subject of promotions. The employer insists upon such control and grounds his position on considerations of efficiency; but he listens carefully to the contrary arguments of the union and responds to them. In the end no agreement on this subject can be reached. The union's final position is that all terms and conditions of employment including promotions must by law be subject to joint union-management control unless both parties otherwise agree.

The employer also proposes to the union a clause providing that before the union may call a strike over any issue that might arise in the future, it will take a secret ballot among all employees in the unit on the company's last offer, and in the event a majority of employees reject the company's last offer, the company will have an opportunity, within 72 hours, of making a new proposal and having a vote on it prior to any strike. The union refuses to bargain at all over this ballot clause, insisting that it relates to the internal affairs of the union, a subject that it claims is none of the employer's business. Each time the employer mentions the ballot clause the union representative takes this position. The employer, however, insists that such a provision, or one like it, is essential if there is to be agreement, and continues to demand that the union bargain about its inclusion in the contract.

For its part, the union proposes that the parties negotiate a contract provision concerning pensions for employees. On this subject the employer flatly refuses to bargain, assuming a stance similar to the union's on the ballot clause. The employer's position is that pensions are solely the concern of management and not at all a subject for collective bargaining.

When no agreement can be reached because of the several difficulties, the parties turn to the Labor Board, each asserting that the other has violated its bargaining obligation contained in section 8(d) of the Labor-Management Relations Act. That section, it will be recalled, requires employer and union to bargain in good faith "with respect to wages, hours, and other terms and conditions of employment." Failure to do so is an unfair labor practice.

One can with considerable confidence predict the outcomes in the hypothetical case. First, pensions are a "term and condition of employment" within the meaning of section 8(d). They are, therefore, a mandatory subject of bargaining. During contract negotiations, both parties have a legal duty to bargain in good faith about any mandatory subject raised by one of the parties to the negotiation. The employer thus committed an unfair labor practice.[27]

Second, the ballot clause is not a "term and condition of employment" within the meaning of section 8(d). The Supreme Court has so held. Nor is it an illegal term in that it is interdicted by statute or in some other way contrary to public policy. Accordingly, the ballot clause is what has come to be known as a non-mandatory or permissive subject of bargaining. During contract negotiations the parties, if both agree, may bargain about a non-mandatory subject, but neither party has a legal duty to bargain at all about such a subject. Moreover, and more significantly, it is itself an unfair labor practice for one party to insist upon bargaining about such a subject. Thus, the employer violated the statute when he stubbornly demanded that the union negotiate regarding the inclusion of such a clause in the collective contract.[28]

Finally, there was good faith bargaining about promotions, admittedly a mandatory subject of bargaining. The union's contention that all mandatory subjects must be under joint control is without merit. The employer or the union has every right to bargain hard—but always in good faith—for unilateral or sole control over a mandatory subject. Thus, for example, the employer could bargain for unilateral control of discharges, merit wage increases, or bonuses. By bargaining in good faith for unilateral control over promotions, the employer did not commit an unfair labor practice.[29]

Although the Labor Board at one time took a contrary position, there can be no doubt that this last rule, drawn from the Supreme Court's decision in the *American National Insurance* case, is correct when tested by statutory purpose, and wise when measured against industrial realities. For the Board and the courts to have required joint control of mandatory subjects would have shaped the substantive terms of collective contracts in cases where the employer otherwise would have insisted successfully upon unilateral control.[30] Nor would much progress have been made in the quest for industrial peace, for hard bargaining with possible economic disruption would have centered upon the terms of joint control. In such bargaining the employer would have striven to regain the substance without the appearance of unilateral control.

Moreover, a requirement of joint control unless both parties agreed to the contrary would, as applied to specific subject matter, be unwise for many industries. Management should have an opportunity, if it thinks it important enough, to insist on unilateral control at the potential cost of economic disruption. Its sights are on the particular problems of a particular industry, and on those problems as they manifest themselves in a particular enterprise. This microscopic view is likely to be far keener than the sweeping vision of the Labor Board and federal courts.

Much less clearly correct or undeniably wise, however, are the rules respecting mandatory and non-mandatory bargaining subjects. There is no escaping the question why a company's promotion policy is a "term and condition of employment" while a ballot clause is not.[31] The principal authoritative sources of illumination are two Supreme Court decisions. Let us see how much candlepower they generate.

The *Borg-Warner* case presented the Court with the ballot clause of our hypothetical case; and the Court reasoned that it was not a mandatory subject of bargaining because: "It relates only to the procedure to be followed by the employees among themselves before their representative may call a strike or refuse a final offer." [32] But this hardly is conclusive. The ballot clause must be taken in context. It is part of the total procedure to be followed in future labor-management negotiation. Grievance and arbitration provisions which deal with the procedure for resolving disputes over contract interpretation are clearly mandatory subjects. They do not become partially non-mandatory if they contain language relating "to the procedure to be followed by the employees among themselves."

More to the point perhaps is the Court's conclusion that the ballot clause "substantially modifies the collective-bargaining system provided for in the statute by weakening the independence of the 'representative' chosen by the employees. It enables the employer, in effect, to deal with its employees rather than with their statutory representative." [33] For this special reason, there may be some merit in the Court's holding that a ballot clause is a non-mandatory bargaining subject, although even given this special reason the decision seems doubtful, as Mr. Justice Harlan urged in dissent.

> Since a "no-strike" clause is something about which an employer can concededly bargain to the point of insistence . . . I find it difficult to understand even under the Court's analysis of this problem why the "ballot" clause should not be considered within the area of bargaining described in section 8(d). It affects the employer-employee relationship in much the same way, in that it may determine the timing of strikes or even whether a strike will occur by requiring a vote to ascertain the employees' sentiment prior to the union's decision.[34]

What is important, however, is not the rightness or wrongness of the specific holding in the case, but the fact that the majority opinion offers no general guidance whatever for distinguishing between mandatory and non-mandatory bargaining subjects when the employer is not attempting through contract to establish a procedure for future bargaining directly with employees.

The *Fibreboard* case is the second of the Supreme Court decisions.[35] It involves one aspect of the seemingly ubiquitous problem of subcontracting, or, as it is often called, contracting out. Many companies must decide at various times whether certain jobs can be performed better or more economically by their own employees or by workers of another employer. When faced with this issue, the Fibreboard Paper Products Company reached a decision without consulting its employees' union. It had a study made, the results of which indicated that it would be financially advantageous for it to contract out the maintenance work its own employees had been performing. It thereupon made arrangements with an outside firm that agreed to send its employees to Fibreboard's premises to do the job. The result for Fibreboard's displaced workers was a termination of their employment with the company.

The displaced workers went to the Labor Board insisting that the decision whether to contract out was a mandatory bargaining subject, and that Fibreboard, therefore, had violated its statutory duty by presenting the union with its settled decision on the subject. Fibreboard's obligation, the union contended, was to bargain in good faith with it before reaching any decision. The Company's claim was that contracting out was a non-mandatory subject to which the duty to bargain did not attach. Thus was the issue joined.

The state of decisional law at the time left the issue tendered substantially in doubt. Prior cases suggested that the employer did have a duty to bargain about the consequences of his decision to the affected employees, but whether the decision to contract out the mantenance work was itself a mandatory bargaining subject had been obfuscated by seemingly inconsistent Board opinions. In the case itself, the Board first held for Fibreboard and then changed its collective mind on rehearing.[36] And while the Supreme Court was able to agree unanimously with the

Board's ultimate disposition, Mr. Justice Stewart's concurring opinion suggests it is unlikely that unanimity exists in the high tribunal over the larger problems in the case.

The Chief Justice wrote for the Court. His opinion offers three intertwined reasons to support the ultimate holding against the employer. First, the "subject matter of the present dispute is well within the literal meaning of the phrase 'terms and conditions of employment.'" Second, one

> of the primary purposes of the Act is to promote the peaceful settlement of industrial disputes by subjecting labor-management controversies to the mediatory influence of negotiation. The Act was framed with an awareness that refusals to confer and negotiate had been one of the most prolific causes of industrial strife. . . . To hold, as the Board has done, that contracting out is a mandatory subject of collective bargaining would promote the fundamental purpose of the Act by bringing a problem of vital concern to labor and management within the framework established by Congress as most conducive to industrial peace.

Finally, the Chief Justice suggested that the "conclusion that 'contracting out' is a statutory subject of collective bargaining is further reinforced by industrial practices in this country. While not determinative, it is appropriate to look to industrial bargaining practices in appraising the propriety of including a particular subject within the scope of mandatory bargaining." [37]

Joined to these reasons is a seeming disclaimer of their implications. The Chief Justice insists that the holding is limited to "the facts of this case." But if the reasons supporting the holding are the true grounds of decision—as surely they must be—it is difficult to understand why most subjects that meet the Chief Justice's industrial practice test would not be classified as mandatory. Most subjects that are likely to be raised during collective bargaining can be brought within the literal language of the statute; and the industrial peace rationale applies across the board.

A similar estimate of the majority opinion moved Mr. Justice Stewart to write his concurrence. "Viewed broadly, the question before us stirs large issues," said the Justice. "The Court purports to limit its decision to the 'facts of this case.' But the Court's opinion radiates implications of such disturbing breadth that I am persuaded to file this separate statement of my own view." [38]

The Justice tells us what these large issues are in the concluding paragraph of his opinion: "I am fully aware that in this era of automation and onrushing technological change, no problems in the domestic economy are of greater concern than those involving job security and employment stability." [39] It is perfectly clear that the issues unions try to resolve through collective bargaining reflect the changing nature of technology. And there are a number of ways of describing the issues that modern technology has brought to the bargaining table. One may talk, for example, of job security, efficiency, automation, or manpower utilization. And it is also clear as Secretary Wirtz has told us—without suggesting anything about the legal duty to bargain—that "technological developments have placed severe new strains on collective bargaining. It is one thing to bargain about terms and conditions of employment, and quite another to bargain about the terms of unemployment, about the conditions on which men are to yield their jobs to machines." [40] But Mr. Justice Stewart goes on to insist:

It is possible that in meeting these problems Congress may eventually decide to give organized labor or government a far heavier hand in controlling what until now have been considered the prerogatives of private business management. That path would mark a sharp departure from the traditional principles of a free enterprise economy. Whether we should follow it is, within constitutional limitations, for Congress to choose. But it is a path which Congress certainly did not choose when it enacted the Taft-Hartley Act.[41]

What the Justice here has in mind is far from clear. He speaks as if the duty to bargain about the subjects presented by the new technology meant the end of a free enterprise economy. This might be argued, although it would be dubious indeed, if the duty to bargain were a duty to agree to a sharing of control with the union. But, of course, the duty to bargain is not a duty to agree to anything. Nor, under *American National Insurance,* does it prevent the employer from bargaining for unilateral control of any mandatory subject.

At any rate, Mr. Justice Stewart reads legislative history as requiring the Labor Board and the courts to interpret "terms and conditions of employment" narrowly. His opinion, however, fails to make the case. We are told: "It is important to note that the words of the statute are words of limitation. The National Labor Relations Act does not say that the employer and employees are bound to confer upon any subject which interests either of them; the specification of wages, hours, and other terms and conditions of employment defines a limited category of issues subject to compulsory bargaining." [42] This is inescapably so, but it cannot mean that the words are to be read in a begrudgingly narrow fashion. Nor does it mean that they should be read broadly. The observation that these are words of limitation simply fails to advance the inquiry. The concurring opinion, however, goes on:

The limiting purpose of the statute's language is made clear by the legislative history of the present Act. As originally passed, the Wagner Act contained no definition of the duty to bargain collectively. In the 1947 revision of the Act, the House bill contained a detailed but limited list of subjects of the duty to bargain, excluding all others. In conference the present language was substituted for the House's detailed specification. While the language thus incorporated in the 1947 legislation as enacted is not so stringent as that contained in the House bill, it nonetheless adopts the same basic approach in seeking to define a limited class of bargainable issues.[43]

But the House bill did not pass. Its ultimate rejection perhaps does not mean that the enacted statute rejects "the same basic approach in seeking to define a limited class of bargainable issues." But with all respect, it also surely does not mean that the statute "adopts the same basic approach in seeking to define a limited class of bargainable issues." Realistically, what the statute does is delegate the task of giving content to the open-ended words "terms and conditions of employment" to the Labor Board and the courts. The guidelines for the correct discharge of this delegation will not be found by close attention to bits and pieces of particular legislative history. The guidelines rather must be found in the larger purposes and goals of the statute and the relationship of a duty to bargain to those goals.

This search for guidelines may profit from attending to the effects of the present decisional law, and from inquiry into how far those effects depart from the goals of the statute. What is at stake for labor and management, collective bargaining as an institution, and the integrity of the legal process?

To begin, consider specifically what a decision one way

or the other in *Fibreboard* means. The actual holding in *Fibreboard* means, of course, that the parties must bargain in good faith about contracting out of the sort which occurred in that case. This means that the employer cannot take unilateral action prior to bargaining. It does not mean, however, that the parties must agree; and if they connot agree, the employer may act unilaterally. Moreover, and this is the teaching of *American National Insurance,* the employer has a perfect right to bargain in good faith for unilateral control of future contracting out, should the need arise. And of utmost importance is the fact that the full panoply of legitimate economic force— force not otherwise prohibited by law—is available to both parties.

If *Fibreboard* had held that contracting out was a non-mandatory subject, there would be no duty to bargain in good faith. The employer would be free to act unilaterally. He would be free to act without notice. Moreover, it would seem that under *Borg-Warner* the union could not legally strike in an attempt to block the employer's decision. The union is barred from insisting that the employer bargain over a non-mandatory subject, and the use of economic force is the most sincere method of insisting available to a labor organization.

Naturally enough employers are unhappy with *Fibreboard*. It is with respect to contracting out, plant relocation, the introduction of new machinery, work rules, and similar subjects affecting the job security of employees in the bargaining unit and the efficiency of plant operations that one most often hears today the claim from employers that management's right to manage is being infringed.[44] Clearly employers would like to make decisions without facing a strike, and the *Borg-Warner* rule in part fulfills this desire once a subject is designated non-mandatory. The fulfillment is only partial, both because the illegality of a strike is only a partial deterrent to a strike,[45] and because some of the consequences of these kinds of management decisions—such as whether workers shall have severance pay when employment is terminated—have traditionally been considered mandatory, and therefore subject to strike.[46]

Quite apart from strikes, employers would be pleased not to have to bargain over these kinds of decisions. Sometimes the employer may have to act quickly if he is to act at all, for a business opportunity will not always wait, and economic survival may depend upon quick action. If the employer has to bargain with the union first, it may be too late, even if the employer ultimately gets his way after hard, good faith negotiation to impasse; that is, to a point of no agreement, at which point unilateral action is permissible.[47] But the case of the true economic emergency probably is rare. Where it exists truly, it is entirely consistent with general law and with the administration of the Labor-Management Relations Act in other areas[48] to allow the employer to act first and bargain about the consequences later.

The general problem of unilateral action, of when an employer is freed from his obligation of dealing with the union, however, is aggravated by the difficulty under existing law of determining when an impasse in fact has been reached. One commentator has gone so far as to insist that: "In practice, it is impossible to find any workable criteria which will indicate to the employer how long negotiations must go on before the NLRB will find that an impasse has occurred. The question is further complicated by the fact that an impasse, having arisen, may be 'broken' at any time by a change in circumstances." [49]

There is an additional complication for the employer that should now be noted. Our focus has been upon the duty to bargain at the end of a contract period, when the existing collective agreement runs out and a new agreement must be negotiated. But the employer may desire to contract out work or automate his plant during the term of a collective agreement, and doubt exists under the law as to the employer's right to take unilateral action with respect to a mandatory subject during the term of a collective contract. It would seem that the employer must bargain unless the contract relieves him of the obligation either by giving him unilateral control over the subject, or—at least in some situations—providing for arbitration of the subject as an alternative procedure to collective bargaining. It is very far from clear, however, what language in the contract will accomplish either of these results.[50]

Both at the end of the contract and during its term, it may be costly for the employer to take unilateral action when his duty is to bargain collectively. The Board may order him to undo what he has done and return to the *status quo ante.* Thus, in *Fibreboard,* the employer had to cancel his subcontracting arrangement and reinstate the discharged maintenance employees with back pay.

The lack of clarity in the law, as to the impasse rule and the rule respecting the duty to bargain during a contract term, exerts on employers pressure to bargain and to postpone making business decisions that is plainly improper under the statute. It is pressure resulting from the poor administration of difficult problems, not from the theoretical purposes of the legislation. Poor administration is susceptible to workmanlike repair. The Labor Board by now should have a sufficient body of experience in both of these areas to enable it to clarify its standards.

No amount of administrative improvement, however, can remove one of the sources of employer unhappiness. The obligation to bargain over a subject, quite apart from any obligation to agree, may result in an agreement that is a compromise of the employer's original position. There might be fewer private pension plans today, for example, if the Labor Board and the courts had not held that pensions were a mandatory bargaining subject.[51]

Unions, of course, are happy with decisions of the

Fibreboard sort because the union generally is the party trying to expand the scope of collective bargaining. *Borg-Warner*, the ballot clause case, is the exception to the rule. However, when the Labor Board and the courts designate as non-mandatory a subject about which the union would like to bargain, joy turns to tears. There are a number of such situations. The Board, for example, has not given the decision in *Fibreboard* an expansive reading,[52] and the Supreme Court seems to have suggested that an employer's decision to go out of business is a non-mandatory subject. In a considered statement—but not in a case involving the scope of the duty to bargain as such—the Court observed that "when an employer closes his entire business, even if the liquidation is motivated by vindictiveness toward the union, such action is not an unfair labor practice." [53]

What should be clear in all of this is that the totality of effects which stems from the mandatory—non-mandatory distinction makes law much too important in terms of the statutory goal of freedom of contract. The legal rules condition the substantive content of agreements, and influence the direction and growth of collective bargaining as an institution. This intrusion upon freedom of contract is without any visible justification in terms of other statutory goals. Accordingly, the relevant questions become what went wrong where, and how can the wrong be rectified. Inquiry into these questions will demonstrate the institutional difficulties inherent in the content of the present rules.

The *Borg-Warner* rule, that insistence upon hard bargaining over a non-mandatory subject is itself an unfair labor practice, is indefensible and should be rejected. It, more than any other rule, makes sharp the distinction between mandatory and non-mandatory subjects. The Board and courts determine what are non-mandatory subjects; the *Borg-Warner* rule keeps such subjects from collective bargaining and out of the contract. To this extent, the institution of collective bargaining develops by governmental fiat; the terms of collective contracts through governmental intervention.

The *Borg-Warner* Court insisted, as it had to, that the rule was required by the statute. This is its reasoning: "The company's good faith has met the requirements of the statute as to the subjects of mandatory bargaining. But that good faith does not license the employer to refuse to enter into agreements on the ground that they do not include some proposal which is not a mandatory subject of bargaining. We agree with the Board that such conduct is, in substance, a refusal to bargain about the subjects that are within the scope of mandatory bargaining." [54]

In dissent, Mr. Justice Harlan conclusively disposed of these contentions:

The Act sought to compel management and labor to meet and bargain in good faith as to certain topics. This is the *affirmative* requirement of section 8(d) which the Board is specifically empowered to enforce, but I see no warrant for inferring from it any power in the Board to *prohibit* bargaining in good faith as to lawful matters not included in section 8(d). The Court reasons that such conduct on the part of the employer, when carried to the point of insistence, is in substance equivalent to a refusal to bargain as to the statutory subjects, but I cannot understand how this can be said over the Trial Examiner's unequivocal finding that the employer did in fact bargain in "good faith," not only over the disputed clauses but also over the statutory subjects. . . . It must not be forgotten that the Act requires bargaining, *not* agreement. . . . Here the employer concededly bargained but simply refused to *agree* until the union would accept what the Court holds would have been a lawful contract provision.[55]

Nor is the *Borg-Warner* rule really likely to serve the statutory goal of industrial peace. As one commentator has observed: "If the parties feel so strongly about a proposal that they are unwilling to make concessions, even to obtain a contract covering other matters about which they agree, forcing them to remove the disputed subject from the agenda will leave matters of serious controversy unsettled; unrest, rather than stability, will result." [56]

But retreat from the *Borg-Warner* rule is not enough. Even in its absence the law, as we have seen, would continue to play too important a role in shaping collective bargaining and the collective contract. Perhaps the obvious answer is that the Labor Board and the courts should not concern themselves at all with the subject matter of collective bargaining. Perhaps they should not, in a disputed case, determine whether a subject is a "term and condition of employment." [57] If this were the law—and it would undoubtedly require an amendment of section 8(d)—the role of the enforcing tribunals in this area would be limited to judging whether collective bargaining, whatever its scope, was in good faith. The subject matter about which the parties negotiated would be for the parties alone to decide.

What would be the desirable consequences of such a change? It is at best difficult for Board or court to elaborate wisely the phrase "other terms and conditions of employment." As we have seen, *Borg-Warner* gives no help; nor does the concurring opinion of Mr. Justice Stewart in *Fibreboard*. And if one were to inquire with care into the pronouncements of the several courts of appeals and of the Labor Board itself on the question, one's bewilderment would not be abated.[58] The majority opinion in

Fibreboard is the most promising source of information, and the most authoritative. But its logic sweeps most subjects that are likely to be raised by a union into the mandatory class if they have a basis in industrial practice. There is, however, difficulty with respect to industrial practice resulting largely from the diverse nature of industrial organization.[59] Subjects that in one industry or firm are appropriately handled through collective bargaining may be inappropriate subjects for collective bargaining in another industry or firm. This is as it must be. The steel industry is very different from the trucking industry; the automobile from the textile. The history of bargaining in one firm is not the same as in another. The relations between union and management are variable. Sometimes they are mature and trusting; sometimes infantile and suspicious.

Yet, once the law speaks, once it designates a subject as mandatory, that subject which might not have become a matter for bargaining in some industries tends so to become everywhere. It is difficult for anyone freely to give away something of value that the law has bestowed. It may be especially difficult where the gift is to an organization with a complicated political structure that makes it wise for its officers to show shiny new and different results in the short run.

By contrast, if the law were to stay out, the parties would decide for themselves on the basis of interest, practicality, and economic power what to bargain about. These factors would not be influenced by law. The scope of bargaining would be tailored by the situation for the situation.

However, there are difficulties with this solution. It would allow the strong employer so substantially to limit the scope of collective bargaining as to make virtually impossible the union's continued survival. This would be contrary to statutory purpose. The point is similar to the rationale of a supportive duty to bargain in good faith. It is, of course, less forceful because of the good faith requirement. An employer who declines to negotiate about most standard subjects might well be found not to be acting in good faith. But to place such a burden on good faith asks too much, unless a reasonableness test were to be incorporated into the duty, and that would be even more at war with freedom of contract values.

Moreover, the goal of industrial peace would not be served well by allowing the employer so to limit the scope of bargaining. The Chief Justice's second point in *Fibreboard* is to the point: "One of the primary purposes of the Act is to promote the peaceful settlement of industrial disputes by subjecting labor-management controversies to the mediatory influence of negotiation." [60]

To summarize and reformulate, then, the advantages and difficulties that would result if the Board and the courts were not required to determine whether a subject was a term and condition of employment: First, some of the values that justify freedom of contract would be maximized. The parties alone would decide what subjects were proper for bargaining. They best know their needs; they best can tailor their contract to these needs. Second, law would not be employed in a disadvantageous way. It would not be used to achieve an unwanted uniformity, or to affect the direction of collective bargaining's growth. Third, the Board and the courts would not be asked to make decisions that they are institutionally ill-suited to make. Except at the extreme or margin it is impossible to justify in terms of reasoned elaboration a holding that one subject is, while another is not, a term and condition of employment. What Holmes said of the injunction cases applies with equal force here. "The ground of decision really comes down to a proposition of policy of rather a delicate nature concerning the merit of the particular benefit to themselves intended by the defendants, and suggests a doubt whether judges with different economic sympathies might not decide such a case differently when brought face to face with the issue." [61] However, fourth, the Board and courts by determining whether a subject is mandatory support the conditions necessary for free collective bargaining, for freedom of contract, and in this situation, as the Court in *Fibreboard* has told us, the result is consistent with the congressional quest for industrial peace. This would be lost if government withdrew.

The problem then is to find a way to obtain the advantages that would result if government stayed out, while keeping government enough in the picture to insure collective bargaining and encourage industrial peace. This can be accomplished without any change in the statute. The Labor-Management Relations Act need only be interpreted in a fashion that is more responsive to its goals.

All subjects arguably within the statutory language, "wages, hours, and other terms and conditions of employment," should be mandatory subjects about which the parties must bargain in good faith if one of the parties so desires. Of course subjects for bargaining must be proposed in good faith. A subject may not be raised in order to avoid the bargaining duty.

This interpretation of the duty to bargain is consistent with the industrial peace argument of *Fibreboard,* and with the supportive function of the duty to bargain. It has the happy effect of removing from the Labor Board and courts a task—distinguishing mandatory subjects from non-mandatory ones—which they have been unable to perform satisfactorily, and about which many think it makes no sense to draw distinctions. One illustrious study group suggests that: "In light of the realities of the bargaining situation, distinctions between matters that are subject to 'mandatory bargaining' and those that are not have a hollow ring." [62]

Moreover, if all subjects arguably within the statutory

language were mandatory, the parties on the basis of interest and strength would decide where hard bargaining would take place. As it is now, the legal determination, since it is selective, influences the subject matter in which the parties become interested, and thereby influences the contents of collective agreements. Furthermore, the proposed interpretation would not usually increase the bargaining power of unions or weaken the power of employers. The union would not be given a new and more effective strike weapon, just additional issues over which it might strike. Apart from the fact that the "rank and file" may support a dispute over one subject and not over another (work rules but not wages), a successful strike to compel agreement on a formerly non-mandatory subject must cost the union in terms of what it otherwise might have obtained. Thus, a strike to compel an agreement about pensions may mean that the union has no power left to strike for shorter hours. The major exception to this is where the formerly non-mandatory subject involves, as it did in *Fibreboard,* a complete termination of employment for workers in a bargaining unit. This, however, may be thought to be an additional benefit of the proposed interpretation.

There is one important class of subjects arguably within the statutory language, however, which constitutes an exception to this proposed general rule. In an effort to protect neutral employers, the statute in section 8(e) makes it an unfair labor practice for the parties

> to enter into any contract or agreement, express or implied, whereby such employer ceases or refrains or agrees to cease or refrain from handling, using, selling, transporting or otherwise dealing in any of the products of any other employer, or to cease doing business with any other person.

A subject within this so-called "hot cargo" provision of the statute must be excluded, of course, from the mandatory bargaining class. Observe, moreover, that section 8(e) if read literally would cover a vast number of subjects including a provision barring subcontracting in the *Fibreboard* situation itself. Section 8(e), however, is not to be read literally. It was meant to protect neutral employers, but not at the expense of employees in the bargaining unit. Howard Lesnick provides guidance to an understanding of section 8(e):

> The central question is whether the . . . contracting employer is properly to be regarded as a third party with respect to the union's objective. Is the union seeking his aid for its effect elsewhere, or does it intend the impact . . . simply to relate to the working conditions of the employees of the . . . contracting employer? [63]

Section 8(e) should be limited to situations where the "contracting employer is properly to be regarded as a third party with respect to the union's objective"; where the union is "seeking his aid for its effect elsewhere." The Supreme Court has taken the first step toward such a reading of this troublesome section.[64]

Unquestionably the scope of collective bargaining would expand if the suggested interpretation of the duty to bargain were adopted. And unquestionably a cry of pain would be heard throughout the land from employers and their associations. Neil Chamberlain reminds us of what Charles E. Wilson, in 1948 when president of General Motors, had to say about a union demand that G.M. bargain over pensions:

If we consider the ultimate result of this tendency to stretch collective bargaining to comprehend any subject that a union leader may desire to bargain on, we come out with the union leaders really running the economy of the country; but with no legal or public responsibility and with no private employment except as they may permit. . . . Under these conditions, the freedom of management to function properly without interference in making its every-day decisions will be gradually restricted. The Union leaders—particularly where they have industry-wide power—will have the deciding vote in all managerial decisions, or at least, will exercise a veto power that will stop progress. . . . Competition will be stifled and progress in the improvement of industrial processes which reduce the cost and price of the goods produced by industry will be halted. . . . Only by defining and restricting collective bargaining to its proper sphere can we hope to save what we have come to know as our American system and keep it from evolving into an alien form, imported from East of the Rhine.[65]

Mr. Wilson's rhetoric is timeless. It sounds of today and of the 1806 *Philadelphia Cordwainers* case. Pensions were in the forefront of Mr. Wilson's mind. Today's subjects are plant relocation, subcontracting, automation, and other aspects of efficiency, on the one hand, and job security, on the other. In the conspiracy cases the issues now seem so conventional: wage rates and union security. The subjects that are raised for discussion reflect the changing nature of industrial society. This is as it should be. Collective bargaining is not static and fixed. If it is working properly it is a flexible, dynamic institution, and to the extent that the law does not direct union interest toward particular subjects by selective, rather arbitrary designations—and the proposed interpretation of the statute eliminates this—unions will bring to the bargaining table matters that the leadership believes important to the welfare of employees. This is their function as representatives, and it is what the statute envisions.

Nor need we fear, under the proposed interpretation of section 8(d), that the unions will use the statute to subvert our "American system," to evolve it "into an alien form, imported from East of the Rhine." Mr. Wilson did not know his labor movement. American unionists are not dedicated to changing the social order or the nature of business organization. Union leaders are not driven by the ideology of socialism or syndicalism. Their ambition is not to replace management. Indeed, few institutions are more committed to capitalism than the unions; few have a larger stake in the status quo.

Yet, it may be claimed that certain subjects that unions now want to bargain over, some of the subjects that have been held to be mandatory, and surely subjects that are arguably encompassed by the statutory phrase "terms and conditions of employment," are subjects going to the very essence of the managerial function, are, therefore, distinguishable from the more traditional subjects of collective bargaining, and are thus the business of management and management alone.

Many attempts have been made to conceptualize the management function, and Neil Chamberlain has summarized the three general approaches found in the literature. The first, is "to identify the function of management with decision-making. The business firm is the locus of decisions about what line of products or services shall be produced, on what scale, at what prices, by what methods. The function of management is to make such decisions." The second, suggests that "perhaps management can better be defined as those who have been accorded a legal basis for exercising the decision-making authority. On this approach it is not so much the decisions themselves that identify management as the authority with which decisions are made, an authority which is recognized in the law." The third is the "new philosophy of pragmatic management," which "starts from the view that decisions are not the cerebrations of the top men behind the mahogany desks—at least not only that. Decisions are what get translated into action. And since in the typical business, a completed action is something which has been participated in by a number of individuals, decision-making is actually a group process." [66]

Mr. Chamberlain himself offers a fourth theory. He sees corporate action as a two-step process involving bargaining over corporate decisions among interested individuals and groups both within the corporation and outside of it, and the coordination of the resulting bargains. It is the latter that Chamberlain regards as the essence of the managerial function. He states his position this way:

This task—the coordination of the bargains of all those who compose the business—is the unique function of management. It is an inescapable function within an enterprise, since the various terms demanded by the various component parts of the firm do not somehow coordinate or arrange themselves. It is an isolable function, exercised separately from those who make demands on each other. The bargains which are struck constitute the decisions made within the corporation—the decision-making process is seen as a kind of multilateral bargaining process, involving those whose aspirations are somehow involved in any of the numerous decisions which are constantly being made or remade. But this decision-making process is not the same thing as management, any more than collective bargaining is the same thing as management. Beyond the terms which are demanded, the bargains which are struck, the decisions which are made, is the inevitable necessity of a coordinating authority

who must see to it that the numerous bargains or decisions are somehow made consistent with one another.
It is that coordinating authority which is here identi-
fied as management.[67]

Whatever the insights into the function of management
provided by these several theories, none, save the first, supports the claim that the subject matter of collective bargaining must be limited in law if the essence of the
managerial function is to be preserved. The coordinating
function of management—as Mr. Chamberlain is quick
to observe—is in no way impaired by increasing the scope
of collective bargaining. Unions may participate in bargaining over a greater variety of corporate decisions; they
do not participate at all in "the coordination of the bargains of all those who compose the business." The philosophy of pragmatic management, with its emphasis on group
decision-making, is plainly neutral as to the scope of collective bargaining; and the legal approach, in this context,
is, of course, question begging.

But if the essence of the managerial function is decision-
making plain and simple, then management functions are
impaired when the scope of collective bargaining is increased. In fact, they are impaired when there is collective
bargaining over any subject at all. Indeed, if there is genu-
ine individual bargaining with employees, management's
power to make decisions has been limited. This theory,
therefore, simply is not a discriminating tool of analysis.
As a flat proposition it is totally unrealistic. No corporate
manager has power to make decisions unilaterally; all must
deal with suppliers, customers, and government. At best,
the theory is a modern day rationalization of the views
of the judges in the conspiracy cases. As such, it has been
rejected by the theories supporting collective bargaining
and the policy goals of the Labor-Management Relations
Act.

I have suggested that it is consistent with the statutory

goals of freedom of contract and industrial peace to make mandatory any subjects arguably within the statutory language "terms and conditions of employment." It should be added that such an interpretation comports also with the goal of industrial democracy, an important goal of many who supported legislation for collective bargaining. It was Senator Wagner himself who said:

> We can raise a race of men who are economically as well as politically free. By permitting labor to organize freely and effectively we can convert the relation of master and servant into an equal and cooperative partnership, shouldering alike the responsibilities of management and sharing alike in the rewards of increasing production. . . . To me the organization of labor holds forth far greater possibilities than shorter hours and better wages. Organization plants in the heart of every worker a sense of power and individuality, a feeling of freedom and security, which are the characteristics of the kind of men Divine Providence intended us to be.[68]

The larger purposes or goals of the statute and the relationship of the duty to bargain to those goals indicate, then, that all subjects arguably within the statutory language "terms and conditions of employment" be considered mandatory subjects of bargaining. No claim is made, however—nor can it be—that this interpretation of the statute will result in the attainment of such desirable goals as the maximization of industrial efficiency or of economic growth. Industrial decision-making through collective bargaining, whatever the subject matter, in some situations may be quite inconsistent with these goals. But the Labor-Management Relations Act is not concerned with efficiency and growth. The Labor Board—as presently constituted—the courts of appeal, and the Supreme Court are totally ill-equipped to make decisions based upon such considerations. The problem of accommodating collective bargaining to economic policy, which is centrally related to these issues, urgently demands the rethinking of our national labor policy. This is the subject-matter of a later chapter.[69]

On the other hand, there is no reason to suppose that the suggested reading of the statute will importantly affect the attainment of these economic goals. Consider the contracting out issue. Management has urged that it must be free to act without bargaining in part because of considerations of efficiency. Yet, Margaret K. Chandler's recent study of firm practices suggests that it is far from clear what the effect of *Fibreboard* will be. "In sum," she says, "the luster of management's rights may have been symbolically tarnished by the Board's decisions, but their effect on actual flexibility in the management decision process was less clear. It was erroneous to assume that these pronouncements were being visited upon a management freely conducting a completely rational decision-making process. As a matter of fact even in the absence of the union, management generated substantial sources of restraint within its own organization." [70]

There is an additional claim that cannot be made for the suggested reading of the statute. It will not solve the labor problems caused by the new technology, although these are the problems that are principally responsible for the unions' drive to expand the scope of collective bargaining. Automation no doubt will radically change the nature of industrial organization, and the transitional dislocation of workers should not be underestimated.[71] In the future there may be, as one writer has suggested,

> a decline in the significance of the durable, shielded relationship between industrial supervisor and subordinate. Part of this decline will be attributable to situations in which the supervisor shifts to the role of contract administrator and continuity of employment,

traditionally furnished by the integrated industrial firm, becomes the product of a series of agreements held by an outside bureaucrat, the contractor. Or, in line with greater flexibility in the employment relationship, the industrial worker's primary attachment may be his association with a given technology or industrial process. Thus, he may work interchangeably for an industrial firm, for a contractor, or in the contract division of one firm performing a service function in another.[72]

The transition to this world or some other requires the mighty assistance of government: federal, state, and local.[73] Massive retraining programs, perhaps some form of negative income tax, relocation inducements, "a national computerized job-man matching system," and many other approaches are necessary. Some of the programs, goals, and legislation of the "Great Society," while often dealing with larger problems, and perhaps inefficient in administration, are steps in the right direction. The 1966 Report of the National Commission on Technology, Automation, and Economic Progress is heavy with useful suggestions.[74] But government's role must be one of partnership with management and labor. And if collective bargaining is to be involved in this partnership, it must concern itself with the subjects of the new technology. One can claim—indeed, insist just a little—that the proposed interpretation of the statute offers the necessary legal support for this great adventure in modern American capitalism.[75]

Chapter 3

Freedom of Contract and the Collective Bargaining Agreement

The complex body of law which we have just traced is dedicated to making collective bargaining work. When collective bargaining works, collective bargaining agreements result. The agreement establishes the wages, hours, and other terms and conditions of employment. During its life it is unquestionably the major source of the parties' reciprocal rights and obligations. Yet, to picture the collective agreement as an end point in the employer-union relationship would be misleading, for the agreement is not like a sales contract or an insurance policy. It governs too dynamic a relationship for any such comparison. Harry Shulman, while the distinguished arbitrator for Ford and the United Automobile Workers, suggested this markedly different comparison. The agreement, he said,

> is a means to a greater end. Like the marriage vow, it only launches the parties' life as joint enterprisers. The success of the enterprise, like the success of a marriage, depends upon the satisfactory adjustment of the conflicts and frictions in the day-to-day life of the parties. These adjustments must be made by the parties themselves and require daily cooperation in tolerant and generous consideration of each other's needs and complaints. And it is only by their honest and daily cooperation that the parties can achieve the greater end—an efficient enterprise operating with justice for those engaged in it and for the public welfare. That, indeed, is the ultimate justification for both private enterprise and labor unions.[1]

Mr. Shulman was a practical dreamer of nobility; his vision of daily cooperation, often an unrealized ideal. But the ideal has not been unrecognized by the very parties upon whom it imposes its heavy obligation, an obligation far greater than the one that burdens the parties to most commercial transactions.[2] This becomes abundantly clear, I think, when the techniques that have been developed for the administration of the collective bargaining agreement are contrasted with those generally employed in commercial contract administration.

Consider first the way in which commercial contract disputes of all types and varieties are settled; that is, disputes over the meaning of contractual language, the order of performance, the quality of performance, and so forth. Most disputes are resolved informally by the parties themselves through negotiation. The sense of the contract, as understood by each party, is the principal standard employed as justification for the various claims each asserts. While disputes are over contract meaning, over the rights and duties imposed upon the parties by the document they have signed, the object of a settlement is often continued performance, and the desire for performance may result in the compromise or abandonment of claims based upon the document. In this context all unperformed contracts are works in progress providing flexible guides rather than fixed rules for resolving disputes. The extent of rigidity—the extent to which contractual language controls the settlement of disputes—in any commercial transaction unquestionably varies enormously from contract type to contract type. But private settlement is a form of negotiation; it is not adjudication. It is not a method by which disputes necessarily are resolved in terms of preexisting standards. It may be thought of as either (or both) negotiation in which the preexisting standards supplied by the contract are the principal but not the single guide to settlement, or negotiation where the contractual standards are themselves reshaped by the parties.

This most important method for resolving disputes is not institutionalized in the commercial world by contract or custom. Contracts do not usually contain procedures for ironing out disputes at this informal level, nor does custom dictate, as a general proposition, the procedures to be followed.

If private negotiation fails, however, the contract may provide for arbitration as the means of settlement. Where it does, the arbitrator, a private citizen chosen by the parties, is charged with resolving the dispute by ascertaining the sense of the argreement. His job is to adjudicate. The standards he employs are those supplied by the parties' contract. The contract, of course, must be projected against its commercial background. The sense of any agreement is always more than its language contemplated in isolation. But the sense of the agreement, once determined, is not to be compromised by considerations of expediency, as it well may be at the earlier settlement stage.

Lacking an arbitration provision, the procedures to be followed are dictated by law. And of course the vast bulk of the relatively small number of disputes that are not resolved informally by private negotiation are resolved formally through judicial assistance at pretrial, trial, and appellate levels (quantitatively, each in diminishing importance). Trial and appellate review are adjudications in the sense used here.

Contrast the situation under collective bargaining agreements. Precisely because daily cooperation is such a felt necessity and a continuing problem, the settlement of disputes by negotiation is institutionalized through contract. The so-called grievance procedure is found in almost every collective agreement. A grievance is a complaint made by the union or an employee over something the employer has done that affects one or more employees covered by the agreement. (In some agreements the employer may grieve over union or employee conduct.) An employee may be discharged, allegedly for breaking rules or not following orders; a group of workers may be laid off during a slack period, allegedly in accordance with the seniority provisions of the contract; the employer may fail to pay double rates for holiday work as he allegedly is required to under the contract; the employer may contract out work, allegedly in violation of his written promise. The employer's action in each of these situations may give rise to a grievance. The collective agreement's grievance procedure establishes a defined channel through which the resolution of the dispute may be achieved. The grievance section in the agreement often creates a multistep procedure in which the forum of negotiation moves from shop level union and management officials to high level personnel. Minor problems are to be solved below; the more difficult, at more elevated levels.

While it is difficult to generalize because labor-management relations and grievances themselves are so diverse, it would seem that the settlement of grievances sometimes is achieved less through reliance upon preexisting contractual standards and more upon prudential considerations than often is the case in the commercial world. Moreover, the resolution of grievances through arbitration —which generally is employed when negotiation through the grievance procedure fails to produce settlement—is, as I shall discuss shortly, much less clearly the paradigm of adjudication that one sees (perhaps through innocence) in commercial arbitration. In labor arbitration, considerations of expediency may intrude themselves. Sometimes this is with the blessing of the parties. Sometimes it is not.

Labor arbitration is considerably more pervasive than its commercial counterpart. Ninety-six percent of collective bargaining agreements today provide for some form of grievance arbitration.[3] It is the usual method of resolving most labor disputes during the term of the contract that have not been settled by negotiation in the grievance procedure. Arbitration is often considered, and spoken of, as the final step in the grievance procedure. Grievance arbitration is to be distinguished from the arbitration that sometimes is employed to write afresh one or more of the terms and conditions of employment. Grievance arbitration is a very important institution in American labor-management relations; the arbitration of new contract terms as yet is not.

As in commercial arbitration, the labor arbitrator is chosen by the parties. He may be an ad hoc decision-maker, employed to resolve a particular unsettled grievance, or a permanent umpire selected to hear all disputes subject to arbitration under the collective agreement. Labor arbitrators are paid; for a few arbitration is a vocation. Some professional arbitrators are also university professors; and some professors are amateur arbitrators. Some arbitrators are very able; some are not so able. But able or not, full or part time, ad hoc or permanent, the arbitrator rather than the judge is the important third party decision-maker under collective bargaining agreements. And this is so even though the collective agreement is a contract fully enforceable in the courts.[4]

It should not be assumed, however, that the courts play no role in resolving disputes under collective agreements. To the contrary, in the past few years their role has been very important. Because of the prevalence of arbitration, however, the major domain of the judiciary covers the collective agreement's arbitration provision, the arbitrator's award, and the other great "procedural" clause found in many collective agreements, the so-called no-strike clause (wherein the union agrees, in some or all cases, to refrain from employing economic force during the term of the contract). This seemingly limited domain has proved to be rich with problems of freedom of contract, industrial peace, and the nature of the legal process; problems that are the first cousins of those explored in Chapter 2, and the lineal descendants of many observed in Chapter 1.

BACKGROUND

Before 1957 one could not have said with assurance that the collective agreement was a contract fully enforceable in the courts.[5] Prior to the enactment of the Taft-Hartley Act in 1947 the question of the agreement's enforceability depended upon the diverse laws of the several states, and a determination in a state court often was difficult because of the procedural complexities surrounding a suit against an unincorporated union.[6] Moreover, it was not especially important to know the extent to which a collective agreement was an enforceable contract. From the end of World War II, disputes that arose during contract time were—as they are now—usually channeled through a grievance procedure with arbitration as its terminal step. The courts were not thought of as the alternative or important helper to this private method of settlement. To be sure, in those states that had an arbitration statute,[7] and to some extent under the United States Arbitration Act,[8] suits to compel arbitration or to enforce an arbitrator's award did reach the courts. But these were, relative to the situation today, unimportant exceptions.[9] Accordingly, it could quite properly be said of this period that the administration and enforcement of the labor contract was largely a private, voluntary matter.

Three factors were primarily responsible for this phenomenon. First, labor's experience with the courts in the nineteenth and early twentieth centuries had been unfortunate, as we have seen. In the eyes of the union movement, the judiciary in a grossly unfair way had blocked all meaningful efforts by unions to organize and bargain collectively. Union fear of judges carried over to the new era of government-supported collective bargaining. If alternative methods of resolving a dispute were available to it, therefore, a union was not likely to take its case to court.

The second factor contributing to the former unimportance of judicial enforcement of the collective agreement is closely related to the first. The judicial process was thought by many to be poorly suited to the demands that would be imposed upon it if it were to assume a front-line position in the administration and enforcement of these agreements. For one thing, the intervention of the courts might irritate rather than soothe the parties' continuing relationship. For another, judicial interpretation tends to standardize arrangements. And standardization may be antipathetic to the genius of the collective agreement—its sensitivity and adaptability to the dynamics of industrial life.[10]

Finally, as remarked, it was often difficult for an employer to sue a union in contract. Most unions are unincorporated associations, and the procedural law of many states imposed a heavy burden upon a plaintiff who sought to obtain jurisdiction over such an organization.[11] Naturally enough this probably influenced the quest for alternative methods of enforcement, and these were found in arbitration.

When Congress enacted the Taft-Hartley Act, it was not centrally concerned with the question of judicial enforcement of the collective agreement. Congressional tolerance for strikes and other types of labor disputes, however, was low, and the strike during contract time was one of the many sorts of union activity that came in for censure. Some thought was given to making any such strike an unfair labor practice; but this was not done. Procedures were erected limiting the union's freedom to strike, and the

strike in breach of the collective agreement was itself "left
to the usual processes of law"—whatever they might be.
The procedural difficulties involved in suing a union because it was an unincorporated association, however, did
engage the attention of Congress, and unions were made
suable as entities.[12] The legislative process in the end
produced a seemingly innocuous section providing in
part that: "Suits for violation of contracts between an employer and a labor organization representing employees in
an industry affecting commerce . . . may be brought in
any district court of the United States having jurisdiction
of the parties, without respect to the amount in controversy or without regard to the citizenship of the parties."
But, this section—301 of the Labor-Management Relations
Act—has proved to be far reaching in its impact. Indeed,
the reach given to it by the Supreme Court of the United
States is well beyond any that Congress could have foreseen. The law of the collective agreement has been turned
around. Today it is one of the most rapidly developing
segments of American jurisprudence.

   Textile Workers v. Lincoln Mills[13] is the case that began
this quiet revolution. It was decided by the Supreme Court
in 1957, and it grew out of the effort of a union to compel
an employer to submit grievances to arbitration. The
union brought suit in a federal district court under section 301. It asserted that the employer had promised in
the collective agreement to arbitrate grievances which
arose during contract time; that he had broken this promise, and that, therefore, the court should order specific
performance of the promise to arbitrate. The employer in
turn raised some interesting defenses going to the question
of whether the court had the power to grant equitable
relief in these circumstances.

   The first of these defenses relied on the Norris-La
Guardia Act's prohibition against federal courts issuing
injunctions in labor disputes.[14] But while an order com-

pelling specific performance is quite properly thought of as a mandatory injunction, it is not the type of injunction which is a central concern of the Norris-La Guardia Act, and the Supreme Court ultimately had little difficulty in concluding that the anti-injunction statute did not apply in a suit for specific performance of an arbitration promise.[15]

Much less easily resolved, however, was another of the employer's contentions. At common law in most states the promise to arbitrate was not enforceable by an order of specific performance.[16] This was so whether the promise was contained in a commercial contract or in a collective agreement. Theoretically one might recover damages for breach of this promise, but practically one could never show damages.[17] This state rule was also the federal rule.[18] Some states,[19] and the federal government,[20] had legislation which, for some types of contracts at least, changed the common law rule. But the law of the relevant state apparently could not help the union in *Lincoln Mills,* and there was serious doubt whether the United States Arbitration Act applied to arbitration promises in collective bargaining agreements.[21]

Moreover, it was unclear which body of law governed a suit brought under section 301. The statute appeared to be no more than a grant of jurisdiction to the federal courts. It said nothing about the substantive rights of the parties. The early law—what there was of it—on the subject of rights under the collective agreement was, as noted, of state, not of federal, origin. Nor was it clear whether the law governing the availability of the equitable remedy of specific performance was the law of the forum or the law which created the cause of action.[22]

All of these problems were serious. They had split the lower courts for ten years; they had worried the commentators and disturbed the private orders. All of these serious problems were solved by the Supreme Court in the *Lincoln*

Mills case by judicial fiat. No serious attempt was made by that Court to bridge with reasoned elaboration the gap between question and conclusion. The majority opinion is simply an *ipse dixit*.

The Court held that section 301 was a charter to the courts to develop a federal "common law" of the collective bargaining agreement, and that section 301 itself empowered the courts to grant specific performance of the promise to arbitrate.

Lincoln Mills is a questionable decision by any criterion. It is a decision that seems to be unrelated to legislative purpose. It is a decision that intrudes the federal government into an area of traditional state concern, with serious consequences to the survival of state power. It is a decision that intrudes the courts into labor-management affairs without guidance, and which imposes upon them the task of constructing a mature code of law that must inevitably affect the balance of power between labor and management, and that may or may not reduce combat between them. We shall return to *Lincoln Mills* after looking at some of its progeny, in order to suggest—with hindsight's aid—what the Court should have done, and why.

JUDICIAL REVIEW OF THE PROMISE TO ARBITRATE

The story after *Lincoln Mills* is best begun in the late spring of 1960 when the Supreme Court handed down a group of interrelated decisions clarifying the role of the judiciary in the labor arbitration process. In two cases, a union requested the court to compel an employer to submit a grievance to arbitration. The employer insisted that he had never promised to do so. In the third case, a union sought the court's assistance in forcing an employer to obey an arbitrator's award. The employer's position was that the arbitrator had exceeded his power. Written opinions were filed by the Justices in all three cases.[23] They indicate that, where a collective bargaining agreement contains a general promise to arbitrate grievances, a court is to order arbitration or enforce an arbitration award without serious inquiry into whether the parties agreed to submit the particular grievance to an arbitrator. These opinions have had a significant effect on the law of labor arbitration. The nature of this effect may be understood best by first examining the cases involving judicial intervention prior to arbitration.

Let us take as a model for the problem of judicial intervention prior to arbitration the case of *United Steelworkers v. Warrior & Gulf Navigation Co.*[24] This was one of the three cases with which the Supreme Court was concerned, and it is the case in which the Court produced its major opinion. The underlying dispute was over Warrior's contracting out of maintenance and repair work. This allegedly caused the layoff of several Warrior employees who were represented by the Steelworkers Union. The union charged that the contracting out was in violation of its collective bargaining agreement with Warrior. It asserted that the layoffs resulting from the employer's action were tantamount to a partial lockout, an employer weapon specifically prohibited by the agreement.

Warrior and the union were unable to resolve this dispute through negotiation—that is, under the grievance procedure—and the union called for arbitration. When Warrior declined to arbitrate, the union filed a bill in equity under section 301.

Before the court, the union charged once again that Warrior had broken a promise made in the collective bargaining agreement, claiming this time a violation of the arbitration clause. That clause called for arbitration of unsettled grievances: "If agreement [by negotiation channeled through a multi-step grievance procedure] has not been reached the matter shall be referred to an impartial umpire for decision." The union wanted the court to

compel arbitration of the underlying dispute over contracting out, by ordering specific performance of this promise to arbitrate.

Warrior claimed that the arbitration promise did not
extend to a dispute over contracting out. It asserted that
the collective agreement, if properly interpreted, allocated
to it unilateral control over such decisions. Contracting
out was intended to be "strictly a function of management," and the agreement provided in terms that "matters
which are strictly a function of management shall not be
subject to arbitration."

One well might suppose that a judge when faced with
this dispute over the scope of the arbitration promise
should proceed as he would in an ordinary contract case.
And there is nothing in the Labor-Management Relations
Act to preclude such an approach. In the absence of an
agreement, an employer often must negotiate about contracting out the work done by his employees, but since
Warrior had been free to contract for unilateral control,
the mandatory nature of the subject was now irrelevant to
the judge's task. Summoning all of the skills that training
and experience have given him, the judge, if he were to
proceed in the normal fashion, should consider carefully
the evidence properly presented to him bearing upon the
question whether contracting out is "strictly a function
of management" within the sense of the contract. If it is,
the employer has not broken the arbitration promise and
judgment should be for him. If, on the other hand, contracting out is not "strictly a function of management,"
the employer has broken his promise to arbitrate and the
union's request for an order of specific performance should
be granted.

This appears to be the approach taken by the lower
courts in the *Warrior* case.[25] They held that contracting
out was strictly a function of management, that, accordingly, the arbitration promise had not been broken, and

that, appropriately, judgment should be entered for Warrior.

The Supreme Court reversed. It held that the lower courts had misconceived the judge's role. Said the Court:

> An order to arbitrate the particular grievance should not be denied unless it may be said with positive assurance that the arbitration clause is not susceptible of an interpretation that covers the asserted dispute. Doubts should be resolved in favor of coverage. . . . In the absence of any express provision excluding a particular grievance from arbitration, we think only the most forceful evidence of a purpose to exclude the claim from arbitration can prevail, particularly where, as here, the exclusion clause is vague and the arbitration clause quite broad. Since any attempt by a court to infer such a purpose necessarily comprehends the merits, the court should view with suspicion an attempt to persuade it to become entangled in the construction of the substantive provisions of a labor agreement, even through the back door of interpreting the arbitration clause, when the alternative is to utilize the services of an arbitrator.[26]

Lower courts then are to approach the question of whether to order arbitration armed with a strong affirmative presumption, a very strong presumption indeed.

From the rather murky opinion of the Court, one can extract a dual justification for this new and powerful presumption. First, arbitration serves industrial peace,[27] and the attainment of industrial peace is a major goal of the Labor-Management Relations Act. The affirmative case for this proposition seems simple enough. Unlike commercial arbitration, the alternative to labor arbitration is not likely to be a judicial resolution of the underlying dispute. Theoretically, if the lower courts had been

sustained, the union in *Warrior* could have sued the employer under section 301, on the ground that contracting
out was in breach of the collective agreement. For, theoretically, the lower courts had passed not upon that question, but upon the question whether the arbitration
promise had been broken. Actually, it would have been
surprising if the union had sued. It would either have
accepted the employer's action or have called a strike.
Accordingly, since strike may be the alternative to arbitration, the goal of industrial peace invites a rule of construction that gives generous scope to the arbitration
promise. We shall return to this branch of the Court's
opinion later and in some detail. For in the contract enforcement area, the Court's vision, while sometimes di-
verted, always comes to rest upon the statutory goal of
industrial peace.

Second, the issue before a court in a pre-arbitration
hearing and the issue before an arbitrator hearing the
merits of the underlying dispute usually are intertwined.
And because of the nature of a collective bargaining
agreement, the arbitrator, at least in the first instance, is
a better decision-maker than the judge. Thus, the judge
should defer to the arbitrator; and the strong presumption
in favor of arbitration admirably accomplishes this result.[28]

While the presumption in favor of arbitration may be
stronger than it should be, this second justification for
the Court's holding is essentially correct. In *Warrior,* as in
most pre-arbitration cases, the question for the court in
deciding whether to order arbitration, and the question
for the arbitrator on the merits are, at least in part, the
same question. Central to whether Warrior had agreed
to arbitrate a dispute over contracting out—the question
for the court—is whether under the collective agreement
contracting out is "strictly a function of management."
Central to whether Warrior had broken its promise when

it contracted out work—the question for the arbitrator—is also whether contracting out is "strictly a function of management." Thus, if the arbitrator is better qualified than the judge to decide this question correctly, he should have the first chance to do so.

The claim that an arbitrator is a superior first-line decision-maker relies upon the nature of a collective bargaining agreement and the institutional difficulties that such a document is likely to pose for a court. First, collective bargaining agreements frequently cover a large variety of technical and specialized problems. Nevertheless portions are often drafted in purposely vague terms. Not only must the language be general enough to encompass numerous unforeseen and unforeseeable events, but it must also fail to resolve some present controversies. For the price of present resolution, the price of explicitness, may be a prolonged strike. Second, and closely related, the collective agreement does not exhaust the field. The common law of the jurisdiction—that is, the custom, usage, and practice of the enterprise—still has a direct role to play. Third, and largely as a consequence of the first two points, a collective agreement must be interpreted not only in terms of its specific purpose; it must be fitted into the general body of the law of the enterprise and interpreted in a fashion harmonious with the received traditions and principles of that body of law.

Because of experience and training, because of time and attitude, a good arbitrator is probably better able to cope wisely with this sort of an agreement than is a good judge. The judge's training is likely to make him reject some of what in fact should be closely considered. In the busy world of the district court, the judge's instinct may be to read collective agreements the way he reads commercial contracts and to interpret similar language in very different collective agreements as meaning the same thing. Yet, collective bargaining works reasonably well only because it is adaptable to the diverse needs of diverse enterprises.

Some—perhaps many—arbitrators are not good, and in any given case a judge might perform better. But it is true that the parties themselves name the arbitrator, and thus have some control over the situation. Moreover, experience demonstrates the general weakness of the approach followed by the lower courts in *Warrior*. Prior to the Supreme Court's decision, most judges, when requested to order specific performance of the promise to arbitrate, inquired fully into whether the arbitration promise comprehended the particular underlying dispute. No presumptions were indulged. Close attention to these decisions suggests that the courts were not successful. In the judgment of a number of disinterested observers, the courts often failed to compel arbitration where a more sophisticated study of the underlying problem would have indicated that arbitration was appropriate.[29] Finally, one might suppose that the principal protection against the bad arbitrator is subsequent judicial review of his authority to make the award he has. But there is considerable doubt as to the extent of this protection.

JUDICIAL INTERVENTION AFTER ARBITRATION

Suppose that in *Warrior*, an arbitrator were to decide that contracting out was not "strictly a function of management," and that the employer had violated the collective agreement when he contracted out maintenance work to other employers. Should the employer now be able to get serious judicial review of whether the arbitrator had authority so to hold? While there is room for a difference of opinion (the difference is reflected in subsequent cases in the lower courts[30]), I believe that the logic of the Supreme Court's decisions means that serious review by a court is inappropriate.

In the post-arbitration case decided by the Court, *United Steelworkers v. Enterprise Wheel & Car Corp.*,[31] the employer's principal contention was that the arbitrator had acted beyond his authority in ordering reinstatement of employees after the collective agreement had expired. While the Court's opinion, sustaining the arbitrator, observes that "an arbitrator is confined to interpretation and application of the collective bargaining agreement," and that "his award is legitimate only so long as it draws its essence from the . . . agreement," [32] it also instructs the judges as to their role on review. The Court said:

> The refusal of courts to review the merits of an arbitration award is the proper approach to arbitration under collective bargaining agreements. The federal policy of settling labor disputes by arbitration would be undermined if courts had the final say on the merits of the awards. As we stated in . . . Warrior . . . the arbitrators under these collective agreements are indispensable agencies in a continuous collective bargaining process. They sit to settle disputes at the plant level—disputes that require for their solution knowledge of the custom and practices of a particular factory or of a particular industry as reflected in particular agreements. . . . When an arbitrator is commissioned to interpret and apply the collective bargaining agreement, he is to bring his informed judgment to bear in order to reach a fair solution of a problem.[33]

Of course, in many situations, as the Court recognized in these decisions, a judge cannot possibly pass on the authority of the arbitrator to hold as he did without passing on the merits of the underlying dispute. The issues are intertwined. No magic can separate them. Thus, in *Warrior,* both the issue on the merits and the issue of the arbitrator's authority turn inescapably upon whether contracting out is "strictly a function of management." As much as one may wish otherwise, one must conclude, therefore, that the spirit of the *Enterprise* case precludes a court from making too close an examination of whether contracting out is strictly a function of management, no matter how the issue is raised in a suit to enforce the award.

The nagging question posed by this conclusion is whether such an allocation of function between arbitrator and court—a wise allocation at the pre-arbitration stage— makes sense in a post-arbitration proceeding. The Court's explanation is not satisfactory. It rests principally upon the same argument advanced for judicial abnegation in a pre-arbitration suit, namely, the relatively greater competence of the arbitrator. But while an arbitrator initially may be better able than a court to inform himself about the content of the phrase "strictly a function of management"; while he may have experience which makes it easier for him to understand the relevance of past practices; while he may have a feel for the common law of the enterprise that the judge lacks; and while he may be able to proceed in a more informal and leisurely fashion than the judge in a pre-arbitration hearing, these considerations do not suggest that a court lacks competence to review what the arbitrator has done in light of what the arbitrator has said.

Indeed, the Court at one point tells us: "When the arbitrator's words manifest an infidelity to [his obligation to make an award that 'draws its essence' from the collective bargaining agreement] courts have no choice but to refuse enforcement of the warad." [34] The Court's opinion goes on to say, however, that "arbitrators have no obligation to the court to give their reasons for an award. To require opinions free of ambiguity may lead arbitrators to play it safe by writing no supporting opinions. This would be undesirable for a well-reasoned opinion tends to engender confidence in the integrity of the process and aids in clarifying the underlying agreement." [35] It is not clear why a court could not insist that an arbitrator produce an unam-

biguous and reasoned opinion.[36] True, no such requirement existed prior to *Warrior*; but *Warrior* changed the
relationship between court and arbitrator. Surely *Warrior*
did not exhaust the Court's creative power.

But with or without a well-reasoned arbitrator's opinion,
the question still must be whether it is wise policy for a
court to place the full weight of government behind an
award without giving serious attention to the objecting
party's continuous and insistent claim that it had never
promised to submit the dispute to arbitration in the first
place, and that the arbitrator had exceeded his authority.[37]
The factors that might lead one toward an affirmative
answer to this question are perhaps best developed by con-
trasting the judicial process with arbitration.

The declaration of law through reasoned elaboration of
rules and principles used as standards for adjudication is
perhaps the hallmark of the judicial process. Rules and
principles embody experience which, of course, must constantly be reevaluated by all law-declaring institutions, including the courts themselves. But because courts adjudicate claims in terms of preexisting standards, because the
arguments made to them are arguments about rights and
obligations existing at the time a dispute arose, judicial
law declaration relies substantially less upon the exercise
of discretion by the decision-maker than does law declaration by other kinds of institutions. The executive and
legislative branches of government are plainly institutions
of this latter type; so too administrative tribunals in some
of their activities. Arbitration tribunals, engaged in grievance arbitration, however, are much harder to classify in
terms of the degree to which the decision-maker may legitimately exercise discretion.

On the one hand, we are told by the majority in the
Enterprise case that the arbitrator "does not sit to dispense

his own brand of industrial justice." [38] His power, Mr. Justice Whittaker assumes in dissent, is strictly limited by contract; his task, much the same as that of the judge.[39] On the other hand, the majority tells us—this time in the *Warrior* case—that:

> The labor arbitrator is usually chosen because of the parties' confidence in his knowledge of the common law of the shop and their trust in his personal judgment to bring to bear considerations which are not expressed in the contract as criteria for judgment. The parties expect that his judgment of a particular grievance will reflect not only what the contract says but, insofar as the collective bargaining agreement permits, such factors as the effect upon productivity of a particular result, its consequence to the morale of the shop, his judgment whether tensions will be heightened or diminished. For the parties' objective in using the arbitration process is primarily to further their common goal of uninterrupted production under the agreement, to make the agreement serve their specialized needs.[40]

One private dispute settlement tribunal, established by the International Brotherhood of Electrical Workers and the National Electrical Contractors Association, announced its understanding of the difference between the arbitration and judicial processes in the following terms:

> The Council differs from so-called arbitration boards in that it professes to be a court of justice and not merely a court of arbitration. It proceeds on the theory that arbitration involves compromise, which seems to mean in some minds adding up the claims of both sides of a dispute and dividing the sum by two; while judicial settlement involves the application

of definite and certain principles without any accommodation between the parties.[41]

From a cluster of factors that might account for the divergent views about the role of discretion in arbitration, one seems particularly compelling: there simply is no unitary system of grievance arbitration. Its nature under any collective bargaining agreement depends upon how several factors interact. What, for example, does the collective agreement say? What do the parties want? What does the arbitrator conceive to be the needs of the parties, and how does he perceive his role and the restraints imposed upon him? This latter factor is particularly important, for the arbitrator's conception of his job—if he has one—goes far toward determining the extent to which discretion will shape his award.

Different combinations of answers to these questions result in arbitrations that differ markedly as to the place of discretion in the process. To the extent, however, that the parties themselves control the scope of the arbitrator's discretion, this difference may be desirable. It may even be an important reason for the widespread use of arbitration in labor relations.

Labor arbitration then as a method for resolving disputes, may not always rely solely upon preexisting standards found in the collective bargaining agreement as "implemented and furnished by the common law of the shop." For this reason arbitration may not fit the usual concept of adjudication. Sometimes arbitration may be a method for resolving disputes in which the arbitrator is concerned with such prudential factors as—in the words of the Supreme Court— "the effect upon productivity of a particular result, its consequence to the morale of the shop, his judgment whether tensions will be heightened or diminished." [42] This must mean that the arbitrator will give less than full attention to the terms of the agreement. And while this may be what the parties expect when they choose their arbitrator, how can a court possibly tell on review?

Thus, the Supreme Court's apparent instructions to the lower courts, not to review seriously the authority of the arbitrator after an award (for that would involve serious review of the merits), may reflect the Supreme Court's unwillingness to have the judiciary tamper with what the Court takes to be a satisfactory and frequently highly discretionary process.

But, as sympathetic as one may be with the Court, one cannot blink the fact that it has tampered with the arbitration process and tampered with it substantially. Out of concern for the preservation of one type of consensual arbitration—that which relies heavily upon prudential considerations—the Court has interfered mightily with another type of consensual arbitration, that which relies exclusively upon the preexisting standards supplied by the contract. The Court has made it possible for arbitrators to exercise enormous discretion without regard to the desires of the parties. Indeed, the exercise of such discretion may be directly contrary to what the parties desire. Where arbitrators have such power, one can be sure that from time to time the power will be used. Thus, in this important class of cases, the Supreme Court has upset the reasonable expectations of parties who with words have tried to order the future in that fashion which they deemed, at the time of contract formation, to be best for them. Decisions that have this result undercut the freedom of contract goal of the Labor-Management Relations Act. They impose substantive terms upon the parties to which the parties did not agree.

THE NO-STRIKE CLAUSE AND FREEDOM OF CONTRACT

When one turns from the arbitration promise to the no-strike promise—the other great procedural clause of the collective bargaining agreement—one finds a grosser disregard for freedom of contract values.

Local 174, Teamsters v. Lucas Flour[43] is the case of principal importance. A collective agreement provided in one paragraph for arbitration over "any difference as to the true interpretation of this agreement," and also stated that, "during such arbitration, there shall be no suspension of work." A second paragraph of the arbitration article provided that "should any difference [not covered by the first paragraph] arise between the employer and the employee, same shall be submitted to arbitration." Nothing was said in this second paragraph about work stoppages.[44]

A difference, within the meaning of the second paragraph of the arbitration article, did arise when the employer fired an employee.[45] In protest, the union called an unsuccessful strike. Subsequently, the discharge was upheld in arbitration, and the employer successfully sued the union in a state court for damages resulting from the strike.[46] The Supreme Court granted certiorari, and proceeded to decide the case on the seemingly correct assumption that the union had not expressly promised to refrain from striking over the discharge. The question on the merits to which the Supreme Court addressed itself was whether a union which strikes over an arbitrable dispute is in breach of the collective bargaining agreement even if the agreement does not contain a promise by the union not to strike.[47]

The Court held that the strike was in breach of contract, for the collective agreement "expressly imposed upon both parties the duty of submitting the dispute in question to final and binding arbitration." [48] When such is the case, a no-strike promise is to be implied.

Two claims, unencumbered by reasoning, were advanced in support of this rule. One appealed to the goal of freedom of contract: "To hold otherwise would obviously do violence to accepted principles of traditional contract law." [49] This claim is without the citation of authority. The other, and explicitly the more important claim, appealed to the goal of industrial peace: "Even more in point," said the Court, "a contrary view would be completely at odds with the basic policy of national labor legislation to promote the arbitral process as a substitute for economic warfare." [50] This claim is supported by a citation to *Warrior*; and thus, the arbitration and strike cases are united in purpose by the quest for industrial peace. I shall deal with this aspect of both problems shortly, but first let us see if the *Lucas Flour* rule is responsive, as the Court claims, "to accepted principles of traditional contract law."

Mr. Justice Black dissented in *Lucas Flour*. He argued that the Court's holding marked a departure from the statutory policy which allowed the parties freely to write the substantive terms of their contract. "I have been unable to find any accepted principle of contract law—traditional or otherwise—that permits courts to change completely the nature of a contract by adding new promises that the parties themselves refused to make in order that the new court-made contract might better fit into whatever social, economic, or legal policies the courts believe to be so important that they should have been taken out of the realm of voluntary contract by the legislative body and furthered by compulsory legislation." [51] Mr. Justice Black was clear that freedom of contract demanded a different conclusion from the Court's:

> Both parties to collective bargaining discussions have much at stake as to whether there will be a no-strike clause in any resulting agreement. It is difficult to believe that the desire of employers to get such a promise and the desire of the union to avoid giving it are matters which are not constantly in the minds of those who negotiate these contracts. In such a setting, to

hold—on the basis of no evidence whatever—that a union, without knowing it, impliedly surrendered the right to strike by virtue of "traditional contract law" or anything else is to me just fiction.[52]

Mr. Justice Black surely seems correct. The no-strike pledge is a promise commonly found in collective bargaining agreements.[53] It has never been thought to be an unimportant promise,[54] and accordingly, it is hardly probable that the parties overlooked it or that they assumed that its inclusion in any way would be redundant. Yet the parties did expressly agree to arbitrate the dispute. Might it not be said, therefore, that they must have meant that the dispute was not to be settled by economic combat? Is it not fair to assume that the parties chose arbitration as an exclusive procedure, and in so doing rejected alternative procedures? [55] This argument assumes that the parties established a dispute-settlement procedure that coincides with the Court's, or some other outsider's, notion of a reasonable procedure. It is an argument that might be thought to make good sense if the events that took place in *Lucas Flour* were, at the time of contract formation, remote or unforeseeable. As Lon Fuller has observed, when courts, in finding implied terms in contracts, talk of intention, they frequently are not talking about "conscious and deliberate choice" but rather are discussing "the manner in which current mores and conceptions of fairness can be said to influence the shape and conduct of parties without their being aware of the existence of alternatives." [56] But Mr. Justice Black's unanswerable point is that in collective bargaining agreements the omission of a no-strike clause must itself be taken to be a "conscious and deliberate choice" of the parties.

It may seem stubborn, wrongheaded, and unreasonable for a union to bargain hard and successfully for an arbitration promise and not give up its right to strike. It

may also seem unreasonable, stubborn, and wrongheaded
for an employer to bargain hard and successfully for unilateral control over many of the terms and conditions of
employment and for a no-strike pledge without giving in
exchange a promise to arbitrate.[57] But here, as with the
duty to bargain, the enforcement of reasonable behavior
only can be at a sacrifice. And what is sacrificed here, even
as what would be sacrificed there, is freedom of contract.[58]

On the basis of what has been said thus far, however, it
may be thought, in both *Lucas Flour* and in the arbitration cases, that the sacrifice of freedom of contract resulting from the Court's rules is no more than a short-run
phenomenon. After all, the rules developed by the Court
are rules of construction which can be avoided by explicit
language in the collective agreement. A closely limited
arbitration provision can be written. A no-no-strike clause
may present some grammatical difficulties, but it is not
beyond the competence of the draftsman.

It is, of course, true that it is only in the short run—
only with respect to contracts then in being—that the
Court's decisions upset the reasonable expectations of the
parties. But it is also true that the balance of bargaining
advantage with respect to the particular subjects is shifted
permanently when the law erects presumptions of the sort
found in the arbitration and no-strike cases. For example,
it is likely to be much easier for a union successfully to
resist the inclusion of a no-strike clause in a collective
agreement than it is for a union to obtain a clause permitting a strike over an arbitrable grievance. And in the
negotiation of the agreement, where the focus usually is
on the economic terms of contract, it may be difficult for
the employer successfully to insist on a detailed and explicit catalogue of exceptions to arbitration.

The Supreme Court decisions have shifted the burden

of obtaining contract language that orders the future from union to employer in the arbitration area and from employer to union in the strike area. This ensures that "the new Court-made contract" will, in the words of Mr. Justice Black, "better fit into whatever social, economic or legal policies the courts believe to be so important that they should have been taken out of the realm of voluntary contract by the legislative body and furthered by compulsory legislation." [59]

In these contract enforcement decisions, then, the Court has done exactly what it said, in the good faith cases, should not be done.[60] It has erected a labor policy "on a foundation of government control of the results of negotiation." [61] It has done this for a reason which we have not explored yet in any detail; namely, that the promulgated rules serve the statutory goal of industrial peace.

THE INDUSTRIAL PEACE RATIONALE

The Court's attempt to justify the rules it has fashioned, by insisting that they advance the law's quest for industrial peace, invites speculation along two lines. How important is that aspect of the problem of industrial warfare that the Court's rules seek to regulate; and to what extent are these rules likely to promote peace in industrial relations? [62]

There is little reason to think that strikes, triggered either by the refusal of an employer to arbitrate an arbitrable grievance or by an employer's unilateral action that admittedly is subject to arbitration, are an important source of industrial unrest. Only a small number of arbitration proceedings require judicial intervention, and this was true before the Supreme Court's arbitration decisions.[63] This fact certainly is not surprising; most parties are likely to comply with their agreement, and sanctions usually exist apart from law.[64] The relationship between the employer and the union is a continuing one, the harmony of which might be jeopardized by the failure of one party to stick to its promise. Moreover, if the employer declines to arbitrate, he invites the sanction of self-help in the form of a work stoppage. These deterrents mean that work stoppages are usually not necessary.[65] Nor is a union likely to strike—whether or not it has promised to refrain from doing so—over a dispute that an employer is willing to arbitrate. A strike is too serious and costly. It is too much the ultimate weapon to receive other than the most infrequent use as a means of settling arbitrable grievances. The plain fact is that while industrial warfare increasingly is being perceived as a national economic and political problem,[66] the type of industrial warfare with which the nation is concerned occurs mainly during the negotiation of the collective agreement, not during its administration.

Even if it were otherwise, however, the engaging question would remain whether the Court's generous construction of arbitration and no-strike clauses is likely to be productive of industrial peace. This question should be refined before an answer is attempted. Although there is doubt, one may assume for these purposes that neutral judicial enforcement of the promise to arbitrate and the promise not to strike would further the law's quest for industrial peace by deterring breach of contract. I mean no more by neutral judicial enforcement than enforcement through rules of interpretation that are designed with the single aim of effectuating the sense of the collective agreement, rules that reflect a sympathetic concern for the goal of freedom of contract. With this concession made to judicial enforcement, the question becomes whether the compulsory or noncontractual aspects of the Court's rules further industrial peace. Put another way, are compulsory arbitration of grievances and a compulsory ban on strikes over arbitrable grievances likely to be productive of industrial peace? I venture to answer that they are not.[67]

Consider the *Lucas Flour* rule which by fiat prohibits strikes over arbitrable grievances. Unions are not likely to strike over such grievances; when they do, feelings must be running very high. And when feelings run high is it likely that the consequences will be altered by the legal rule? The answer in part depends upon the sanctions that attach to the legal rule. If we were prepared to use guns to keep people at work, there might be considerable short-run success. Happily we are not. Indeed, legislative policy plainly stated in the Norris-La Guardia Act and properly followed by the Supreme Court in the case of *Sinclair Refining Co. v. Atkinson*[68] forbids the federal courts to issue an injunction to prevent a strike in breach of contract. Nor has Congress shown any inclination to change this law. And a harsh sanction would tax the legal system.[69] It is often difficult for a union to control its members when feelings run high and there are many effective slowdown techniques available to the enterprising worker who is compelled to give up the picket line.[70]

Consider the rule in *Warrior* and *Enterprise* that forces an employer to arbitrate a dispute he has not agreed to arbitrate. The union would not have struck over the dispute unless it considered that dispute very serious. Now, if the employer is ultimately successful in the arbitration, is there reason to suppose that the union will be contained if it would not have been contained in the absence of the arbitration? Perhaps, but there is hardly any certainty one way or the other. Moreover, arbitration may accomplish no more than to postpone economic combat to the time of contract renegotiation. This is a likely consequence if the ultimate result of the compulsory arbitration is a decision against the employer and the issue is one about which he feels strongly.

The point, at least in part, is that it is misleading to think of a collective bargaining agreement as an ordinary contract for a fixed term. Many commercial contracts are

just that; and after the term is over, the association is
ended. A collective bargaining agreement, however, is one
episode in a continuing, joint history of a firm and union.
It is a temporary calm in a restless, shifting relationship.
Accordingly, to attempt to compel the employer or the
union during contract time to yield on a deeply felt issue
about which it never consented to yield is not to resolve
that issue. Rather—if it has any consequence at all—it is
to delay ultimate resolution to a time when the parties are
freed from governmental constraints.[71] At that time, the
time of contract renegotiation, economic combat may be
the means of decision.

The Supreme Court, however, shows no sign of abandoning industrial peace as the rationale for its contract enforcement decisions. It seems that now more than ever
one can expect this misplaced faith to guide judicial
action. The case of *John Wiley & Sons v. Livingston*[72] is
a striking example. It involved the question whether a
relatively large, unorganized corporate employer which,
after a merger, had integrated into its working force a
minority group of employees, must arbitrate about such
things as the survival of those employees' seniority rights
under a collective agreement between a union and the
smaller, merged corporation. The Court conceded that
"the principles of law governing ordinary contracts would
not bind to a contract an unconsenting successor to a contracting party." [73] But the Court was nevertheless quick
to order arbitration, and principally upon the following
ground: "The transition from one corporate organization
to another will in most cases be eased and industrial
strife avoided if employees' claims continue to be resolved
by arbitration rather than by 'the relative strength . . .
of the contending forces.' " [74] How arbitration here serves
industrial peace is nowhere explained. One might well
suppose that if a minority group of employees is to be
treated differently from the majority, the consequences

will be industrial unrest, not peace. And while it may be that the sense of the collective agreement when properly understood requires that the obligation to arbitrate survives the merger, the Court made no attempt to interpret the agreement before it.

The Court does tell us:

> Employees, and the union which represents them, ordinarily do not take part in negotiations leading to a change in corporate ownership. The negotiations will ordinarily not concern the well-being of the employees, whose advantage or disadvantage, potentially great, will inevitably be incidental to the main considerations. The objectives of national labor policy, reflected in established principles of federal law, require that the rightful prerogative of owners independently to rearrange their businesses and even eliminate themselves as employers be balanced by some protection to the employees from a sudden change in the employment relationship.[75]

This is true, and it should impose on the employer contemplating merger a duty to bargain over the subject with the union representing its employees.[76] That far, and for the reasons canvassed in the preceding chapter, the "objectives of national labor policy" go. But the Court, in an unpromising quest for industrial peace, should not impose upon anyone a court-made contract that better fits "into whatever social, economic, or legal policies the courts believe to be so important that they should have been taken out of the realm of voluntary contract by the legislative body and furthered by compulsory legislation."

THE APPROPRIATE ROLE FOR LAW[77]

Our analysis of the contract enforcement cases discloses the need for law reform, and suggests at least one direction that such reform might take. Judicial enforcement of the collective agreement should concern itself less with effectuating the statute's goal of industrial peace—a job at which the courts must be unsuccessful—and more with preserving its ideal of freedom of contract. Experience teaches that the sense of the collective agreement is a more appropriate standard in adjudication than the one the courts in fact have employed. Accordingly, *Lucas Flour* should be overruled.

As for arbitration, a happier solution than the present one is to have serious judicial review of whether the parties agreed to arbitrate a particular dispute in a post-arbitration proceeding. This does not mean, of course, that the court should hear arbitration cases *de novo*. It does mean that the arbitrator should be required to write a reasoned and unambiguous opinion, and it does mean that the court should review the arbitrator's award to determine whether it is reasonable in light of the language of the collective agreement, projected against its industrial background and revealed in the opinion of the arbitrator.

If we review what the Court has done it will become clear that this much reform is required, not because this suggested approach is more consistent with wise labor policy, but because present law violates the integrity of the judicial process. Under present law the major function of courts in the labor arbitration area is not to resolve particular disputes through the application of general and reasoned principles. Rather, it is blindly to approve and make official the actions of private decision-makers whose authority to decide is frequently itself the issue in dispute. The Court has instructed the judges that in the garden variety case they need accept no responsibility. Although one party insists from the beginning that he never agreed to arbitrate the particular dispute, that the arbitrator has exceeded his authority, and although this is the issue tendered the court, the judge is to order arbitration and enforce an award without ever seriously examining this issue. It seems to me quite improper, where contempt of court and ultimate imprisonment may be at stake, for a court so to rubber-stamp the decision of a private arbitrator.

But while the suggested reform eliminates this difficulty, it has a substantial drawback which invites consideration of a more radical solution. Serious judicial review will have the inescapable effect of converting labor arbitration into a more uniform decision-making process. It will tend to eliminate that type of arbitration which the Supreme Court so strenuously endeavored to preserve: arbitration in which reliance is not placed solely upon preexisting standards supplied by contract, but also upon prudential considerations related to a changing industrial environment. Of course, the parties still can have this type of arbitration if they stay away from the courts, but an arbitrator who may be reviewed is likely to be restrained in his exercise of discretion, and if the courts are available, they are likely to be used, no matter how much discretion the losing party originally desired the arbitrator to exercise.

Harry Shulman, whose extensive experience as an arbitrator was in an industrial situation that apparently called upon him to employ considerable discretion, may have had this consideration, among others, in mind when, as Dean of the Yale Law School, he delivered the Holmes Lecture at Harvard. Speaking before *Lincoln Mills,* but after the enactment of section 301, he said:

Arbitration is an integral part of the system of self-government. And the system is designed to aid management in its quest for efficiency, to assist union leadership in its participation in the enterprise, and to secure justice for the employees. It is a means of making collective bargaining work and thus preserving private enterprise in a free government. When it works fairly well, it does not need the sanction of the law of contracts or the law of arbitration. It is only when the system breaks down completely that the courts' aid in these respects is invoked. But the courts cannot, by occasional sporadic decisions, restore the parties' continuing relationship; and their intervention in such cases may seriously affect the going system of self-government. When their autonomous system breaks down, might not the parties better be left to the usual method for adjustment of labor disputes rather than to court actions on the contract or on the arbitration award? [78]

While there may be some cost in the law's strategic retreat from this area of labor relations—neutral enforcement, as suggested earlier, to some extent may promote industrial peace—the administration of collective agreements went quite well for many years without any extensive aid from the courts. This slight cost seems worth the considerable gain of flexibility in contract administration, a flexibility that it is not possible fully to preserve under a regime of positive law.

The great shame is that the present regime of law is the product of an unthinking act by Congress and a theoretically unsound decision by the Supreme Court. Section 301 of the Labor-Management Relations Act was not a piece of thoughtful legislation. Enacted in 1947, it was responsive to the understandable, but basically simple-minded and generalized notion that a collective bargaining agreement, like a sales contract or an insurance policy, should be judicially enforceable. The disadvantages and difficulties of imposing a judge-made system of positive law at this point in the collective bargaining process was never canvassed by the legislature. Congress merely passed a vague statute delegating the whole problem to the courts.

Congress sometimes must be saved from itself. Section 301 was legislation which, when given a broad interpretation, was to work a major change in labor policy; a change that had not been considered by Congress. The Supreme Court knew this when it was called upon to elaborate the statute in the *Lincoln Mills* case. Accordingly, it would seem that its obligation then was narrowly to construe the statute—to hold, for example, that equitable relief was not available—in order to contain the statute's unfortunate effects, and thereby to further the major purposes of the entire federal scheme of labor-management relations. This, and a candid opinion explaining its actions, was the Court's obligation to Congress, whose legislative prerogative would not have been compromised had its enactment been treated in such an institutionally responsible fashion.

Part III

The Employee in the Collective Structure

Chapter 4

Collective Bargaining
and the Individual

Collective bargaining's effect on the individual worker concerns the law today no less than it did at the time of the early conspiracy cases. Then, seeing little merit in allowing workers to organize, the courts extended full legal protection to the individual worker who stood out against the union. To protect the individual, law simply crushed the collective movement, or did its best to do so. Today, because of the majoritarian bias inherent in collective bargaining—its commitment to democratic and egalitarian values—there must be some sacrifice of individual freedom. Without that sacrifice there cannot be effective representation of the mass of employees, and without such representation, the future for any democratic society may be bleak. But within the collective framework, the dissenting individual must be protected, and all those represented must be saved from negligent or corrupt representatives. Accommodating the interests of the dissenter and those of the majority is always difficult. The hallmark of a truly democratic society is its unwillingness to give up easily either majority rule or individual freedom. In the labor field this has proved to be a difficult accommodation. It has and continues to demand of all concerned with formulating and effectuating labor policy—Congress, the Board, the executive, the courts, and the parties—great understanding and ingenuity.

While early nineteenth-century rhetoric professed to protect the individual's freedom of contract, the Labor-

Management Relations Act enshrines aggregate freedom of contract. The union of a majority of employees in an appropriate unit is the exclusive bargaining representative of all employees in the unit, and the minority worker may not represent himself or be represented by another union in negotiating his terms and conditions of employment. Some few individuals might be able to obtain better compensation by bargaining on their own, but permitting them to do so would disrupt the workings of the system.[1] And thus the statute, as interpreted by the Supreme Court, makes it an unfair labor practice for employers to negotiate directly with individual members of a bargaining unit. Section 8(a)(5) requires employers to bargain with majority unions on mandatory subjects; to bargain with individuals would be to fail to bargain with the union.[2] In its *J. I. Case Co.* opinion—a labor law landmark—the Court tells us why individual bargaining is objectionable:

> advantages to individuals may prove as disruptive of industrial peace as disadvantages. They are a fruitful way of interfering with organization and choice of representatives; increased compensation, if individually deserved, is often earned at the cost of breaking down some other standard thought to be for the welfare of the group, and always creates the suspicion of being paid at the long-range expense of the group as a whole.[3]

In addition, the Court's opinion signals one source of friction that makes government protection of the dissenting individual necessary.

> The workman is free, if he values his own bargaining position more than that of the group, to vote against representation; but the majority rules, and if it collectivizes the employment bargain, individual advantages or favors will generally in practice go in as a contribution to the collective result.[4]

That some employees may have to give up favored treatment within the unit seems inevitable, yet, opposition to the majority union must be protected (indeed, encouraged) and this requires that government restrain the union from discriminating against anti-union employees. And those who voted against union representation may not be the only minority in need of protection from the union. Racial minorities, workers in specialized job categories, and those who oppose the established union hierarchy also may need government's protection.

Modern labor law has struggled to provide such protection without undercutting union effectiveness. Several approaches can be observed. First, specific statutory provisions have been enacted dealing with the relationship between job rights and union membership. Second, a general duty of fair representation has been fashioned by the Supreme Court—the union of the majority must represent all employees fairly. This duty is enforced by an agency of the government—court or Labor Board—that judges actions taken by the collective bargaining representative in the negotiation and administration of the collective agreement. Third, the employee may have some rights under the collective bargaining agreement that he can enforce if the union unfairly declines to do so. Fourth, the courts first, and then the Congress, have attempted through law to create or to maintain within unions a climate conducive to fair representation, and, in furtherance of our labor policy, beyond this to industrial democracy.

JOB RIGHTS AND UNION MEMBERSHIP

The statute forces some employees to accept representation by a labor organization that is not of their choosing. An unwanted union of the majority represents dissenting employees in all important job-connected matters. The economic power of the union might accomplish this irrespective of statute. The law, however, makes majority rule national policy. But the Labor-Management Relations Act does not compel union membership as a matter of policy; it only permits union and employer to negotiate a statutory union shop.[5] Workers may be required by contract to join the union within thirty days after they have been hired. Membership then becomes a contractual condition of continued employment. Because representation costs money, the union shop is of great importance to the union. And since the union represents all, the proposition that all should pay for the representation is compelling. The rhetoric of the labor movement claims that there is no room for the free rider.[6]

Yet there is nothing in the free rider rationale of compulsory membership to suggest that an employee's relationship with his union should control success in his job.[7] And the statute attempts to separate the two. It provides that:

> no employer shall justify any discrimination against an employee for nonmembership in a labor organization (A) if he has reasonable grounds for believing that such membership was not available to the employee on the same terms and conditions generally applicable to other members, or (B) if he has reasonable grounds for believing that membership was denied or terminated for reasons other than the failure of the employee to tender the periodic dues and the initiation fees uniformly required as a condition of acquiring or retaining membership.[8]

Clause (B) means that an employee can break every union rule in the book (to be distinguished from legitimate provisions in the collective contract), be expelled from the union, and under the statute retain his job if he tenders his dues to the union. Good union membership, as it were, and job rights are separated, or at least that is the statute's aim.

Union rhetoric claims that this statutory protection is misguided. If unions are to function as effective representatives, the argument runs, and to fulfill their role in establishing industrial democracy they must be able to demand loyalty. This can be accomplished best by tying job rights to good union membership.[9]

But the position places too little value on the right of vigorous protest by deed as well as word. Protest may be salutary not only because it tends to right wrongs but also because it can contribute to the long-run stability of the organization. If the protest is idiosyncratic, it is institutionally harmless because it will not attract support; yet it may still provide a psychological release mechanism for individuals. Protest that reflects group unhappiness, however, is likely to attract support which may induce gradual adjustment within the organization. And gradual adjustment is institutionally important because it conduces to the organization's long-run stability. Without gradual adjustment (and muzzling protest by tying job rights to good union membership would decrease its likelihood), pressure may build up and ultimately cause a major explosion that will injure or destroy the organization.[10]

Worker protest, of course, would be even more effective if the worker, without losing his job, could refuse to pay dues. But such a rule would encourage some workers to ride free simply to save money. This would have little institutional utility, and how could one distinguish between a principled dissenter and a cynical free rider?

Yet, the statute tolerates this type of free rider. It specifically permits states to enact legislation prohibiting the union shop.[11] Some twenty states have right-to-work laws in one form or another. Having nothing to do with the right to work, these laws are inappropriately named.

Their principal effect has not been to cripple unions, as the labor movement claims, but unjustly to shift the cost of representation. Those who support the union must pay more than they otherwise would. Some who as a legitimate protest would like not to pay dues must do so because their state has not enacted a right-to-work law. Inequality thus is introduced into a system designed to promote its opposite. In the end, after all, someone does have to pay for the free rider.[12]

The problem of job rights and union membership is broader than right-to-work laws, free riders, and union shop agreements; the statute attends to the broader problems. In sections 8(a)(3) and 8(b)(2) it makes it an unfair labor practice for an employer to discriminate and for a union to cause an employer to discriminate "in regard to hire or tenure of employment or any term or condition of employment to encourage or discourage membership in any labor organization." Permission to negotiate a statutory union shop is an exception to these provisions.

There is a considerable body of technical learning concerned with the interpretation of sections 8(a)(3) and 8(b)(2). In sum, the sections, as they relate to the encouragement of union membership, mean that in the negotiation and administration of the collective agreement, the union cannot legally bargain to the disadvantage of nonunion employees. For bargaining purposes, nonmembers must be treated the same as members. Moreover, discrimination may not be practiced against a bad union member in order to encourage him to follow the union rules; and this is so whether or not there is a union shop agreement.[13]

Observe that in these provisions the statute is sharply limited in its protection. As the Supreme Court has put it in a leading case:

The language of section 8(a)(3) is not ambiguous. The unfair labor practice is for an employer to encourage . . . membership by means of discrimination. Thus this section does not outlaw all encouragement . . . of membership in labor organizations; only such as is accomplished by discrimination is prohibited. Nor does this section outlaw discrimination in employment as such; only such discrimination as encourages . . . membership in a labor organization is proscribed.[14]

Limited though it is in scope, the statutory protection could be important if it were skillfully managed in the various industrial situations that give rise to problems. But skill has not always been the Labor Board's long suit. Nor have the courts always had the necessary skill. The union hiring hall is one industrial situation where natural opportunities for discrimination have made the problems exceedingly delicate. Here, the rights of the individual, the needs of the industry, the claims of policy, and the nature of the legal process intertwine in subtle fashion.

In some industries the standard model of many employees working regularly for a single firm is inappropriate. It will do well enough for the steel or automobile industries, but not at all for maritime, trucking, or construction. In these latter industries, one finds the worker employed now by one firm, now by another, moving about as demand for his labor shifts and changes. For both the employer and the worker this presents in an acute form the continuing problem of bringing supply into harmony or equilibrium with demand. How can the employer find the worker; the worker a job? Moreover, for the worker, the goal of employment security cannot be achieved through the accumulation of seniority with a single employer as often it can for his counterpart in manufacturing. Indeed, most of the problems involved in rationalizing the employment relationship are accentuated where workers as a matter of course do the same or similar jobs for several employers.[15]

The task of bringing worker and job together has yielded to various solutions. One is the shape-up (as described in testiomony before the Senate Labor Subcommittee):

> Under a shape-up system which still exists in some ports, what the men do is to come down to the docks and gather around and try to get a job. A hiring boss, a stevedoring boss, gets up in front of them and selects the men he wants to put on. . . . They have a rough idea when ships are coming in and they try to pick up a job. The men usually form a sort of half-circle, which is called a "shape," and they are selected for work in that way. . . . It is quite clear . . . that what develops in this kind of situation is that a man who has an "in" gets selected. That can mean many things. It can mean a man who kicks back part of his salary. It can mean a man who buys a drink for someone in a saloon. It can be a man who cashes his check in a certain place. . . . The selection is completely in the hands of the immediate boss over the operation.[16]

The union hiring hall, however, is the most common solution in many industries. It is an employment agency run by the union. Usually it is established through collective bargaining and at least some of the provisions respecting its operation are often incorporated in the collective agreement.

The hiring hall not only has the potential for bringing the worker and the job together—of supplying labor to the employer—but of rationalizing the employment relationships by building multi-employer seniority into a job referral system. But this will work well only if all employees who are hired by employers using the hall are referred through the hall. This in turn creates a substantial problem because it gives crucial power over employment opportunities to union officials.

The union is legally required to make referrals from the hiring hall without discriminating in favor of the good union man as against the bad union man or the non-union man; for discrimination based on such factors will encourage union membership. This legal requirement may tax the union official (saint though he is) responsible for running the hall.[17] Since the situation can breed discrimination, the question for the Labor Board and the courts is how the exclusive hiring hall—a useful institution—can be separated from the illegality that may accompany it.

The Labor Board's initial answer was straightforward and ineffective. In each case the individual had to prove discrimination. And this case by case approach was coupled with the Board's standard remedy: a cease and desist order; an order requiring the respondent to post notices promising no further discrimination; and an order requiring the reimbursement of the worker for the monetary loss he had suffered as a result of the union's discrimination.[18]

In time, however, the Board came to see that this approach was not effective. It simply did not root out the illegality inherent in the exclusive hiring-hall situation. As the Board said in the decision that overturned its prior approach:

From the standpoint of the working force generally —those who, for all practical purposes, can obtain jobs only through the grace of the Union or its officials—it is difficult to conceive of anything that would encourage their subservience to union activity, whatever its form, more than this kind of hiring-hall arrangement. Faced with this hiring-hall contract, applicants for employment may not ask themselves what skills, experiences, or virtues are likely to win them jobs. . . . Instead their concern is, and must be: What, about themselves, will probably please the Unions or their agents? How can they conduct themselves best to conform with such rules and policies as Unions are likely to enforce? In short, how to ingratiate themselves with the Union, regardless of what the Employer's desires or needs might be.[19]

The new assault stimulated by this view was two-pronged. First, in the *Mountain Pacific* case the Board declared that the hiring-hall provision of a collective agreement would be held invalid on its face unless it contained language which, in the Board's judgment, tended to cleanse the hall of its inherent illegality. Said the Board:

We believe, however, that the inherent and unlawful encouragement of union membership that stems from unfettered union control over the hiring process would be negated, and we would find an agreement to be nondiscriminatory on its face, only if the agreement explicitly provided that: (1) Selection of applicants for referral to jobs shall be on a nondiscriminatory basis and shall not be based on, or in any way affected by, union membership, bylaws, rules, regulations, constitutional provisions, or any other aspect or obligation of union membership, policies, or requirements. (2) The employer retains the right to reject any job applicant referred by the union. (3) The parties to the agreement post, in places where notices to employees and applicants for employment are customarily posted, all provisions relating to the functioning of the hiring arrangement, including the safeguards that we deem essential to the legality of an exclusive hiring agreement.

If, in the operation of a hiring hall that comports with these requirements and is therefore lawful on its face discriminatory acts occur, they are, of course, violations of the statute, both by the union which refers or refuses to refer on a discriminatory basis, and by the employer who has delegated the hiring authority to the union.[20]

Second, the Board put teeth—the teeth of a saber-toothed tiger—into its sanctions by applying what came to be known as the *Brown-Olds* remedy: All dues collected in connection with an illegal hiring hall, within a six-month period prior to the filing of the unfair labor practice, were to be returned to the employees.[21]

On review in the Supreme Court, the two-pronged attack on the evils of the hiring hall was beaten back by the Justices. The Board, the Court held, had acted beyond its statutory authority. The difficulty with the *Brown-Olds* remedy was that it was unrelated to any proven offense. It may be, as the Board insisted, that some old union members would have quit the union but for the fear of the consequences generated by the illegally run hiring hall. But it is highly unlikely that the illegality of the hall affected the conduct of very many union members. And thus the general reimbursement of dues ordered by the Board hardly could be considered compensation for injuries incurred through union illegality. In the case striking down the *Brown-Olds* remedy, the Supreme Court was clear about this.

The Board has broad discretion to adapt its remedies to the needs of particular situations so that "the victims of discrimination" may be treated fairly. . . . But the power of the Board "to command affirmative action is remedial, not punitive, and is to be exercised in aid of the Board's authority to restrain violations and as a means of removing or avoiding the consequences of violation where those consequences are of a kind to thwart the purposes of the Act." . . . Where no membership in the union was shown to be influenced or compelled by reason of any unfair practice, no "consequences of violation" are removed by the order compelling the union to return all dues and fees collected from the members; and no "dissipation" of the effects of the prohibited action is achieved.[22]

The primary law created by *Mountain Pacific* raised difficulties of a different nature, some of which the Supreme Court undertook to consider in *Local 357, Teamsters v. NLRB*.[23] The union maintained a hiring hall for casual employees, that is, employees who did not work regularly for any particular trucking firm. The collective agreement between the union and the California Trucking Association, which established the hall, failed to satisfy the *Mountain Pacific* requirements, but did provide that:

> Casual employees shall, wherever the Union maintains a dispatching service, be employed only on a seniority basis in the Industry whenever such senior employees are available. An available list with seniority status will be kept by the Unions, and employees requested will be dispatched upon call to any employer who is a party to this Agreement. Seniority rating of such employees shall begin with a minimum of three months service in the Industry, irrespective of whether such employee is or is not a member of the Union.[24]

Notwithstanding this no-discrimination pledge, the Board held that the hiring-hall provision was unlawful on its face because it did not follow the *Mountain Pacific* formula.

There would seem to be two difficulties with the Board's decision. First, the Board never really justified its *Mountain Pacific* standards sufficiently to qualify them as rigid rules rather than general guides. Without an explanation that draws upon the Agency's specialized understanding of discrimination in hiring halls—if in fact such understanding exists—it becomes difficult for a court to accept the proposition that any departure from *Mountain Pacific* warrants the Board holding a contract illegal irrespective of the reasonableness of the efforts made by the parties to avoid encouraging membership.

Second, the unfair labor practices centrally involved— sections 8(a)(3) and 8(b)(2)—are not neutral as to the blameworthiness of employer or union. With some exceptions the courts have insisted—and rightly so in view of the legislative record—that the Board prove that encouragement of union membership was the motive for, as well as the effect of, employer or union action; and that the action was not, therefore, motivated by an independent business purpose.[25] And this is so even though the encouragement itself may be inferred from whatever action the union or employer has taken; for example, the negotiation of a hiring-hall contract. As the Court in *Teamsters* suggests, any union-run hiring hall is likely to encourage membership. Indeed, the very existence of the union as exclusive bargaining representative may well have this effect.[26]

Accordingly, it does seem highly improper to hold, as the Board did, that a union and employer are guilty of unfair practices requiring proof of motive without ever attempting the proof. A decision under sections 8(a)(3) or 8(b)(2) tends to stigmatize the defendant unless it is understood that motive is not in fact, but only in legal fiction, an element of the unfair practice. But it would be both difficult and improper for the Board to promote such an understanding given the statute's legislative history and its judicial gloss.

The odd thing about the *Mountain Pacific* performance is that the Board did not undertake to regulate the hiring hall with the available set of unfair labor practices that, as a general proposition, do not require proof of motive.[27] Section 8(a)(1) provides that it is an unfair practice for an employer "to interfere with, restrain, or coerce employees in the exercise of the rights guaranteed in section 7"; and 8(b)(1)(A) makes it an unfair practice for a union to "restrain or coerce" employees in the exercise of such rights. Section 7 grants employees "the right of self organization, to form, join, or assist labor organizations, to bargin collectively." It also grants employees "the right to refrain from any or all of such activities."

When 8(a)(3) and 8(b)(2) practices are found, it generally has been assumed that the 8(1) offenses also are made out. For, apart from the statutory union shop, the right freely not to join a union is one of the rights guaranteed by section 7. And—union shop or not—so is the right, so far as employment is concerned, to disregard union rules, to be a bad union member. Thus, sections 8(a)(1) and 8(b)(1) were involved in the hiring-hall cases, but the Board did not consider them centrally important. And given the Board's approach this was correct. The 8(1) sections, however, have a function quite apart from sections 8(a)(3) and 8(b)(2) that could have been deemed centrally important for the hiring-hall problem. The 8(1) sections permit the Board to regulate business practices that are free of any improper motive, when the Board finds that the practices restrain or coerce employees in the exercise of their section 7 rights.[28]

The leading case is *Republic Aviation,* in which an employer had a general rule prohibiting all solicitation on his property.[29] During a union campaign to organize Republic's employees, the rule was enforced against employees who solicited for the union during their lunch hour. For violating the rule, they were discharged. The rule was in aid of plant efficiency, and its enforcement in the particular case was held to have been motivated by that business purpose. Restraint of employees in the exercise of their section 7 rights, however, was the inescapable consequence; and the Supreme Court held that the Board had the power to accommodate employee section 7 rights with the general property rights of the employer. Republic's no-solicitation rule was too broad. A narrower rule, one limited to working time, while still in fact a restraint, would be permissible. Here, as elsewhere, the statute could not wisely have been read literally; the task was to balance the needs of employees and the realities of business organization.

The principle of *Republic Aviation* is surely correct, although it must be said that the Board rarely makes the case for drawing lines where it does. But lines must be drawn, and fairly definite ones at that, if the statute is to be administered with even tolerable efficiency.[30]

The approach of *Republic Aviation* is relevant for the hiring hall. The hall serves a legitimate business purpose as an employment agency providing employees with some degree of job security. By encouraging union membership, however, it restrains employees in the exercise of their section 7 right "to refrain." Some accommodation is necessary, and under 8(1) it can be made without concern for motive. Perhaps something like the *Mountain Pacific* requirements achieve an acceptable result. If they do, efficient administration of the statute requires that a set of newly fashioned requirements be enforced as rules. But before that is possible, not only must the 8(1) approach be employed, so that the motive problem will be put to rest, but the relationship of the new requirements to the fact of employee restraint must be elucidated with some specificity and persuasiveness. One is entitled to ask this much of a specialized administrative agency, for this much is its most important reason for existence.

The question of remedy, however, remains. Subsequent to the demise of *Brown-Olds,* the Board had occasion to work out a creative remedy in a nasty case. Local 138 of the Operating Engineers ran a hiring hall in a vigorously and persistently discriminatory fashion. In the *J. J. Hagerty* case (the fourth case in which the operation of the hall was called into question) the Board, in addition to the standard remedy, ordered the union to develop an objective, nondiscriminatory referral system in conjunction with and subject to the approval of the Regional Director, and to keep permanent records of its operation, which were to be made available on request to the Director's agents.[31] While the first part of the order was struck down by the Court of Appeals—it seemed to require the negotiation of a hiring hall, or at least to bring the Agency too much into the bargaining process—the record-keeping portion was enforced.[32]

J. J. Hagerty is distinguishable from most cases in that a pattern of illegality is patent; but it is within the power of the Board to require record keeping in a hiring-hall situation where illegal discrimination has been proven. However, in order to fit the remedy to the offense, it would be appropriate to allow the union to show—where such is the case—that the discrimination was an isolated event. Moreover, where there is a pattern of discrimination, it seems to me entirely appropriate for the Regional Director to retain a veto over hiring-hall arrangements. Here, freedom of contract may have to yield some to the protection of the individual.

The combination, then, of these additional remedies in discrimination cases with the suggested section 8(1) approach would help achieve the statutory protection of the individual without impairing the utility of the exclusive union hiring hall. As we shall see, preserving useful institutions while protecting the individual is a goal which the solution to the hiring-hall problem shares with the solution to most other problems in this area of labor law.

It is extraordinary, if one thinks about it for a moment, that neither the Labor-Management Relations Act nor its counterpart, the Railway Labor Act, has an express provision requiring that the union of the majority exercise its power to represent all employees in a unit with absolute fairness and impartiality. That this is the case speaks rather badly for the Congress of the United States which did write into law the majority rule concept.[33] This congressional lapse, however, was to afford the Supreme court in *Steele v. Louisville & N.R.R.*, a 1944 case, a brilliant opportunity to display the creative art of statutory interpretation.[34]

The Brotherhood of Locomotive Firemen and Enginemen, the exclusive bargaining representative of the Louisville's white and Negro firemen, had a collective agreement with the railroad that discriminated against Negroes in the unit, because they were Negroes, in matters of seniority and promotion. The Negroes, none of whom was in the Brotherhood because the Brotherhood chose to be for whites only, sued the parties to the agreement. Alleging a right to fair representation which had not been respected, they sought to enjoin operation of the discriminatory agreement and, while unsuccessful below, they were able to gain a unanimous decision from the Supreme Court.[35]

In his masterly opinion for the Court, Mr. Chief Justice Stone produced a three-string bow, and each string propelled the Court to establish a duty of fair representation within the interstices of the Railway Labor Act. First, the statute's ultimate policy goal, the achievement of industrial peace, would hardly be served if the majority representative could ignore the interests of the minority group. Stripped by statute of the power to represent themselves by direct peaceful negotiation with their employer, the "only recourse of the minority would be to strike, with the attendant interruption of commerce, which the Act seeks to avoid." [36] Since legislation should be read to serve congressional purpose, the statute had to be read as imposing on the majority union a duty of fair representation.

Second, the statute would raise serious constitutional questions if it were interpreted to empower a majority union to represent a minority group of workers in total disregard of those workers' interests. Congress through the statute made the majority union the exclusive representative of all workers in the unit. It is highly questionable whether Congress can affirmatively grant a union power to regulate non-consenting individuals in an arbitrary manner. As a matter of the equal protection of the law, Congress itself could not legislate to the disadvantage of the Negro firemen because they were Negroes. Accordingly, there is reason to suppose that Congress could not delegate to the union a power which it does not itself possess. [37]

This constitutional question may not be quite as simple as it seems—in a subsequent chapter we shall return to consider it—but under any circumstances the underlying constitutional question is a serious one which is to be avoided by the Court if possible. Congress should not be taken to have legislated in a manner that trenches this closely upon the constitutional rights of individuals if a different interpretation is possible. And, unless it is inescapable, the Court ought not either to legitimate a constitutionally questionable statute by giving it the imprimatur of constitutionality, or, on the other hand, exercise its sovereign prerogative by declaring the legislature's work unconstitutional. The language of an enactment should be very plain indeed, the congressional will entirely unambiguous, before either of these courses is adopted as the appropriate judicial response. [38]

No such unambiguous statement of congressional will confronted the *Steele* Court. The statute was silent on the question of union power. An interpretation that bypassed the constitutional issue was, therefore, required of the Court, and, of course, the qualification of power by the duty of fairness provided a satisfactory judicial route to this result.

Third, labor statutes cannot be read in isolation. No statute can. Each new piece of legislation must be woven into the fabric of existing law. The textures must be matched so that the feel and look are uniform even though the garment may now be altogether different. This is not a job for the legislative process alone. It is a joint under-taking, and the court's role must be at once imaginative and sensitive: imaginative in discerning the direct purpose of the statute—the goals upon which the legislative eye is fixed—and sensitive to the values embodied in existing law, values reflecting the traditions of a people. Congress can surely reject these received values if they are not en-shrined in the Constitution; but just as surely it ought not to be understood to have done so unless it has been direct and unambiguous in the language it has employed. For Congress, the branch of government closest to the people, must take the major responsibility for sharp departures from the received traditions of the people.

It is this canon of statutory interpretation that moved the Court to say:

> The fair interpretation of the statutory language is that the organization chosen to represent a craft is to represent all its members, the majority as well as the minority, and it is to act for and not against those whom it represents. It is a principle of general appli-cation that the exercise of a granted power to act in behalf of others involves the assumption toward them of a duty to exercise the power in their interest and be-half, and that such a grant of power will not be deemed to dispense with all duty toward those for whom it is exercised unless so expressed.[39]

The first branch of the holding in *Steele*, then, is that the union of the majority has a statutory duty to represent fairly all employees in the bargaining unit. The second branch of the holding had to deal with the content of that duty, at least to the extent of determining whether the Brotherhood had failed fairly to represent the Negro firemen. Here this task was not taxing. Said the Court: "We think that the Railway Labor Act imposes upon the statutory representative of a craft at least as exacting a duty to protect equally the interests of the members of the craft as the Constitution imposes upon a legislature to give equal protection to the interests of those for whom it legislates." [40] And it is perfectly plain that no legislature could act toward the Negro firemen the way the Brotherhood had without violating the Constitution.[41]

Observe, however, what the Court is not deciding. *Steele* does not hold that the equal protection clause of the Constitution applies to the Brotherhood of Locomotive Firemen and Enginemen. The equal protection clause regulates state action—including, through the due process clause, the actions of the United States itself. It would require some rather sophisticated doctrinal analysis of the most far-reaching constitutional, and, therefore, fundamentally political, sort to equate Brotherhood action to state action.[42] Perhaps the equation is possible, but the Court was careful not to attempt it. The equal protection clause was employed as an analogy, not as a constitutional requirement. By analogy it served as a standard with which the Court was able to inform itself as to the meaning of fairness in the industrial setting with which it was concerned. And a perfectly splendid analogy it was! A legislature may not draw distinctions on the basis of color; such distinctions are barred absolutely. Labor unions when negotiating collective agreements are engaged in essentially legislative activity, prospectively establishing the terms and conditions of employment. Nothing in the union's structure or function suggests that it should be held to a less exacting standard of conduct in its legislative activities than state or federal legislatures. Indeed, as we shall see, a higher standard is called for.

Steele radiates beyond its narrowest holding. Of course it applies to the Labor-Management Relations Act.[43] And the statutory duty of fair representation runs to union members as well as non-members,[44] even though the full force of the industrial peace argument—perhaps the weakest string in the Court's bow anyway—may not be present. The union meeting, while not usually effective, is a peaceful forum for minority protest; but the other reasons for the duty compel the result. Since the member, by withdrawing his consent to union representation, by quitting the union, cannot change the fact of union representation —that can be done only by majority action—it is the statute that subjects the member to the majority rule doctrine. The avoidance and harmonizing canons of statutory interpretation require that the resulting union power be hedged about by a duty of fair representation.

Moreover, the union must represent all employees fairly in the administration of the collective agreement as well as in its negotiation. In *Conley v. Gibson,* where the union discriminated against Negroes by not supporting their contract claims, the Supreme Court met and appropriately overcame the technical difficulty with extending the union's duty to the grievance procedure. Mr. Justice Black spoke for the Court:

> The respondents point to the fact that under the . . . Act aggrieved employees can file their own grievances . . . or sue the employer for breach of contract. Granting this, it still furnishes no sanction for the Union's alleged discrimination in refusing to repre-

sent petitioners. The . . . Act, in an attempt to aid collective action by employees, conferred great power and protection on the bargaining agent chosen by a majority of them. As individuals or small groups the employees cannot begin to possess the bargaining power of their representative in negotiating with the employer or in presenting their grievances to him. Nor may a minority choose another agent to bargain in their behalf.[45]

And Justice Black reminds us further: "Collective bargaining is a continuing process. Among other things, it involves day-to-day adjustments in the contract and other working rules, resolution of new problems not covered by existing agreements, and the protection of employee rights already secured by contract. The bargaining representative can no more unfairly discriminate in carrying out these functions than it can in negotiating a collective agreement."[46]

The *Steele* doctrine has important application in Labor Board representation proceedings as well as in the negotiation and administration of the collective agreement, that is, in situations like *Steele* itself and *Conley v. Gibson.* But it was not until 1964, twenty years after the decision in *Steele,* that the Board seemed fully to recognize the extent to which the doctrine should affect its determination of whether a union may serve as exclusive bargaining agent.[47]

The statutory authority for the Board to weigh a union's ability to discharge its duty of fair representation is perfectly plain. The duty may reside in the interstices of many sections of the statute, but nowhere more obviously so than in section 9, dealing with representation proceedings, for that section announces majority rule: "Representatives . . . selected . . . by the majority of employees . . . shall be the exclusive representatives of all the employees."

Given the authority, then, the representation question

of central importance is whether a union that discriminates in membership, either by an outright bar of Negroes or by placing them in a segregated local, should be recognized by the Labor Board as the exclusive bargaining representative under section 9. The case against recognition is that unions which refuse to admit Negroes continue to discriminate in collective bargaining. This has been established by a continuous line of cases since 1944.[48] One reason for continued discrimination is apparent: an employee who is not a full union member has no voice in the political processes of the union. This means that he cannot participate in the choice of leadership. It also means that he cannot contribute to the formulation of the union's collective bargaining policies, or vote to approve or reject contracts that will regulate his industrial life. Membership is by no means a guarantee of fair representation. Unions tend to be oligarchies, and even in democracies, majorities discriminate against minorities. But experience and available evidence suggest that there can never be fair representation without membership.[49]

There are two minor technical difficulties, however, with the conclusion that the Board should not extend section 9 recognition to a "jim crow" union. First, the Court in *Steele,* without the benefit of twenty years of experience, was able to say that the union had "the right to determine eligibility to its membership." But even in 1944 it was also said that "the union is required to consider requests of non-union members of the craft and expressions of their views with respect to collective bargaining with the employer and to give to them notice of and opportunity for hearing upon its proposed action." [50] But these are words without substance in the absence of membership, for union leadership bent upon discrimination is not likely to give any weight to the minority employee who has no political power in the organization because he has no vote.

The second difficulty was mentioned and answered by

the trial examiner in the celebrated *Hughes Tool* case, where one of the issues was the decertification (removing the union as statutory bargaining representative) of a Jim Crow union. Examiner Reel had this to say in his generally excellent opinion:

> I am, of course, aware of the proviso to Section 8(b)(1) (A) stating "That this paragraph shall not impair the right of a labor organization to prescribe its own rules with respect to the acquisition or retention of membership therein." But this proviso goes only to the Union's freedom from liability under Section 8(b)(1)(A), and sheds no light on its right to representative status or certified status under Section 9. In this connection it must be remembered that we are dealing at this point, not with unfair labor practices, nor even . . . with actions to compel admission to membership, but solely with the powers and policies of the Board with respect to certification of unions which practice discriminatory racial policies in determining eligibility for membership.[51]

Mr. Reel announced, on reasoning smiliar to that advanced here, the principle that a union that bars or segregates Negroes cannot serve as statutory bargaining representative. And in its 1964 *Hughes Tool* opinion, the principle was approved by the Board in this terse paragraph: "We hold that the Board cannot validly render aid under Section 9 of the Act to a labor organization which discriminates racially when acting as a statutory bargaining representative." [52]

One wonders why the Board took twenty years, the time between *Steele* and *Hughes Tool,* to reach this conclusion. It was not for lack of professional urging. During the years many disinterested commentators had argued the position to the Board.[53] The unhappy fact is that the National Labor Relations Board failed during those twenty years to perform its task properly, to display the courage required of it, to provide leadership in the fight against discrimination; and leadership, nothing less, was what the statute required. Indeed, it was not until the civil rights movement caught up with the fair representation doctrine that the Board accepted its responsibility. At this point in time it would have taken misguided courage not to have decided the fair representation question as the Board did in *Hughes Tool*.

THE CIVIL RIGHTS ACT OF 1964

It is ironic that *Hughes Tool* was decided in the same year that Congress enacted Title VII of the Civil Rights Act.[54] That statute, with its forthright rejection of union privilege to bar membership on the basis of color, is a source of law that one would suppose the Board would have been pleased to have when it decided *Hughes Tool*. For if there were any doubt about national labor policy and racial discrimination—which there should not have been—Title VII puts that doubt firmly to rest.

Section 703(c), which became operative in July 1965, provides:

It shall be an unlawful employment practice for a labor organization—(1) to exclude or to expel from its membership, or otherwise to discriminate against, any individual because of his race, color, religion, sex, or national origin; (2) to limit, segregate, or classify its membership, or to classify or fail or refuse to refer for employment any individual, in any way which would deprive or tend to deprive any individual of employment opportunities, or would limit such employment opportunities or otherwise adversely affect his status as an employee or as an applicant for employment, because of such individual's race, color, religion, sex, or national origin; or (3) to cause or attempt to cause an employer to discriminate against an individual in violation of this section.

Title VII is much more than a union anti-discrimination statute. It is a full-blown fair employment practice act with provisions making it illegal for employers and employment agencies to discriminate on grounds of race, color, religion, sex, or national origin.[55] Moreover, in its application to unions the statute's ultimate remedy is direct. *Hughes Tool* made it possible for the Board to deny recognition as exclusive bargaining agent; but the strong union, able to impose its will on an employer, may not need such recognition. Under Title VII, however, a court can, should all else fail, order a union to admit an aggrieved employee to membership.[56]

Yet, while the primary rights created by the statute are far-reaching and generously conceived, and the ultimate remedy direct and substantial, the enforcement procedures, unless wisely developed by the courts and Department of Justice, can be very unsatisfactory and thereby make the statute more promise than fulfillment.

Title VII creates the Equal Employment Opportunity Commission which, when it has reasonable cause to believe that the statute has been violated and after giving state and local agencies a chance to deal with the problem, must try through "conference, conciliation, and persuasion" to right the suspected wrong.[57] The Commission, however, does not have an enforcement arm; unlike the Board it is not an adjudicatory tribunal. Its job is to negotiate. When negotiation fails it is the aggrieved individual who may go to court, and the individual must start fresh for nothing "said or done during and as a part of the [Commission's] endeavors may be made public . . . or used as evidence in a subsequent proceeding." [58] In the individual's suit, the court may appoint counsel, and, if the case is of general public importance, allow the Attorney General to inter-

vene. As to remedy: "If the court finds that the respondent
has intentionally engaged in or is intentionally engaging
in an unlawful employment practice . . . the court may
enjoin the respondent from engaging in such . . . practice, and order such affirmative relief as may be appropriate." It also may allow a reasonable attorney's fee.[59]

The difficulty with this procedure is that it calls upon
the individual to carry the burden of his cause, and this
at a time when he is likely to be discouraged. For while
there is some doubt, he probably must wait until after the
Commission has tried unsuccessfully to negotiate a settlement.[60] This is likely to be some time after the alleged
offense; the suit may itself be time-consuming, and it may
cost the individual money, which he may not have. Without
support from a group such as the NAACP Legal Defense
Fund, these enforcement provisions are bound to deter the
individual in his fight against discrimination.

However, in section 707, the statute authorizes the Attorney General to seek an injunction where he has reasonable cause to believe that any person or group is engaging
in a "pattern or practice of resistance." Labor unions
which practice racial discrimination would seem to fall
squarely within section 707. The wise employment of that
section by the Justice Department,[61] and the Labor Board's
new approach to fair representation in its section 9 proceedings, together with the pressure on unions in enterprises that deal with the government and are barred by
executive order from discriminating in employment opportunities,[62] give new hope in the fight against racial discrimination still practiced by a small but ugly and important segment of the labor movement.[63]

FAIR REPRESENTATION AND ECONOMIC DISCRIMINATION

The cases make plain what is implicit in *Steele*: nonracial discrimination too may violate the union's duty of

fair representation.[64] But while distinctions in a collective agreement that turn upon race can readily be branded as unfair, economic distinctions often should be judged as entirely fair. Indeed, some distinctions are essential. No one would suggest, for example, that wage differentials between skilled and unskilled workers necessarily violate the union's duty of fair representation. To the contrary, a failure to discriminate would be a breach of duty. On the other hand, a situation easily can be imagined in which an economic distinction has no legitimate basis in industrial experience, and can be explained only as a disregard of the interests of a minority group by the majority union. An obvious example is the union which, subsequent to an organizational campaign, negotiates a collective agreement providing inferior seniority rights for employees who, as the evidence demonstrates, happened openly to oppose unionization.

A leading case involving the duty of fair representation in a nonracial context is *Ford Motor Co. v. Huffman,* decided in 1953 by the Supreme Court.[65] Huffman and other similarly positioned employees of Ford were laid off under the seniority clause of a collective agreement that Ford had negotiated with the United Automobile Workers, the exclusive bargaining representative. The clause in effect dated an employee's seniority either from the time he was hired or from the time of his induction into the armed forces, whichever provided him with the greater employment security. This meant that Huffman, who had been hired by Ford before his induction, had less seniority than employees who started work at Ford after Huffman, but who had entered the armed forces before Huffman had commenced his work at Ford.

Claiming that this seniority clause was negotiated in violation of the Auto Workers' duty of fair representation, Huffman sought to enjoin Ford and the union from enforcing it to his disadvantage. He was ultimately unsuccess-

ful. The union had not violated its duty of fair representation, and the Court was quite clear as to why this was
so. First, public policy favored "crediting employees with
time spent in military service in time of war or national
emergency." The Selective Service Act, which provided for
such credit if a worker were employed before induction,
constituted one of several manifestations of this public
policy, all of which the Court was able to draw upon in
determining what fair representation meant in the particular industrial setting. Other manifestations of the announced public policy were the Veterans Preference Act,
which provided that credit for military service be given by
every civilian federal agency, whether military service pre-
ceded or followed civilian employment, and the report of
a Labor Department committee, which urged private employers voluntarily to follow the same approach "at least
for purposes of job retention." [66] Second, industrial practice—the practice under other collective bargaining agreements—was consistent with the Ford-UAW seniority clause,
as several briefs filed with the Supreme Court made clear.[67]

Because of the clear-cut public policy favoring veterans'
preference, the task of the Court in giving content to fair
representation—the relevant standard of decision—was not
difficult in *Huffman*. But what of the case—the standard case—where there is no clear evidence of public
policy? [68] The plain fact is that there is little authoritative
learning about this ordinary case, whether it involves the
negotiation or administration of the collective agreement.
Moreover, little serious attention has been given to the
development of standards appropriate for judging economic distinctions fair or unfair.

The *Steele* case, it will be recalled, did produce one standard which, as best one can tell from the terminology employed in subsequent opinions, seems to have found great
favor. "We think," the Court said, "that the . . . Act imposes upon the statutory representative of a craft at least as

exacting a duty to protect equally the interests of the members of the craft as the Constitution imposes upon a legislature to give equal protection to the interests of those
for whom it legislates." [69] Analogy to the equal protection
clause works well enough where distinctions are drawn
upon the basis of color. They are banned absolutely. The
test for economic discrimination under the equal protection clause, however, is the reasonableness, rationality, or
absence of arbitrariness of the classifications drawn by the
state.[70] And it is difficult to judge irrational, unreasonable,
or arbitrary economic distinctions that arise in collective
bargaining.

Suppose, for example, that company B is acquired by
company A, and that B employees go to work at A where
they are outnumbered ten to one. The union in A, which
is the representative of a majority of employees, is certified
by the Board as exclusive representative. If it and the company negotiate a collective agreement treating all of the
former B people as new employees for seniority purposes,
has the union violated its duty of fair representation to the
old B workers? With slight variations, this situation appears again and again in our industrial jurisprudence.[71]
Here the classification established by the collective agreement can hardly be held arbitrary in the constitutional
sense. Since the seniority of some employees had to be reduced, the union simply chose an arrangement which was
the least damaging to the seniority status of the greatest
number of employees in the unit. In the economic area the
equal protection clause demands no more of the states.
However, the wisdom of allowing unions to exercise the
kind of discretion that the states can exercise in the economic area is extremely questionable. The equal protection analogy may be a starting point, but there is no reason
why it should be the limit of regulatory power as well.

The metaphor that likens a collective bargaining agreement to public legislation can be at least as misleading as

an attempt to equate the agreement to a commercial contract. It is useful when employed to disabuse the uninitiated of naive beliefs, but should not be taken seriously as describing the union's duty of fair representation in the economic area. The metaphor when used this way preposterously misrepresents the status of labor unions in our society by suggesting that their collective bargaining decisions should be accorded the same respect under federal law as the decisions of state legislatures. They should not for at least two reasons.

First, the states are not institutions that have been delegated power by the federal government; it is the other way around. The labor union, by contrast, is the beneficiary of delegated federal power, and a responsible government must be intensely concerned with the way in which a private organization exercises this type of power.

Second, and more important, one of the justifications for the Court's employment of reasonable or rational as the standard for review of state economic decisions under the equal protection clause is the democratic nature of state government. To the extent that all the citizens of a state are able to participate through their representatives in the formation of governmental decisions, and to press their point of view through the pressure groups to which they belong and through the franchise which they may exercise every two or four years, to that extent judicial safeguards properly should perform a limited role—protection against patently outrageous economic decisions. Most of us, most of the time, are more deeply committed to democracy than we are certain about the wisdom of a judicial elite. But I would suggest that we would trust the judicial elite more if the decision under review were the product of an oligarchy rather a democracy. We would have to, even if it meant a serious impairment of efficiency.

State governments, of course, do not fully achieve the democratic ideal, but in most respects they do approximate it considerably more successfully than most labor unions. While union constitutions proclaim a commitment to democracy, and while the law—which we shall examine in the next chapter—in its conception goes as far as law can to make democracy a reality, the conditions necessary for democratic union government are often glaringly absent. Both theory and experience teach skepticism. Oligarchy, not democracy, is the rule in labor unions.

There are many theoretical and empirical studies which make this point.[72] One of the most useful is Seymour Martin Lipset's little essay on union government in his *Political Man*.[73] Mr. Lipset traces and catalogues the conditions and factors that pull against internal union democracy and push toward oligarchy. Among the more important are: (1) The tendency of the modern union to become bureaucratic, to adopt "a system of rational administration." This may result from the necessity of dealing with bureaucratic managerial structures, from the variety of services performed by the union, and, one would suppose, from a general drive for efficiency and order. While unions have no monopoly on bureaucracy—this they surely share with state governments—the consequences for union democracy are serious: "knowledge and skill of union operation gradually become available only to members of the administrative elite"; "by increasing the power of the administration over local units, the officials reduce the source of organized opposition"; "as control over decisions shifts away from the local levels, there is a decrease in membership participation and interest in local affairs." [74] These antidemocratic effects of bureaucracy in unions must exist in government as well, but in unions, it would seem, they are aggravated by the other factors and conditions that militate against democracy.

To return to Mr. Lipset's catalogue, (2) The leadership of a union tends to monopolize communication about internal union matters, both political and economic, for the leadership is in control of such channels for disseminating information and opinion as the union newspaper and the union meeting. (3) The leadership tends to have a monopoly of the political skills necessary for effective leadership. With rare exceptions there is no opposition party as such in a union. Unions are notoriously one-party governments. Those in power sharpen their manipulative and rhetorical skills; the worker with a latent political flair has little opportunity in the organization to develop his talent except as part of the establishment. And the skills of the leader are admired by the worker, and give status that few haves are pleased to share with have-nots. (4) Union leaders have good jobs relative to the worker in the plant. They are paid more and, as suggested, they enjoy higher status. Accordingly, they are at the least reluctant to give up their jobs. This means that they are likely to employ their considerable skills to block opposition. Moreover, should one lose office, he usually will seek employment outside the union movement where his manipulative and rhetorical skills may be put to use. Since the ousted leader usually does not return to the plant, he is not likely to be in a position to form an opposition party within the union. (5) Finally, since unions must compete with other organizations and activities for membership participation, the existence of an oligarchy often means the unions lose out. Oligarchy contributes to apathy and apathy to oligarchy.

Democracy in unions is more myth and aspiration than it is reality, and thus it is highly inappropriate to test the economic decisions of unions, when such decisions are challenged by affected workers, with a standard developed to judge the relatively democratically made economic decision of the states. The equal protection clause is an inappropriate analogy because it serves as a check on an altogether different institution. Yet language which calls to mind the standard of equal protection is most often employed by those courts that are aware that there is a problem in giving content to the duty of fair representation. Indeed, in *Huffman* itself the Supreme Court announced a standard that sounds much like equal protection, but happily qualified it by introducing an honesty and good faith test. Said the Court: "A wide range of reasonableness must be allowed a statutory bargaining representative in serving the unit it represents, subject always to complete good faith and honesty of purpose in the exercise of its discretion." [75] And in the recent cases of *Humphrey v. Moore*,[76] and *Vaca v. Sipes*,[77] the Court reaffirmed this statement of the standard. It also may be thought to have suggested in *Humphrey* that some procedural protection must be afforded the disadvantaged employees, that is, that they must have notice of the union's position and some opportunity to present their case. But *Humphrey v. Moore* indicates that the protection thus to be afforded is minimal and the requirements imposed upon the union easily complied with; and *Vaca v. Sipes* provides little insight into what reasonableness means in the fair representation context. Moreover, while the good faith and honesty test of *Huffman* is sound, it affords little protection to the individual. The absence of good faith or honesty is difficult to prove, and their presence in no way insures that the union's decision is substantively what it ought to be. To be generous with the Court, it simply is not clear where the Court is going with the duty of fair representation, but it does seem, if language is any evidence, that even that august body is taken in more than it ought to be by the equal protection analogy.

To some extent, perhaps, this can be explained by considering again the equal protection clause as applied to the economic decisions of the states. One reason for requiring no more than that state decisions be reasonable or rational is the democratic nature of the state decision-making process; but another is the institutional limitations of the courts. They are not well equipped to pass on the wisdom of a state's economic decisions. This latter rationale for the limit on the scope of judicial review under the equal protection clause—unlike the former—is applicable to court review of union decisions. Courts are not well equipped to evaluate the wisdom of a union's collective bargaining decision. This point, of course, has been made in other contexts several times in these pages.[78] And yet, should it lead here to judicial restraint, it may leave the individual inadequately protected.

FAIR REPRESENTATION AND THE NATIONAL LABOR RELATIONS BOARD

If the courts are not institutionally well equipped to protect the individual, perhaps the duty of fair representation should be enforced by a different institution. Can any governmental agency, no matter how specialized, do more than pass upon the rational nature of distinctions drawn in the collective bargaining process without seriously jeopardizing the process of collective bargaining itself? The difficulty is one that we have encountered before. Collective bargaining is a vital institution only so long as it is capable of adjusting to the complicated and changing demands of modern industrial society; only so long as it can accommodate itself to all industries and firms and to the ever-shifting conditions and problems within these industries and their subdivisions. This flexibility could be lost if a governmental agency became seriously involved in reviewing collective bargaining decisions. Such involvement, moreover, would place decision-making responsibility in the hands of those less well qualified than the parties to judge the needs of the parties; it would shift power from the private to the public sector; and it might tax the institutional capacities of even a specialized agency. In earlier chapters, I have argued against such interference by government with the statutory goal of freedom of contract. My earlier arguments, however, had a component that here is absent. In the arbitration, no-strike, and duty to bargain situations, governmental interference with freedom of contract is virtually without purpose. The stated purpose, industrial peace, is illusory. But governmental interference with freedom of contract to achieve fair representation is purposeful. To protect the individual, freedom of contract must yield; but if the standards that are developed for this purpose are drawn from an industrial context, the effect on collective bargaining need not be too hurtful.

The task of developing and applying standards is not easy; neither was the job of the Labor Board in the mid-thirties. It had to make sense out of the unfair labor practice provisions and out of the representation provisions of the Wagner Act. Responsibility for establishing the appropriate bargaining unit and for infusing meaning into the requirement of the duty to bargain forced the Board into a continuing examination of collective bargaining practices. A meaningful administration of the duty of fair representation would intensify this examination. For the principal standard to be applied in such cases should come from collective bargaining practices; and this is why the job should devolve principally upon the Board rather than the courts.

Collective bargaining, or more accurately the union's practice of collective bargaining, in part reflects the expectations of employees. In turn the employees' expectations are created by past practices viewed from the perspective of a present and perhaps changing industrial society. Each employee has expectations. He anticipates from his own experience and the experience of others that the union, if it is doing its job, will, when representing him in the negotiation and administration of the agreement, treat him in a particular way or ways relative to other employees in the unit. Since a particular employee may be unreasonable, single expectations are not in themselves important in creating standards. There is, however, a sense of the employee community on these questions which is significant for decision-making. Indeed, in most disputes between a union and an individual the expectations of the employee community may be the most important source of law available to an adjudicatory tribunal in determining whether a union has complied with its obligation to represent all employees fairly.

The expectations of the employee community vary with the nature of the interest at stake. Back pay, for example, is of a different and higher order than position on a seniority ladder. Seniority is important, but the expectation is not that seniority is immutable.[79] A right to back pay probably would be so considered. The extent of reliance, as well as the nature of the interest, is an important related factor which influences the intensity of expectations. The union in bargaining for seniority in the first collective agreement would have more freedom than in bargaining for changes of status after a system of seniority had been established. And, of course, in the administration of the collective agreement, the sense of the contract is the single most important source of employee expectations.[80]

Perhaps an illustration will make the standard clearer. In the situation where company A acquired company B, and the B employees were treated as new employees for seniority purposes, the union, under the expectation standard would be in breach of duty. Although position on the seniority ladder is subject to revision, bargaining for its total elimination seems clearly outside the expectations of the employee community. Some sort of dovetailing accordingly would be required to comply with the duty of fair representation.

Often it will not be easy to determine what employee-community expectations are in a given case. But is it really asking too much of the Board? Are not most decision-making bodies expected to perform similar tasks of similar difficulty? Courts are constantly trying to discover what a reasonable man in the position of the plaintiff or defendant would have done or would have thought. Judges are generalists. When their reasonable man comes from a specialized community they may be in trouble, and that is why they should not be charged with the principal task of administering the duty of fair representation. The Labor Board member, however, is a specialist, or soon becomes one after appointment. The expectations he must ascertain under the suggested approach belong to the community with which he is paid to become familiar. He has all of the aids necessary—a specialized bar, the use of expert testimony, official notice, a learned staff, and continuing exposure to the problem. We make too much of judging if we suggest that this task is institutionally too great.

Employee-community expectation, while the principal standard for deciding questions of fair representation, should not be the only standard employed. Coupled with it should be the good faith-honesty standard of *Huffman* ("complete good faith and honesty of purpose in the exercise of its discretion"). Moreover, clear public policy, such as the *Huffman* Court found with respect to veterans' preferences, and which a tribunal should find in the sex, religion, and national origin provisions of Title VII of the Civil Rights Act of 1964, should inform the meaning of fair representation. Furthermore, other labor legislation is itself useful. The Labor-Management Reporting and Disclosure Act, for example, seeks to protect political dissent within unions. Accordingly, should a union discriminate in collective bargaining against unsuccessful political dissenters, it would, in my judgment, violate its duty of fair representation.[81]

Although, since the 1962 *Miranda Fuel Co.* case, the Labor Board has claimed the statutory power to adjudge a union guilty of an unfair labor practice for violating the duty of fair representation, it has not made very substantial progress in giving content to the fairness standard in the economic area. Perhaps this is because of the internal battle over the threshold question of statutory power. Opinion has been deeply divided on the Board and elsewhere as to whether a violation of the duty of fair representation is, under existing law, an unfair practice (to be distinguished from a judicially cognizable offense and a relevant consideration in Board representation proceedings).[82]

The affirmative case seemingly is simple. Not only does the duty reside in the interstices of section 9, but as well in those of section 7. The brief for the Labor Board in a Court of Appeals case testing the question of statutory power—a case in which the Court sustained the Board's position—put the position this way: The duty of fair representation is

embodied in Section 7, for its guarantee to employees of the right "to bargain collectively through representatives of their own choosing" necessarily encompasses the employees' right to have their chosen collective bargaining representative fulfill its duty to act as a representative in a fair and impartial manner. Furthermore, Section 8 provides a prohibition against union conduct which may restrain or coerce an employee in the exercise of this Section 7 right. When a union which enjoys the status of exclusive bargaining representative of all the employees in a bargaining unit refuses to act on behalf of those it represents, or takes hostile action against any segment of those employees for irrelevant, unfair or invidious reasons, and by either this inaction or action adversely affects employees' terms and conditions of employment, the union not only breaches its statutory duty to be a fair and impartial representative; it also restrains

and coerces the affected employees in the exercise of
their guaranteed Section 7 right to bargain collectively
through their chosen agent, for such action or inaction
deprives them of the full measure of representation
which they are guaranteed and thus violates the prohibition of Section 8(b)(1)(A).[83]

Moreover, the Board has held that a violation of fair
representation constitutes an unfair labor practice under
section 8(b)(3), which imposes a duty to bargain in good
faith on the union.[84] To my mind this latter contention is
more difficult successfully to maintain, for it requires acceptance of the proposition that the union's duty to bargain in good faith is a duty that governs the relations
among union and employees. The traditional understanding of section 8(b)(3) has been that it regulates only the
relationship between union and employer.[85] Section 8(b)(1)
poses no such problem, for in terms it limits union conduct vis-à-vis employees.[86]

But the contention that a violation of the duty of fair
representation is an unfair labor practice at all does present difficulties as the Board minority has made plain.
Their position, however, rests upon a number of mis-
understandings: One is the effect of legislative silence; another, the relationship between an administrative agency
and Congress. In *Hughes Tool,* the minority—Chairman
McCulloch and Member Fanning—said:

Section 7 was part of the Wagner Act which in its
unfair labor practice section was aimed only at employer conduct. The Wagner Act also contained the
present Section 9(a). It hardly seems reasonable to
infer, in these circumstances, that Section 7 contained
a protected implied right to fair representation against
the bargaining representative, when the entire Wagner Act did not make any conduct by a labor organization unlawful. Section 7 was continued substantially

unchanged in the Taft-Hartley Act except for the addition of the "right to refrain" clause, which is not material to our problem. Although the Taft-Hartley Act added union unfair labor practices to the list of prohibited conduct, neither the Act nor the legislative history contains any mention of the duty of fair representation, despite the fact that the *Steele* [and other] decisions were well known, having issued three years previously. Again, although in the interval between the dates of the Taft-Hartley and Landrum-Griffin Acts, there were additional court decisions and articles by learned commentators in the law journals dealing with the legal problems of fair representation, Congress made no change in the wording of Section 7, and ignored the problem completely in adding a "Bill of Rights" section. . . . If Congress had really intended that violation of the duty of fair representation should be an unfair labor practice, it would seem that the 1959 revision afforded it an opportunity to clear up the uncertainty. Instead it remained silent. We do not believe that realistically this silence can be interpreted as in any way favorable to the contention that the right to fair representation is a protected Section 7 right.[87]

And the minority went on:

What we are confronted with is an important question of policy which should be resolved not by logomachy, but by a careful weighing of alternatives in the light of the ends to be achieved. Where specific statutory rights or prohibitions are not involved, should enforcement of the duty of fair representation be left to the courts, to the Board, or both? In such circumstances, should cases of breach of this duty insofar as they involve race discrimination be treated differently from breaches involving nonracial factors?

If a separate agency is created to handle the task of eliminating employment discrimination by unions and employers based on race, should the Board have a duty in this field? If so, what should it be? To ask these questions is to appreciate that the problem with which we are presented is legislative to be resolved by Congress and not by an administrative body whose duty it is only to administer the law which Congress has written.[88]

The congressional silence argument of Messrs. McCulloch and Fanning, if it is an attempt to use silence to prove the Board majority wrong, is totally misguided. It assumes that when Congress fails to act affirmatively it must be understood to have acted negatively. This simply is a contrary to fact assumption. The fact is that Congress did not act at all. There was no consideration of the matter, let alone a vote. Why should one conclude, therefore, that legislative inaction should be read to halt the normal growth of law (and for the purpose of testing the legislative silence argument, one must assume that the normal growth of law, but for legislative silence, would result in reading fair representation into section 7). I should suppose that Congress can halt the normal growth of law only by affirmative action, only by passing a statute. Thus, congressional silence is simply irrelevant; simply a method for avoiding the majority's contentions.

The minority's second argument is also wrong, and plainly so. There is an obligation—if our legal system is to work—on the part of all adjudicatory tribunals constantly to reexamine legal doctrine and to participate in the growth of law. Legislatures cannot possibly shoulder the entire responsibility for the law's development and adaptation to a changing world, and this is just as true of enacted law as it is of common law. Congress in particular cannot handle the myriad problems that arise in the administration of our vast network of regulatory statutes. The agencies and the courts must make the statutes work if it is within their institutional competence to do so. Of course, the major policy lines must be supplied by Congress. Of course, the adjudicatory tribunals must effectuate legislative policy and harmonize special law with the general jurisprudence of our legal system. Agencies and courts must be imaginative, creative, elaborators of congressional policy. Nothing less is required of them.

With respect to fair representation these fundamental principles require the conclusion that violation of the union's duty is an unfair labor practice. To sustain this conclusion on the technical level, the Board's brief, quoted above, is adequate. The duty of fair representation is not an explicit statutory requirement. The Supreme Court in *Steele*, true to the fundamental principles of an adjudicatory tribunal, read the duty into the statute. It resides comfortably in the interstices of section 7 as well as section 9.

On the more jurisprudential level, there are two compelling reasons for the conclusion thus permitted by the statutory language. First, in the economic area the duty of fair representation creates a meaningful right only if the principal task of administration is given to a specialized agency capable of elaborating its content through the continuing process of "litigating elucidation," as Mr. Justice Frankfurter once called it.[89] The Labor Board is institutionally fit to elucidate; the courts much less so. This may have been unclear at the time of *Huffman*; today it is perfectly clear. An adjudicatory tribunal is required to strive mightily to provide a remedy which will make a primary right a meaningful right. For if it fails to do so it fails to effectuate the legislative will, which, in the absence of strong contrary evdence, must be understood to desire a remedy appropriate to the right it has fashioned. Anything less than this comes close to attributing political fraud to the legislature.[90] Of course, there are exceptions to this proposition, but they are few and have no relevance here.[91]

Second, the quest for an appropriate remedy, which is the responsibility of the Board and the courts, is particularly urgent in view of the general concern for the individual and his interests manifested by Congress in such legislation as the Labor-Management Reporting and Disclosure Act. That statute, which we shall examine in the next chapter, deals with the individual within the union. But it, and its legislative history, is a powerful expression of the need for governmental protection of the individual employee in the collective system. This spirit of concern should not result in the creation of new primary rights by adjudicatory tribunals—that is for Congress—but it is a source of law which permeates and infuses our national labor policy with its spirit, and demands of adjudicatory tribunals an increased sensitivity to the whole range of remedial problems involving the individual and the collective bargaining process. This does not mean that the Board and the courts in shaping remedies should become callous to the other policy goals of the Labor-Management Relations Act, but those goals can be accommodated to a Board-administered right of fair representation.

One of the important subsidiary questions raised by locating the duty of fair representation within section 7 of the Labor-Management Relations Act is whether the Board's jurisdiction is exclusive, or whether the courts concurrently have power to adjudicate alleged violations of the duty—a power which once was theirs alone. It is generally true that the Board's jurisdiction over unfair labor practices is exclusive. Thus, for example, if a union were to engage in picketing that allegedly was an unfair practice, only the Board could make the determination and, if appropriate, grant relief. A federal court, in an action by the employer, would have no original jurisdiction. Nor would a state court, unless the picketing was a threat to community peace.[92] Many reasons support this doctrine, not the least important of which is the comparatively greater competence of the Board (a competence that stems in part from a sustained involvement with the problem) in developing decisional standards. It is better able through constant adjudication to elaborate the duty to bargain in good faith, for example, than are courts through episodic encounters; and, moreover, it is desirable that standards be elaborated and applied with uniform effect upon the regulated parties.[93]

These considerations strongly suggest that in the economic area the Board should have exclusive jurisdiction over the duty of fair representation; but there are counter-considerations which require attention. First, exceptions exist to the Board's exclusive jurisdiction, and the exception most relevant to our present problem occurs when conduct is alleged to constitute both an unfair labor practice and a breach of the collective bargaining agreement. A strike, for example, in certain circumstances, may constitute an unfair labor practice. It also may appear to be in violation of a collective agreement. If so, a court, in a suit brought by the employer, has jurisdiction under section 301 to try the case, notwithstanding the unfair labor practice.[94] Second, it has been held that employees as well as unions and employers may sue for breach of a collective bargaining agreement under section 301,[95] and, given the exception of contract suits to the general rule of exclusive jurisdiction, one might well suppose that where fair representation and employee rights under a collective agreement overlap, the courts retain their section 301 jurisdiction.

The relationship between fair representation during the administration of the collective agreement and employee contract claims under section 301 is intimate, as reflection upon the institutionalized nature of contract dispute settlement makes plain. A collective agreement, while a contract between a union and an employer, establishes the wages and working conditions of the employees. When a dispute arises during contract time over working conditions—that is, when the employer takes questionable action to the disadvantage of particular employees—the dispute is processed, in the typical case, by the union on behalf of the affected employees through the grievance procedure, and ultimately to arbitration. At any time, however, a dispute may be settled by the union and the employer. That is the purpose of the procedure. But any such settlement may raise a question as to whether the union, in agreeing to the settlement, has violated its duty of fair representation. This is particularly true if the union agrees that the employer acted properly. In addition, the action of the employer which precipitated the dispute in the first place may raise questions as to whether the employer has broken his contractual obligations to the affected employees.

Powerfully influenced by this relation between section 301 and the duty of fair representation, the Supreme Court in *Vaca v. Sipes* held that, even if the Board has jurisdiction over the duty, the courts retain their jurisdiction.[96] Moreover, while the Court failed explicitly to hold that breach of the duty was an unfair labor practice cognizable before the Board, that conclusion seems warranted by the tone and thrust of the Court's opinion. It seems clear, therefore, that Board and courts have concurrent jurisdiction in this important area of the law. Much less clear is the desirability of this development. The problem requires that we ruminate about employees rights in collective agreements, and ask when an employee should be allowed to sue an employer under section 301.

In his concurring opinion in *Humphrey v. Moore*—a leading case concerned with the rights of individual employees under a collective agreement—Mr. Justice Goldberg pinpointed the disutility of allowing individuals to challenge union and management decisions through contract litigation under section 301 of the Labor-Management Relations Act.[97] The case involved the seniority rights of workers who were scheduled to be laid off when their employer acquired another firm and the union and employer agreed to dovetail seniority lists. The Court majority, in holding against the complaining workers, treated the case both as one by individual employees under the collective agreement and as one involving an alleged violation of the union's duty of fair representation. Said Mr. Justice Goldberg:

> mutually acceptable grievance settlement between an employer and a union . . . cannot be challenged by an individual dissenting employee under section 301(a) on the ground that the parties exceeded their contractual powers in making the settlement. . . . The parties are free by joint action to modify, amend, and supplement their original collective bargaining agreement. They are equally free, since "the grievance procedure is . . . a part of the continuous collective bargaining process," to settle grievances not falling within the scope of the contract. . . . In this case, for example, . . . the contracting parties [employer and union] were free to resolve the dispute by amending the contract to dovetail seniority lists or to achieve

the same result by entering into a grievance settlement. . . . There are too many unforeseeable con-
tingencies in a collective bargaining relationship to
justify making the words of the contract the exclusive
source of rights and duties.[98]

And Justice Goldberg also said: "The employer's interest
[in a settlement made with the union] should not be lightly
denied where there are other remedies available to insure
that a union will respect the rights of its constituents." [99]

There is much to be said, and much has been said, for
this point of view. It represents a logical extension of the
general arguments I have made in earlier chapters concerning the flexible nature of a collective agreement and
the appropriate role of law in contract enforcement and
enforcement of arbitration awards that follows from this
and from the nature of the legal process. While such matters are important, however, they are less important than
protecting the individual, and thus Mr. Justice Goldberg's
approach is unacceptable unless it is coupled with an
expanded duty of fair representation as advocated in this
chapter.

The polar alternative to such a development of fair
representation—an alternative consistent with protecting
the individual—is to allow the individual extensive rights
under the collective agreement both at the informal stage
of dispute resolution, that is, in the grievance procedure,
and in arbitration or before the courts.[100] As Clyde Summers has shown in his perceptive article on this subject,
several types of situations will arise, each of which requires
careful discrimination by a decision-making tribunal in
determining the relative interests of union, employer and
employee.[101] Thus, for example, the union may be perfectly willing to process an individual's grievance, but the
individual, out of distrust, may wish to handle his own
complaint. And this may occur at any stage of the griev-

ance procedure, at arbitration, or in a judicial proceeding. The union in a different situation may proceed halfheartedly or decide to drop a grievance after the early stages, and for a variety of reasons going to its view of the merits of the employee's claim, or to the employee's color, his political activities within the union, or the union's interest in other grievances and its belief that it must trade off one grievance for another if it is to maximize the welfare of all. In still a different situation, the union may—and again for a variety of reasons—decline to have anything to do with an employee's grievance. Moreover, in any of these situations the grievance may call into question provisions of various sorts in a collective agreement. Some may be quite explicit, some purposely ambiguous or inadvertently so, some may have important implications for the subsequent administration of the agreement, some may have none. And, of course, the collective agreement may be silent on the question, the issue being unforeseen, purposely omitted, or unforeseeable due to changes in the industrial environment.

The law could be elaborated in a way that would be sensitive to these myriad distinctions, as Mr. Summers has shown, and such a development should meet, in part at least, the objections raised by Mr. Justice Goldberg.[102] But it would result in a body of substantive law which through contract litigation evolved principles and rules similar in content to those which should evolve through a sensitive elaboration of the duty of fair representation. For the underlying question posed by the two conceptually different approaches, is in fact the same; namely, to what extent are union decisions, participated or acquiesced in by management, to be limited by the interests of affected employees?

Two reasons suggest that protection of the individual is better achieved through an expanded duty of fair representation as earlier proposed. First, the substantive issues are only partially contractual in nature. Perhaps they can be forced into the contractual mold, but it would take some hard pushing. The underlying problem is the total relationship of employee to his union and to his job. The collective agreement does not begin to exhaust these relationships, while the content of the duty of fair representation necessarily encompasses it all. The point is that fair representation is the direct route; contract enforcement, the circuitous one. And even for the most skillful traveler a circuitous route sometimes leads up a blind alley.

Second, the courts are not skillful travelers. The contract route means that the body of substantive law will be developed by the judges and the arbitrators. The courts have failed for understandable institutional reasons in economic fair representation cases. They are likely to fail when facing the exact same problems in the doctrinal context of contract. Nor is arbitration promising. The difficulties of the individual's direct participation in arbitration—how is the arbitrator chosen, who pays him—can yield to inventive solution;[103] but the bias of the arbitration fraternity toward the institutional interests of labor and management cannot. Arbitrators, who in standard cases are paid by labor and management, survive only so long as they please labor and management. In most of the cases where the individual is on his own, the pleasure of labor and management does not lie in the successful resolution of the individual's cause.[104]

The Supreme Court in *Vaca v. Sipes*[105] declined to choose between the two routes—contract or fair representation—for protecting the individual during contract time. Rather, it preserved fair representation and individual suits under section 301. In so doing, however, it may have seriously undercut both. For while the Court saw the relationship between the duty of fair representation and the section 301 action, it probably did not see clearly enough. It virtually ignored the content of the duty except to affirm the *Huffman* formulation. It said little about the bearing of the collective agreement upon the duty's content.

Yet, the terms of the collective agreement should importantly influence the content of the duty; and they would, were the standard formulated in terms of the expectations of the employee community (what the agreement says influences employee expectations) as I have urged. The relationship between the terms of agreement and fair representation is much more doubtful where the standard is phrased in constitutional language.

The relationship which the Court did see between fair representation and individual suits under section 301 makes the content of the duty—the standard to be applied —critical. For the Court stated:

> We think . . . the employee may seek judicial enforcement of his contractual rights [in a suit against the employer under section 301] . . . if . . . the union has sole power under the contract to invoke the higher stages of the grievance procedure [and this is the usual situation, or will be after *Vaca*], *and* if . . . the employee-plaintiff has been prevented from exhausting his contractual remedies by the union's *wrongful* refusal to process the grievance.[106]

By *"wrongful"* the Court means that the union has broken its duty of fair representation, for it went on to say:

> It is true that the employer in such a situation may have done nothing to prevent exhaustion of the exclusive contractual remedies to which he agreed in the collective bargaining agreement. But the employer has [broken the contract] . . . which could be remedied through the grievance process to the employee-

plaintiff's benefit were it not for the union's breach of its statutory duty of fair representation to the employee.[107]

In the typical situation, the employee can proceed against the employer if, but only if, he can show that the union is in breach of its duty of fair representation. Thus the utility to the employee of his contract right depends upon the content of the duty of fair representation. And the content of the duty remains decidedly in doubt.

Moreover, in many cases where the union acts in good faith, proof that the union has failed in its duty proves *a fortiori* that the employer has broken his contract, for no matter what the content of fair representation is, it cannot impose on the union a duty to be right (to decide the way a court would in a section 301 case) on every grievance. For example, if an employee is discharged and the union in good faith decides not to pursue the grievance through arbitration—decides that the discharge was justified under the collective agreement—that decision would not under any test be a breach of duty if the union's conclusion about the sense of the contract accorded with the expectations of the employee community. And this is so even though a court, if it had a chance, might interpret the contract in the employee's favor.

Under these circumstances, one is constrained to wonder what the advantage is of retaining employee actions under section 301 where the agreement establishes the usual grievance procedure and requires arbitration. A section 301 action, if it awards damages to the employee, is rather unfair to the employer who, although wrong, acted in good faith in the first place and then entered a settlement in good faith with the union. Nor would it seem to be of much benefit to the employee if the union were fully accountable. But that may be the rub, as we shall see.

There are four types of situations to be considered: (1) The union is in breach of its duty in not processing or continuing to process the grievance, and the employer is in breach of contract. (2) The union is in breach of its duty (it did not act in good faith), but the employer is not in breach of contract. (3) The union is not in breach of its duty; the employer is in breach of contract. (4) Neither is in breach. On no theory can the employee expect redress in situation 4. Under *Vaca,* he is barred in situation 3. In situation 2, the section 301 action, by hypothesis, is worthless. In situation 1, the union's breach of its statutory duty is a central cause of the employee's harm, and one would think, therefore, that the union should be fully liable in damages for the injury. And this should be true whether the employee proceeds in a court or the proceeding is before the Board.

There may, however, be some difficulties with granting full relief in situation 1 if the union is the only defendant. Affirmative relief, such as reinstatement of a discharged employee, requires jurisdiction over the employer. This can be obtained in a judicial forum by the individual's section 301 action. The employee's difficulties can be eased by allowing him to proceed against both union and employer in a suit combining breach of contract and fair representation. The Board, on the other hand, while it has jurisdiction over the union—since breach of fair representation is itself an unfair labor practice—may not have jurisdiction over the employer, for breach of the collective agreement is not itself an unfair labor practice. And unless the union caused the employer to break the agreement, as it did in the *Miranda Fuel* case, or the employer settled the dispute in bad faith, there may be no employer unfair practice and thus no power in the Board to issue an affirmative order against the employer.[108] What the Board can do in such a case, however, is order the union to process the grievance through arbitration.[109] In that case, of course, the arbitrator should not award the employee back pay. He should just order reinstatement, for, on my assumption, the Board would have issued a full monetary award against the union. This result would seem fair to the employer who settled in good faith with the union.

The envisioned procedure before the Board and arbitrator has its drawbacks: it is not as expeditious as the judicial proceeding; and it exposes the employee to an arbitrator, who, under the circumstances, is less likely, on the average, to be disinterested than is the judge.[110] But in my judgment this is outweighed by the fact that the existence of such a procedure before the Board makes it unnecessary to provide individuals with a judicial forum under section 301, and that, in turn, makes it unnecessary to reject, as did the Court in *Vaca v. Sipes,* the considerations that press for exclusive Labor Board jurisdiction over the duty of fair representation.

The *Vaca v. Sipes* Court rejected more than that, however. It rejected the proposition that the union is fully liable for the monetary harm suffered by the employee in situation 1. It failed to explain why the union should not be liable fully. Nor was it clear about the extent of the union's liability. This much did the Court say:

> The governing principle . . . is to apportion liability between the employer and the union according to the damage caused by the fault of each. Thus, damages attributable solely to the employer's breach of contract should not be charged to the union, but increases if any in those damages caused by the union's refusal to process the grievance should not be charged to the employer.[111]

This principle has a variety of unfortunate consequences. First, it is unfair to the employer who settles a dispute

with a union in good faith. True, after litigation it is
determined that he broke his contract, but that might
have been in doubt at the time he acted. Moreover, at
the time of settlement, he may have had no idea that the
union was failing fairly to represent the employee. This
would likely be the case, for example, if the union had
been moved not to process the grievance because of internal union tensions involving the employee.[112]

Second, the Court's approach may have undermined the
duty of fair representation. It simply is not clear what the
union is liable for. But, if its liability is minor, breach
will not be sufficiently deterred by law and this will be
ironic indeed. The rhetoric of the *Vaca* opinion proclaims
the importance of the duty in the scheme of national labor
policy.[113] So important a primary obligation deserves a
remedy with teeth. Perhaps enough remain; one cannot be
sure. If the union is liable in, say a discharge case, for back
pay from the time it broke its duty until judicial or
agency decision, the law's delay may make the remedy
substantial.

Third, the Court's decision on damages makes the
judicial rather than the administrative forum even more
attractive than it otherwise would be. And this is unfortunate, for I must insist that the Court is wrong when it
tells us that "it can be doubted whether the Board brings
substantially greater expertise to bear on these problems
than the courts." [114] It cannot be doubted that in the
fair representation area experience is the best teacher.
Exclusive jurisdiction in the Board would have ensured
the experience that the several district courts (judge and
jury) and their state court counterparts cannot hope to
obtain. And it would have ensured that the duty on the
union to represent employees fairly was uniform throughout the fifty states.

Thus must one conclude that out of the deepest concern for the individual in the collective structure, and the flexibility of that structure, the Court has fashioned a remedial scheme which can work well only if the lower court judges are more than most able men. Unhappily, there is nothing in our history to suggest they are, or are likely so to become.

Chapter 5

The Individual and
His Union

The principal claim of Chapter 4 is that government through law has an inescapable obligation to protect the individual worker from unfair collective bargaining decisions made by the majority union. The claim rests partially upon the same argument as that advanced in 1959 by the Senate Labor Subcommittee which advocated governmental regulation of some aspects of internal union affairs:

> Under the National Labor Relations and Railway Labor Acts the union which is the bargaining representative has power, in conjunction with the employer, to fix a man's wages, hours, and conditions of employment. The individual employee may not lawfully negotiate with his employer. He is bound by the union contract. In practice, the union also has a significant role in enforcing the grievance procedure where a man's contract rights are enforced. The Government which gives unions this power has an obligation to insure that the officials who wield it are responsive to the desires of the men and women whom they represent.[1]

When used to justify the regulation of internal union affairs—regulation that protects the member from unfair union discipline, insures his right to speak in dissent and to oppose the leadership, guarantees fair and frequent elections, and generally insists upon the ideal of democratic union government—the argument encounters objections different from but at least as forceful as those discussed in the last chapter. There the emphasis was on governmental review of union collective bargaining decisions, and the major objection to any affirmative proposal, such as a duty of fair representation—surmountable though it is—was seen to be the effect of review upon a regime of free collective bargaining, of freedom of contract and the values of private ordering. The objections that must be surmounted in order to justify governmental regulation of internal union affairs, on the other hand, consist of doubts as to how successful such regulation can be, what such regulation is likely to cost society, and whether the cost is worth the gain. That the Labor-Management Reporting and Disclosure Act provides substantive regulation in fact does not make these questions any less deserving of close attention.

However, before considering these questions, it is well to be clear that while governmental regulation of internal union affairs seeks, among other things, to achieve fair representation by providing a climate within the union conducive to full membership control and hostile to top-down rule, it cannot, no matter how successful it may be, protect the minority from the majority. And accordingly, regulation of internal affairs cannot be thought of as an alternative to governmental review of union collective bargaining decisions. A predominantly white and fully democratic Brotherhood of Locomotive Firemen and Enginemen, with the Negroes enjoying full participation rights, would still have discriminated against Steele and the other Negro firemen.

To turn then to some of the objections to governmental regulation of internal union affairs: one starts with the fact that union government usually falls far short of ideal democracy or even of the democracy one generally finds in state governments. For the several reasons adumbrated in the last chapter—bureaucracy, one-party government, status differentiation between leader and member, apathy, and so forth—unions have a powerful propensity toward oligarchy, a condition which it is difficult to reverse, and which there is no reason to think federal legislation has reversed. Oligarchy is the natural result of union growth and of the functions unions perform. Unless unions are to be changed completely, it is the realistic model of union government. Moreover, this lack of internal democracy does not necessarily destroy the contribution of labor unions to political democracy which depends upon group representation as well as the individual franchise, free speech, and a two-party system. As Mr. Lipset has suggested: "Even the most dictatorial union is a better protector of workers' economic interests, and of political democracy within the larger society, than no union, provided that the union is not a tool of either the state or the employer." [2]

Union independence from the state is an additional consideration which may influence one's judgment as to the wisdom of legal intervention into internal union affairs. The value of autonomy is the benefit of power diffusion which is so important to the health of a democracy. Of course, fair representation and other methods of protecting the individual trench upon this value. But one might ask —to the extent that these direct techniques protect the individual from economic abuse by the union—why additional regulation is necessary. To put this another way, once job rights and union membership are separated—and this is the thrust of sections 8(a)(3) and 8(b)(2) and in part the aim of fair representation—why should government be concerned with the internal affairs of a union any more than it is with the internal affairs of a country club?

Finally, if government succeeds in making unions more democratic, may it not thereby reduce the public responsibility of union leadership? Union members are likely to demand results in the short run. There is a constant pressure for immediate economic gain through collective bargaining. The leader who may find himself ousted if he fails to satisfy his constituency—unlike the politically entrenched official—is forced to respond affirmatively to such pressure even though his response may be contrary to the long-run best interests of industrial relations or to the goal of wage-price restraint, so often these days alleged to be in the public interest.[3]

Answers to these objections must candidly recognize their partial validity. Law cannot eliminate oligarchy, but it can protect dissent and encourage a leadership that is more responsive to the rank and file. And this is important both for the dissenter and for the long-term well-being of the union. As earlier remarked, bottled-up dissent that is symptomatic of widespread displeasure may eventually explode and destroy an institution. Dissent that is heard and tolerated may lead to evolutionary change within the union, change that makes for long-run institutional stability.[4]

Leadership which is more responsive to the rank and file may be less responsible from a public point of view. There is inescapably a tension here, but because of the conditions that give rise to oligarchy, conditions that law cannot change markedly, the tension is not increased very much by governmental regulation of internal union affairs. However, tension between public responsibility and membership desire is a major problem in every modern capitalistic state and one to which we shall recur in the chapter on bargaining settlements and economic policy.[5]

As to the value of autonomy, labor unions are not country clubs as these pages surely have made plain. Nor can the law of sections 8(a)(3) and 8(b)(2) plus the duty of fair representation fully separate job rights from union membership. The individual in his relationship with the union is more the concern of government than the individual in his relationship with a country club because the union usually is much more important to an individual's economic well-being, and economic well-being is today a central area of concern for government.[6]

These answers constitute defensive positions assumed in response to serious objections to governmental regulation. They are necessary but perhaps not sufficient reasons for intervention into internal union affairs. It remains to make the affirmative case. That case, it seems to me, turns upon what may be called the morality of promise-keeping and the obligation of government through law to protect the reliance and expectational interests generated by the making of certain types of promises.

The myth and aspiration of the labor movement have always been the democratic ideal. This is reflected not only in the rhetoric of the movement, a rhetoric that has proclaimed industrial democracy and its necessary concomitant union democracy, but also in the broad outlines of all labor organizations' written constitutions and in such documents as the A.F.L.-C.I.O. codes of ethical practices which insist upon a model of democratic union government.[7] This commitment, it will be recalled, has provided in turn powerful ammunition to the advocates of legislation protecting unions and promoting collective bargaining. The Wagner Act is the principal example.

Union democracy then is the promise that has been held forth by the unions to the working man and the public alike. It is the promise which in part is responsible for the political support and public acceptance of the unions. It is the promise of worker participation in industrial government, of manhood in emasculating industry, of control over one's destiny in a machine-run society. It is an important element in the moral case that has been made by and for the labor movement. The social sciences may demonstrate that democracy can never be achieved; but no matter. The ideal must be pursued by union leaders, and when it is not, when union leaders are shown to be uninterested in the quest, there is a shock of betrayal, and a

demand for reform, which often means for law. The Mc-
Clellan Committee hearings in the Senate during the late
1950s were a dramatic and highly publicized example of
such disclosure and its consequence.[8] While the hearings
centered on corruption rather than on lack of democracy,
they dwelt to some extent with the latter, and more significantly, they exposed to public view some hair-raising
examples of union leadership devoted to private gain and
callously indifferent to anything else. The Labor-Management Reporting and Disclosure Act of 1959 was the consequence.

As so often is the case with American law, however, the
courts rather than the legislature were the first governmental forum invited to offer assistance to those most
directly affected by the immorality of promise breaking.
My aim is to explore some institutional aspects of the
judicial response before turning to the 1959 statute.

SOME ASPECTS OF THE COMMON LAW

Over the years the courts have been called upon from
time to time to umpire the relationship between unions
and their members. Judicial aid has been requested in a
variety of situations ranging from alleged financial dis-
honesty by union officials,[9] through complaints concerning
the process of electing union officers and the disciplining
of members by the union,[10] to the control of the local
union by its parent international.[11] The courts have had
a difficult time, and the attitude of courts in different states
and within the same state has not always been uniform;
but very often the courts have endeavored to hold unions
to a democratic ideal.[12] This can be seen perhaps most
clearly in the area of union discipline. The object of
inquiry into that subject here is not to attempt a restatement of the substantive and procedural law that has been

developed, but rather to attempt to formulate a theory in justification for this observed trend.[13]

Union discipline is essential to union survival and effectiveness. Without sanctions dues may go uncollected, bargaining standards unobserved, and collective economic action for naught. Yet union discipline too may be used to dominate political opposition and suppress unwanted dissent. Members who speak out, members who try to capture control of their organization may find themselves suspended for their troubles. In such cases the courts at common law, when called upon, usually will protect the member by ordering his reinstatement. Thus, in his exhaustive study of New York cases, Clyde Summers found that: "The conduct which has in fact received the broadest judicial protection is the exercise of democratic rights within the union. The courts have envisioned unions as democratic institutions, and although seldom articulate, have bent the theories, case by case, to place freedom of speech and assembly beyond the reach of union discipline." [14]

The question of first importance is whether courts should perform in this way, whether in protecting the democratic ideal and limiting the disciplinary power of unions they are properly functioning as adjudicatory tribunals. This is to ask whether their judgments are fair as between the parties, whether, in other words, they are applying appropriate preexisting standards. This in turn invites consideration of what the standards for decision are in these cases and the source of those standards.

The place where inquiry begins is the constitution and bylaws of the union. The constitution purports to be the instrument that sets forth the obligations of the members and the authority of the organization. Any marked departure by the organization from the terms of the constitution which disadvantages a member is unfair to the member.

He is entitled to expect that the union will comply with its own provisions. Accordingly, it is not surprising that in adjudicating claims of improper discipline, the courts turn to the union's constitution. It is said to be the principal standard against which disputed conduct is judged; often it is considered a contract between the union and its members. The classic statement is found in *Polin v. Kaplan*:

> The constitution and by-laws of an unincorporated association express the terms of a contract which define the privileges secured and the duties assumed by those who have become members. As the contract may prescribe the precise terms upon which a membership may be gained, so may it conclusively define the conditions which will entail its loss. . . . This is not to say, however, that a court will decline to interfere, if an expulsion has been decreed for acts not constituting violations of the constitution and by-laws, and not made expellable offenses thereby, either by terms express or implied. In such an instance, the expulsion is not within the power conferred by the contract. Accordingly, the proceedings will be set aside and the associate restored to membership.[15]

When one turns to this contract, to the constitution of the union, one finds that in the vast majority of situations there is constitutional language which reasonably might be read to permit union discipline of members who seek boldly to speak or act in dissent. According to a study of 158 unions with a total of 16.9 million members conducted by the Bureau of Labor Statistics in 1963:

> Every constitution that contained a reference to grounds for discipline provided at least one general or "catchall" prohibition that did not explicitly define the behavior outlawed. . . . In 13 unions, these gen-

eral clauses were the only type found, while in 139 constitutions they were added to other prohibitions, more specific in nature.

Certain general prohibitions, in practice, could be as definite and precise as a specific prohibition. For instance, the offense most prevalently cited or proscribed, "violate the constitution," could be defined by reference to specific constitutional provisions. Other general phrases such as "conduct unbecoming a member" or "bringing the union into disrepute" were perhaps far less determinate. . . . Other equally broad but less prevalent catchall clauses prohibited "malfeasance, misfeasance or nonfeasance," violating the "duties, obligations, and fealty of a member," and "any dishonorable act." [16]

Yet the courts find ways to protect the member. One method is by close attention to procedural niceties. The B.L.S. study describes the typical union constitutional procedure in discipline cases:

The variation in the patterns of procedure stems largely from the multiple form of union government. As a general rule, the local union was the body with plenary original jurisdiction, while the international union, in cases involving members and local union officers, had a more limited original jurisdiction, restricted, in the main, to emergency situations and offenses against the international union. . . . The multiple levels of government thus gave rise to two basic patterns of trial procedure—one for trials originating at the local level, and one for trials originating at the international level. As to the former, a typical pattern was as follows: (1) Filing of charges by a member or local officer; (2) service of charges on, and notice of trial to, the accused; (3) trial before the local governing body; (4) decision by the membership as to guilt or innocence; (5) appeal to a district council or other intermediate body, if any; (6) appeal to the international executive board; and (7) appeal to the international convention. . . . As to trials originating at the international level, the following general pattern prevailed: (1) Filing of charges by an international authority; (2) service of charges on, and notice of trial to, the accused; (3) trial before, and decision by, the international executive board; and (4) appeal to the convention.[17]

Of course, it is appropriate for courts to insist upon compliance with the letter of constitutional procedure; however, courts go well beyond this. For one thing, in discipline cases involving political dissent they look closely for bias on the part of union tribunals.[18] While bias is always a problem and often difficult to discover, it becomes an acute problem here for it is the union establishment that is in charge of the disciplinary process and that establishment is not apt to be disinterested.

But the courts go beyond to impose upon the unions judicial notions of fair procedure.[19] Can one justify this? What is the authority of the judiciary to impose external criteria of procedural fairness? The answer, I think, is to be found in the widespread and general community acceptance of the requirements necessary for a fair adversary proceeding. The acceptance grows out of extensive experience with many forms of adjudication—administrative as well as judicial—experience that is codified in codes of procedure and concepts of procedural due process needing but slight adaptation to fit the union situation. Received experience, in other words, is directly relevant to union adjudication, for its object is the same as that of all adjudications; namely, determining whether there has been a departure from preexisting substantive standards and norms of conduct. The procedural standards, then, are

community standards, and in this case they are being administered by judges, who qualify as experts in such matters.

The courts also impose external substantive standards.
One method is through interpretation of union constitutional provisions.[20] While interpretation is required
whenever a document comes before a court, the question
is why ambiguous provisions should be read to protect
members in their speech and associational activities. To
carry forward the contract metaphor, it might be thought
that the constitution is not a negotiated contract, but one
unilaterally imposed on a not very free worker; that is,
a contract of adhesion.[21] While this is certainly true, it
only means that it is inappropriate for a court to rely too
heavily upon the document in order to determine what
is fair between the parties; it does not itself suggest how
the court should determine fairness.

It is clear also that the problem of determining fairness,
of finding the appropriate standard for adjudication, is
present in an even more acute fashion where the court
really has no choice on the basis of constitutional language
but to find for the union. And yet the courts often will
find against the union. Unhappily they often do so by
saying that they are interpreting the constitution.[22] This
misdescribes the process, may mislead the parties and
subsequent judges, and does little to enhance respect for
law. Sometimes courts are admirably candid as was the
New York court in *Madden v. Atkins*: "If there be any
public policy touching the government of labor unions,
and there can be no doubt that there is, it is that traditionally democratic means of improving their union may be
freely availed of by members without fear of harm or
penalty. And this necessarily includes the right to criticize
current union leadership and, within the union, to oppose

such leadership and its policies. . . . The price of free expression and of political opposition within a union cannot be the risk of expulsion or other disciplinary action." [23]

The search, however, is for an external standard with which to judge fairness between member and union whether the task is conceptualized properly as the application of public policy (the nature of that policy must be determined) or, often improperly, as the interpretation of contract. I suggest that the courts have been justified at common law in protecting the individual in his democratic pursuits and that the standard they have applied stems from the very same ideal of union democracy that justifies legislation.

The democratic myth and aspiration of the union movement, expressed in the general structure of union constitutions, in the rhetoric of the labor movement, and in the political acceptance of collective bargaining and the legislative scheme that supports it, constitutes a general holding forth—a promise—to the member and the public by the unions which importantly conditions fairness between member and union. This conclusion is backed by the fact that the member does not read the constitution with care if he reads it at all. Nor is he able to project specific provisions forward to concrete cases. His expectations root, and rightly so, in the document's general structure, in the general holding forth, in the grand design of unions, collective bargaining, and industrial democracy.[24]

Observe, moreover, the nature of the public involvement. The holding forth of democracy by the unions is a promise made to the public as well as to the member. As remarked, public acceptance of unions in part rests upon it. Thus, it is appropriate in this situation to view the member, to some extent, as a representative of the public. And thus, there is more here to consider than one to one fairness between the parties. Fairness between the parties is, of course, centrally important, but because of the public nature of the promise and the public's response thereto, the individual's claim need not rest on his particular expectations; that is to say, he need not prove his own understanding of the union's undertaking. Nor may the union reject the obligation that flows from the general undertaking.[25]

What the courts have done in the area of union discipline is characteristic of the judicial response to the task of finding external standards in "contractual" relationships where the contract alone is unsatisfactory. The *Lockwood* case,[26] discussed in Chapter 1, is another example; so too the automobile cases.[27] The latter, while seemingly very different, are perhaps most analogous to the union discipline situation. It will be recalled that they involve the legal effect of promises made by a manufacturer, and contained in the contract of sale, dealing with the liability of the manufacturer for injury resulting from defective automobiles. Courts have paid less and less attention to the exculpatory terms of such promises (or warranties as they are called) which, like union constitutions, are written by one party and accepted by another who has little choice and who is not likely to read or understand. The growing trend is toward strict manufacturer's liability—that is, liability irrespective of language or negligence—for injury resulting from defective automobiles. One might well justify these cases, as I have attempted to justify the union cases, in terms of a general holding forth. Here it is a holding forth by the manufacturers in their sales campaigns of an automobile that is safe to drive. This holding forth is a major factor in determining fairness between purchaser and maker, and creates a community morality, departure from which the courts may properly consider a violation of community standards appropriately enshrined in law.[28]

As with unions, so with safety and automobiles: the courts acted first and the legislature followed right along.

For the automobile industry, Congress created a new administrative agency to promulgate safety standards.[29] For unions, it enacted a comprehensive statute with far-ranging objectives.[30]

THE LABOR-MANAGEMENT REPORTING
AND DISCLOSURE ACT OF 1959

The Labor-Management Reporting and Disclosure Act conveniently may be thought of as a two-part statute. One part is addressed to the problems of financial malpractice and other forms of corruption in unions. It relies principally upon reporting and disclosure by unions of their practices and financial affairs, and upon investigation by the Secretary of Labor. It also places upon union officers federally enforceable fiduciary responsibilities relating to union financial matters. This part of the statute need not concern us here. It deals with a specific aspect of the general problem of dishonest officials in positions of trust and gives little light on the problems with which we have been concerned. The other part of the statute attends to problems of union democracy.[31] In considering it, it may be helpful to summarize some of what has been said already.

The statute followed hard upon several years of highly publicized Senate committee hearings that revealed extensive corruption in a small number of unions, but the hearings also resulted in the renewal of interest in unions and in their appropriate role in society.

The promise of union democracy—proclaimed in the rhetoric of the labor movement, and employed in advocacy of collective bargaining legislation—had not adequately been achieved in practice. The conditions necessary to support democratic union government do not often exist. Nor is it realistic to think that law can do much to change this. But law can protect dissent and encourage a leadership that is more responsive to the membership. It can reinforce the democratic aspiration of the union movement which has been so important to acceptance of collective bargaining. And this is what the union democracy provisions of the 1959 statute do, and in terms would seem to do very well.

The statute is long and complicated. Title I, the "Bill of Rights for Union Members," is divided into five subsections, the most important of which deal with equal rights of members, members' freedom of speech and assembly, and members' protection against improper union disciplinary action. These subsections are not written as rules but as broad principles to be elaborated by courts in adjudication. Here, as with most titles of the statute, there is not only the desire to protect the union member but to accomplish this without unduly restricting the union.[32]

Thus, the equal rights subsection provides: "Every member . . . shall have equal rights and privileges . . . to nominate candidates, to vote in elections or referendums . . . to attend membership meetings, and to participate in the deliberations and voting upon the business of such meetings, subject to reasonable rules and regulations in [the union's] constitution and bylaws." [33]

The freedom of speech and assembly subsection is broadly phrased, but also qualified in order to protect the union in its legitimate activities. It reads:

Every member . . . shall have the right to meet and assemble freely with other members; and to express any views, arguments, or opinions; and to express at meetings . . . his views, upon candidates in an election . . . or upon any business properly before the meeting, subject to the organization's established and reasonable rules pertaining to the conduct of meetings: *Provided,* That nothing herein shall be con-

strued to impair the right of a labor organization
to adopt and enforce reasonable rules as to the
responsibility of every member toward the organization as an institution and to his refraining from
conduct that would interfere with its performance
of its legal or contractual obligations.[34]

The disciplinary subsection adds little to the common
law, and its major failing is the absence of any attempt
to deal with the problem of the biased tribunal.[35] The
subsection reads: "No member of any labor organization
may be fined, suspended, expelled, or otherwise disciplined
except for nonpayment of dues by such organization or
by any officer thereof unless such member has been (A)
served with written specific charges; (B) given a reasonable time to prepare his defense; (C) afforded a full and
fair hearing." [36]

Enforcement of the Bill of Rights is by private suit in
a federal district court. The member must show, however,
that he has attempted to exhaust "reasonable hearing
procedures (but not to exceed a four month lapse of time)
within" the union.[37]

Finally, it should be noted that the protection afforded
by the Bill of Rights does not replace but is in addition
to common law protection.[38]

Title III regulates trusteeships, that is, any device by
which an international union suspends the autonomy of
a local. The title attempts with considerable skill to safe-
guard local union autonomy, so necessary to the hope of
union democracy, while permitting central control where
there is local corruption, inefficiency, or suppression of
members' rights.[39]

The election title of the statute, Title IV, goes far in
the primary duties it places upon unions. The statute
regulates the frequency of elections: An international
union "shall elect its officers not less often than once every

five years either by secret ballot among the members in good standing or at a convention of delegates chosen by secret ballot." [40] A local union "shall elect its officers not less often than once every three years by secret ballot among the members in good standing." [41]

The statute has provisions to insure honesty in balloting. It gives candidates the right to have observers at the polls and at the counting of the ballots, and it requires that ballots and records be preserved for one year.[42]

The statute protects the political rights of members in the election process. Members are to have reasonable opportunity to nominate candidates, and "every member . . . shall have the right . . . to support the candidate . . . of his choice, without being subject to penalty, discipline, or improper interference or reprisal of any kind." [43] And, "each member in good standing shall be entitled to one vote." [44] He is also entitled to notice of the election; and, subject to reasonable qualifications uniformly imposed, "every member in good standing shall be eligible to be a candidate and to hold office." [45]

Finally, the statute goes as far as law can to limit the the advantages a union officer has over his challenger. Thus, section 401(c) provides that a union

> shall be under a duty, enforceable at the suit of any bona fide candidate for office . . . in the district court . . . to comply with all reasonable requests of any candidate to distribute by mail or otherwise at the candidate's expense campaign literature in aid of such person's candidacy to all members in good standing . . . and to refrain from discrimination in favor of or against any candidate with respect to the use of the lists of members, and whenever such [union] or its officers authorize the distribution by mail or otherwise to members of campaign literature on behalf of any candidate or of the [union] itself with reference

to such election, similar distribution at the request
of any other bona fide candidate shall be made by such
[union] and its officers, with equal treatment as to
the expense of such distribution.

And in section 401(g) the statute provides that: "No
moneys received by any [union] by way of dues, assessment,
or similar levy, and no moneys of an employer shall be
contributed or applied to promote the candidacy of any
person in an election. . . . Such moneys . . . may be
utilized for notices, factual statements of issues not involving candidates, and other expenses necessary for the
holding of an election."

Title IV, in terms, provides for a postelection remedy.
After a member has exhausted the union's internal remedies, or has spent three months trying, he may file a
complaint with the Secretary of Labor. "The Secretary
shall investigate . . . and, if he finds probable cause to
believe that a violation . . . has occurred . . . he shall,
. . . bring a civil action against the labor organization as
an entity in the [appropriate] district court." [46] For the
court to take affirmative action, it must find either "that
an election has not been held within the time prescribed
[by statute], or . . . that the [statutory] violation may
have affected the outcome of an election." [47]

The statute also provides in section 403 that:

No labor organization shall be required by law to
conduct elections of officers with greater frequency or
in a different form or manner than is required by its
own constitution or bylaws, except as otherwise provided by this title. Existing rights and remedies to
enforce the constitution and bylaws of a labor organization with respect to elections prior to the conduct
thereof shall not be affected by the provisions of this
title. The remedy provided by this title for challenging
an election already conducted shall be exclusive.

With this sketch of the statute in view, it is profitable, I think, to examine two cases which have placed before the courts centrally important problems concerning the law's role in the quest for union democracy, and which illustrate as well some important questions of joint lawmaking by Congress and the courts.

The first case is *Salzhandler v. Caputo*.[48] The controversy there was one episode in a continuing political struggle within a New York local of the Painters Union. Salzhandler was the union's financial secretary. In a leaflet circulated to the union membership he accused its president, Isadore Webman, of financial irregularities, calling him, among other things, a "petty robber," and "most unworthy of any trust." Webman brought disciplinary charges against Salzhandler, and the trial board established by the District Council of the Union, found that Salzhandler's "unsupported accusations" violated the union's constitution which prohibited "conduct unbecoming a member," "acts detrimental to . . . interests of the Brotherhood," "libeling, slandering . . . fellow members [or] officers of local unions," and "acts and conduct . . . inconsistent with the duties, obligations and fealty of a member."[49] Salzhandler was suspended from the union and barred from all meetings and participation for a period of five years.[50]

He brought suit against the union in a federal district court alleging that he had been deprived of rights guaranteed by section 101(a)(2), the Freedom of Speech and Assembly subsection of the statute's Bill of Rights. The district court dismissed the complaint, holding that the union's "Trial Board's conclusion that the leaflet was libelous was sufficiently supported by the evidence." The court, moreover, "made an independent finding that the statements were, in fact, libelous."[51]

The Court of Appeals, however, reversed. The court said: "We hold that L.M.R.D.A. protects the union member in the exercise of his right to make such charges without reprisal by the union; that any provisions of the union constitution which make such criticism, whether libelous or not, subject to union discipline are unenforceable; and that the Act allows redress for such unlawful treatment." [52]

The union had contended with much plausibility that in elaborating the free speech protection afforded union members by section 101(a)(2), the court should look for analogy to the first amendment of the United States Constitution; "that just as constitutionally protected speech does not include libelous utterances . . . the speech protected by the statute does not include libel and slander." The analogy certainly is suggested by the statute's legislative history. Senator McClellan, the original sponsor of Title I, introduced his measure by saying: "We should give union members their inherent constitutional rights, and we should make those rights apply to union membership." [53]

But the court rejected the too easy constitutional analogy on the basis of institutional reality.

> The analogy to the First Amendment is not convincing. . . . the Supreme Court recognized the possibility that state action might stifle criticism under the guise of punishing libel. However, because it felt that abuses could be prevented by the exercise of judicial authority . . . the court sustained a state criminal libel statute. But the union is not a political unit to whose disinterested tribunals an alleged defamer can look for an impartial review of his "crime." . . . The Trial Board in the instant case consisted of union officials, not judges. It was a group to which the delicate problems of truth or falsehood, privilege, and "fair comment" were not familiar. Its procedure is peculiarly unsuited for drawing the fine line between criticism and defamation, yet, were we to adopt the view of the

[union], each charge of libel would be given a trial de novo in the federal court—an impractical result not likely contemplated by Congress.[54]

The court is unquestionably correct in judging that internal union tribunals, particularly in this kind of case, lack disinterestedness. And, as has been remarked, it is unfortunate that Congress, when spelling out the elements of a fair trial in Title I, did not attempt to deal with the problem of bias. But the court might itself have done something about this. It might have suggested that in the absence of union reform—for example, the establishment of an impartial public review board, similar to the one created by the United Automobile Workers—the court would resort to a trial de novo.[55] A trial de novo is neither unusual nor impractical. Indeed, the absence or inadequacy of a union trial record often has made it necessary at common law.[56]

But quite apart from the nature of the union tribunal, the results in *Salzhandler* on the facts of that case seem perfectly correct.[57] In another context, the Supreme Court has said of the first amendment, that it reflects "a profound national commitment to the principle that debate on public issues should be uninhibited, robust, and wide-open." [58] Without doubt, the free speech section of the statute reflects a similar commitment to debate over union issues. Uninhibited, robust, and wide-open debate on public issues should not be deterred by the law of defamation, and the Supreme Court has taken steps to see that it will not be.[59] Such debate on union issues should not be deterred by union discipline and *Salzhandler* holds out the promise that it will not be.

The language of the *Salzhandler* court, however, would seem to go too far. It appears to protect from union discipline a member who knowingly makes false statements as well as someone like Salzhandler himself, who, as far as one can tell, wrote in good faith. In *New York Times v. Sulli-van,* a case decided after *Salzhandler* and one not involving unions, the Supreme Court said that the first amendment required "a federal rule that prohibits a public official from recovering damages for a defamatory falsehood relat-ing to his official conduct unless he proves that the state-ment was made with 'actual malice'—that is, with knowl-edge that it was false or with reckless disregard of whether it was false or not." [60] Uninhibited, robust, and wide-open debate of union issues by union members requires no more. It is difficult successfully to argue that defamatory state-ments made with "actual malice" deserve protection in view of the union's interest in deterring such statements through disciplinary proceedings. But, because of the na-ture of union tribunals, where actual malice is an issue, the union should have to make its case in a trial de novo be-fore the court. I do not think that this would overwork the judges or clog beyond endurance the federal courts.

The second case is *Calhoon v. Harvey,*[61] and it too in-volves the Bill of Rights of union members; but more important, it raises questions concerning the Election Title and the relationship between Title I and Title IV of the statute.

The case was brought in a federal district court by three members of District No. 1 of the National Marine Engi-neers' Beneficial Association, who alleged that the union's bylaws and constitution infringed "the right of members [of the union] to nominate candidates" [62] in violation of section 101(a)(1), the Equal Rights subsection of the stat-ute's Bill of Rights. "The union bylaws complained of de-prived a member of the right to nominate anyone for of-fice but himself. The . . . constitution in turn provided that no member could be eligible for nomination or elec-tion . . . unless he had been a member of the national union for five years and had served 180 days or more of seatime in each of two of the preceding three years on vessels covered by collective bargaining agreements with the national or its subsidiary bodies." [63] The three members asked that "the union be enjoined from preparing for or conducting any election until it revised its system of elections so as to afford each of its members a fair opportunity to nominate any persons 'meeting fair and reasonable eligibility requirements for any or all offices to be filled by such election.' " [64]

After mixed results below, the plaintiffs lost in the Supreme Court. The Court said:

> All that section 101(a)(1) guarantees is that "every member of a labor organization shall have equal rights and privileges . . . to nominate candidates, to vote in elections or referendums of the labor organization . . . and to participate in the deliberations and voting . . . subject to reasonable rules and regulations in such organization's constitution and bylaws." Plainly, this is no more than a command that members and classes of members shall not be discriminated against in their right to nominate and vote. . . . The complaining union members here have not been discriminated against in any way and have been denied no privilege or right to vote or nominate which the union has granted to others. . . . Whether the eligibility requirements set by the union's constitution and bylaws were reasonable and valid is a question separate and distinct from whether the right to nominate on an equal basis given by section 101(a)(1) was violated.[65]

This is a strange interpretation of section 101(a)(1). And it is especially surprising for it to have been made by a Court which, when dealing with the equal protection clause of the United States Constitution—the closest analogy to section 101(a)(1)—has "recognized the subtle ways by which election rights can be removed through discrimination at a less visible stage of the political process"; a Court which, in "scrutinizing devices designed to erode the franchise . . . , has shown impatience with arguments founded in the form of the device." [66]

Certainly the Court's holding is not compelled by the vague language of section 101(a)(1), and yet its consequences would seem to militate against its adoption unless so compelled. Mr. Justice Stewart, speaking of the Court's holding in his separate opinion, makes clear what those consequences are. "After today, simply by framing its discriminatory rules in terms of eligibility, a union can immunize itself from pre-election attack in a federal court even though it makes deep incursions on the equal right of its members to nominate, to vote, and to participate in the union's internal affairs." [67]

Moreover, I should have thought that a principal source to which the Court would have turned for guidance in its task of elaborating the vague provisions of section 101(a)(1) was the Election Title of the statute. The specificity with which Congress described the primary rights of members during the election process and the generous nature of those rights should have impelled the Court to avoid its excessively narrow interpretation of section 101(a)(1). But the extraordinary fact is that the Court looked not to the primary rights established by Title IV but to the remedies therein provided, and drew inferences as to other remedies on the basis of legislative silence, inferences which are fundamentally inconsistent with the legislation Congress did enact and with the history of its enactment.

After describing Title IV, the Court made its point this way:

> It is apparent that Congress decided to utilize the special knowledge and discretion of the Secretary of Labor in order best to serve the public interest. . . .

In so doing Congress . . . decided not to permit individuals to block or delay union elections by filing federal-court suits for violations of Title IV. Reliance on the discretion of the Secretary is in harmony with the general congressional policy to allow unions great latitude in resolving their own internal controversies, and, where that fails, to utilize the agencies of Government most familiar with union problems to aid in bringing about a settlement through discussion before resort to the courts.[68]

Thus, the Court seems to conclude not only that section 101(a)(1) provides only the most limited protection, but also that preelection relief of any kind is sharply limited, if it exists at all.[69]

When one turns to legislative history, however, one is forced to wonder whether the Court was attending to the statute that Congress enacted, or to the original Kennedy-Ervin Bill which was the bill referred to the Senate Labor Subcommittee. That bill provided for exclusive postelection relief through the Secretary of Labor and the courts.[70] It would have barred federal and state courts from granting individuals preelection relief. But it had been strongly urged upon Congress that postelection relief would fail fully to protect the member, and that, indeed, common law experience showed that preelection relief was the only effective kind.[71] This meant that the bill as written would have reduced rather than increased the law's protection of democratic election processes within the unions. Section 403, however, was amended, and in the statute Congress enacted provides that existing "rights and remedies to enforce the constitution and bylaws of a labor organization with respect to elections prior to the conduct thereof shall not be affected by the provisions of this title."

While it is far from clear what this language means,[72] it is perfectly clear that the availability of any form of preelection judicial relief seriously undercuts the Court's position. In terms of the logic of that position it makes very little difference whether the preelection relief is in a state rather than a federal court, or turns on the union's constitution rather than directly on the statute. If the Supreme Court is serious, it would have read out of the statute the saving clause of section 403, and while there have been situations where a similar course was appropriate,[73] this hardly is such a case.

The legislative history does not end with the amendment to section 403. The major case against the Court's interpretation is in the history of Title I, as Mr. Justice Stewart demonstrates:

> What now constitutes Titles II through VI of the Act was substantially contained in the original bill presented to the Senate by Senator Kennedy. Title I, first introduced by Senator McClellan, was the product of doubt that the bill went far enough in guaranteeing internal democracy in union affairs. The concept of Title I—its stress on equal rights and judicial protection—was the subject of great controversy both in the Senate and in the House. Repeated attempts were made by represesntatives of organized labor, among other groups, to have the strict mandate of this so-called Bill of Rights modified, or eliminated altogether. Despite these efforts to remove Title I, it endured, and indeed was amended to provide stronger remedial provisions than those contained in the original version. As originally introduced, section 102 would have required an aggrieved union member to make his complaint to the Secretary of Labor, exactly the remedy provided by Title IV. The Kuchel amendment, however, substituted the present provision permitting suit by an aggrieved member in a federal district court. When Senator Kuchel introduced this change, he commented: "Here is one of the major

changes in the proposal. The Amendment of the Senator from Arkansas provided that the Secretary of Labor might, on behalf of the injured or aggrieved member, have the right to litigate the alleged grievance and to seek an injunction or other relief. We believe that giving this type of right to the aggrieved employee member himself is in the interest of justice. . . ." Senator Clark of Pennsylvania noted that the Kuchel amendment "takes the Federal bureaucracy out of this bill of rights and leaves its enforcement to union members, aided by the courts." . . . Nonetheless, the Court finds a "general congressional policy" to avoid judicial resolution of internal union disputes. That policy, the Court says, was designed to limit the power of individuals to block and delay elections by seeking injunctive relief. Such an appraisal might have been accurate before the addition of Title I, but it does not explain the emphasis on prompt judicial remedies there provided.[74]

This then is the history of the statute enacted by the Congress. That history, it seems to me, answers the Court's contentions, as Mr. Justice Stewart has shown; but it is instructive now to consider what one must assume if he is to decide, as the Court did, that congressional purpose was substantially to limit preelection relief. It must be assumed, as one commentator put it when describing the position of some opponents of preelection remedies, that "while union democracy is desirable, it should not be purchased at the price of seriously weakening the functioning and efficiency of the union as an organization . . . that valid personal claims may disrupt the union as effectively as frivolous ones, and that while a preelection remedy might provide greater justice for the individual member, the ultimate cost of disrupting the union would be borne by the entire membership." [75]

While it is far from clear that preelection relief is in fact more disruptive than postelection relief—consider the cost of holding a new election and of undoing and redoing—it is perfectly clear that it is much less effective and that, as the history shows, Congress knew this. It knew that a union might disregard many of the primary rights guaranteed its members by Title IV without possibly affecting the outcome of the election, the statutory test for postelection relief. It knew that the object of running for union office often is not unattainable victory but earnest protest, and that where protest is the point only preelection relief can put a member, improperly kept off the ballot, on to it. Moreover, Congress knew of the common law experience. In the words of Clyde Summers: "Study of the cases emphasizes the importance of judicial intervention before the voting. Lawyers who have been involved in these cases agree that preelection remedies are the only ones of any practical value. Correction of defects prior to the voting gives the members that to which they are entitled—a fair and honest election in the first instance." [76]

Accordingly, to find as the Court does that the purpose of Congress was to limit effective preelection relief comes very close indeed to charging Congress with misrepresentation. In accents strong and clear Title IV proclaims the primary rights of the members to a fair and democratic election, and then, as the Court has it, makes an utter mockery of those rights by denying their effective enforcement. This is what the Court has held, and for it to have done so is a great sadness. Congress ought not to be read as making promises and then not fulfilling them, as acting in so slick and deceptive a fashion. This is no way to read statutes, to make law, or to coordinate two of our three branches of government; and that, after all, is more important than the right to run for union office.

Part IV

Labor and Politics

Chapter 6

Unions and
Political Power

Writing in 1960, a close student of money in American politics estimated that the United Automobile Workers' "campaign-connected expenditures" totaled about $3,000,-000 in 1956.[1] And in 1957 a Report of the Senate Special Committee to Investigate Political Activities, Lobbying, and Campaign Contributions found that:

> The United Steelworkers of America, AFL-CIO . . . has been active for over 20 years on Federal and State levels in supporting or opposing legislation of interest to labor.
>
> The Steelworkers maintains a Washington office for its legislative department, consisting of around 7 employees, 3 of whom are registered under the Lobbying Act. From January 1, 1956, to June 30, 1956, the cost of the department was $51,334.81. These funds come from union dues.
>
> Apart from direct contacts with Congress on legislation of interest to the union, the legislative department conducts summer schools on legislative activities and assists the membership throughout the country on legislative problems. There is close liaison with union representatives on legislative matters, and visits to Washington by such representatives to provide additional knowledge and information and to contact Members of Congress.[2]

Organized labor's involvement in politics, as these facts and figures suggest, is extensive. And while this involvement is not through an independent party or part of a radical movement, it nevertheless is productive of great anxiety in some quarters. "This could be a decisive year in the history of America," said Cola G. Parker, the president of the National Association of Manufacturers, in 1956. He went on:

> It is the year in which organized labor leadership has proclaimed an all-out effort to elect a Congress, and if possible an Administration, which will do the bidding of the handful of men who have the effrontery to claim the American working man as their chattel and possession—who have the gall to say that they, and they alone, speak for American working people. Even many of their own members are unwilling captives, and their total enrollment represents only about one-quarter of the nation's work force.
>
> What I'm telling you is not news. There has been no effort to conceal their power-grab from the nation. Heady with the power they already possess by virtue of holding millions of American working people within the iron grasp of compulsory unionism, the leaders of organized labor boldly announce their intention of seizing political control of the country.
>
> As I say, this is not news to this audience. Nor is it news to anyone who reads the papers. But what appalls me is the stark indifference—and indifference which is alarming—which prevails all over the country. As I read the situation, the people are relying on business and professional men to meet and turn back this challenge to their political traditions.[3]

And it was also in 1956 that Barry Goldwater introduced a bill in the Senate providing merely that "every officer of a labor organization who consents to the making of . . . any contribution or expenditure, directly or indirectly . . . in connection with any election, primary election or caucus . . . shall be fined $100,000 or imprisoned for two years." [4]

Yet it would be wrong to suppose either that felt anxiety over labor's political role is limited to labor's antagonists, or that anxiety over the role of interest groups in the political process is limited to labor alone.[5] Congress, for example, and state legislatures too, have been anxious about the political activities of organized labor, and every other organized interest group in society. Nor is the phenomenon new. Anxiety over the role of groups—or as Madison and his generation sometimes called them, factions—in the political life of the country is, as remarked in Chapter 1, as old as the nation itself.

Madison dealt with faction in the Tenth *Federalist.* The "friend of popular governments," he said, "never finds himself so much alarmed for their character and fate as when he contemplates their propensity to this dangerous vice." [6] The vice was called not only "faction," but also " 'party,' a 'spirit of insubordination,' 'mobocracy,' or most succinctly 'anarchy' ".[7] The fear of faction was not less than fear for loss of freedom or for the demise of established government; generally for both.

And thus the judge in the labor conspiracy case wrote from respectable tradition (while applying an inappropriate standard of decision): "If [the Union faction] was tolerated," he said, "the constitutional control over our affairs would pass away from the people at large, and become vested in the hands of conspirators. We should have a new system of government, and our rights be placed at the disposal of a voluntary and self-constituted association." [8] Unlike Madison, however, the judge was perhaps unprepared to accept the inevitability of faction in a free society.

Because Madison saw the "latent causes of faction . . . sown in the nature of man . . . ," in the "zeal for different opinions concerning religion, . . . government, and many other points . . . ," and most importantly, in "the various and unequal distribution of property . . . ," he held that the causes of faction could be removed only "by destroying the liberty which is essential to its existence"—a "remedy that is worse than the disease"—or "by giving to every citizen the same opinions, the same passions, and the same interests"—an "expedient . . . as impracticable as [the destruction of liberty] would be unwise." Since the cause of faction could not wisely or practicably be removed, the task for the political theorist was to devise means to control "its effects." And this the makers of American constitutional government had done: "In the extent and proper structure of the Union . . . we behold a republican remedy for the diseases most incident to republican government." [9] But Madison, prescient as he was, could not have foreseen the growth of corporate business after the Civil War or the development of organized labor that came thereafter.

The development of American capitalism in the post-Civil War nineteenth century is history well known. The resulting concentration of economic power in the "enormous industrial combines," and the massing of great wealth in the hands of a few, bred fears that generated reform pressures leading to such noble experiments as the Sherman Anti-Trust Act of 1890, and a federal income tax law in 1894.

Nor were reform pressures generated alone by the concentration of economic power or by the gross inequality of income. For the political process, which Madison had seen as shielded from the "mischief" of faction by the structure of the new Republic, was threatened with capture. Elihu Root in 1894 told the New York Constitutional Convention: "I believe that the time has come when something ought to be done to put a check to the giving of $50,000 or $100,000 by a great corporation toward political purposes upon the understanding that a debt is created from a political party to it." [10] A joint committee of that

State's legislature, guided by Charles Evans Hughes, after investigating the life insurance companies, reported in 1906: "The frank admission that moneys have been obtained for use in State campaigns upon the expectation that candidates thus aided in their election would support the interests of the companies, has exposed both those who solicited the contributions and those who made them to severe and just condemnation." [11] And two eminent contemporary historians, Samuel Eliot Morrison and Henry Steele Commager, tell us: "Politics was largely a Punch and Judy show, but though the puppets and even the voices changed, the hands that held the strings were the same. Business ran politics, and politics was a branch of business." [12]

That business "ran politics, and politics was a branch of business" meant that unions were not then a significant force in government. Not only were they a faction too small to pull the strings, but from the tail end of the nineteenth century until the coming of the New Deal the preeminent view in the federation that was to dominate the labor movement was "voluntarism": a doctrine which advocated governmental abstention from the labor sector, and which called for qualified and restrained participation by labor in the political arena.[13] The voluntarism of the American Federation of Labor stands in contrast to earlier and later union involvement in the political process, and to the views of other labor organizations at that time.

The movement toward voluntarism, however, was itself gradual. At its inception the A.F.L. favored public works, nationalization of the telegraph and other positive state actions. Moreover, the sentiment for political restraint which was becoming dominant in the Federation between about 1899 and 1904, could not find anything approaching full expression because increasing employer and governmental hostility forced the labor movement to involve itself in political activties. It was only after passage of the

Clayton Act in 1914 that the A.F.L.'s dominant political attitudes were permitted full expression in the Federation's Convention resolutions. But the A.F.L. at no time was out of politics. Samuel Gompers, its president, for one, rejected the suggestion with some heat: "It is not true, as some carping critics allege, that the American Federation of Labor is a non-political organization." [14] It stood ready to reward its political friends and punish its political enemies, or at least to try. And there was always support for intervention of a negative kind, such as that manifested by the 1906 Bill of Grievances[15] seeking relief from the labor injunction and from the application of the Sherman Act to unions. Moreover, there were demands for the restriction of immigration and for the exclusion of the Chinese. Nor did voluntarism prevent the dominant craft unions from working with Republican machines in cities like Detroit and Philadelphia and with the Democratic machine in New York. The concerns of the unions included licensing and apprenticeship laws, help in strikes, and the winning of political influence for obtaining contracts.[16]

But voluntarism, in its limited form, was important to the A.F.L.'s leaders who felt that the reforms advocated by some through the use of social legislation could be achieved far more rapidly by collective bargaining. Vice President Duncan made the point briefly at the Federation's Convention in 1902: "Why wait for the slow process of law when we can exert a sure and certain economic power?" [17] Moreover, substantial involvement in the political process, it was thought, would place too great a burden on the unions' organizational strength with the result that issues affecting the immediate welfare of workmen would be subordinated to the object of getting votes.[18]

The leadership also feared political domination, and that it should have is understandable: throughout its history the labor movement has had to resist attempts at capture by such groups as single-taxers, anarchists, and communists. Voluntarism perhaps was dictated too by the diversity and mobility of the American labor force.[19]

Thus, the turn of the century and subsequent reform pressures to cleanse the political process did not root in anxiety over workingmen's factions. Nor did initial legislative action deal with the unions. The first congressional enactment imposing restrictions on group money in politics was directed at the corporation: "It shall . . . be unlawful for any corporation whatever to make a money contribution in connection with any election at which Presidential . . . electors or a Representative in Congress is to be voted for or any election by any State legislature of a United States Senator." [20] This was 1907. In the years following, Congress frequently returned to these problems.[21] It required disclosure by contributors and congressional candidates; placed limits on the amounts that congressional candidates could spend in seeking nomination and election; and in 1925 it codified and revised its legislation in the Corrupt Practices Act.[22] That act, among other things, tightened the restraints on corporations. Nor was this all. The Hatch Act amendments of 1940 sought to limit the campaign donations of individuals and groups.[23] Yet many of these measures, and those which were to follow, were the product of a good deal of doubt and uncertainty as to what regulations, if any, would be beneficial to the political process. And this doubt and uncertainty are reflected in the structure and language of the statutes, which often duck, through ambiguity or omission, the major policy decisions.

Some of the laws passed from 1907 to 1940 imposed restraints on union activities, along with the activities of other groups and individuals, but it was not until 1943 that labor organizations were subjected to the type of statute that long had applied to corporations. By that time the unions had both established themselves in the economic area and changed their political orientation, and dramatically so. 1936 is generally seen as the turning point in labor's political involvement. A year earlier the Committee of Industrial Organization had been established within the A.F.L. (in 1937 it was expelled, and in 1938 it organized on a permanent, independent basis). The leaders of the C.I.O. were ambitious for labor on the economic front—their mission was to organize the unskilled and semiskilled along industrial lines—and they saw the relationship between economic success and political action. Despite the fact that the A.F.L. officially retained its traditional policy of voluntarism, a total of over $770,000 was reported as labor's political expenditures for that year[24]—some eight times the money raised by the A.F.L. during the prior thirty years.[25]

In the year following, a Senate Committee proposed drastic restrictions affecting "all organizations, associations or enterprises, incorporated or otherwise whose aims or purposes are the furtherance of group, class or special interests." [26] But it was when congressional tempers had been roused by the long-threatened strike of the United Mine Workers in the wartime spring of 1943 that legislation, in the form of the Smith-Connally Act, was enacted. While directed primarily to the problem of strikes, Smith-Connally also contained provisions regulating the use of union money in federal elections.[27] These provisions are similar in nature to existing law which we shall shortly examine.

Hard on the passage of the Smith-Connally Act, the C.I.O. set up the Political Action Committee under the chairmanship of Sidney Hillman, president of the Amalgamated Clothing Workers. The P.A.C. account soon came to some $650,000, the bulk of which was spent in the 1944 elections.[28] The C.I.O. and P.A.C. acted upon the legal advice of Lee Pressman, general counsel of the C.I.O. who was able in a legal opinion to find in the thicket of the Smith-Connally Act a comfortable area for union political activity.[29] We shall find that such a comfortable area exists under the law today.

CAMPAIGN CONTRIBUTIONS AND EXPENDITURES

There are two major pieces of contemporary national legislation concerned with organized labor's participation in the political process. One is the 1946 Federal Regulation of Lobbying Act which is a statute requiring individuals and organizations to file reports of their spending with the Clerk of the House of Representatives if they solicit, collect, or receive money for the principal purpose of influencing federal legislation.[30] This statute—and there are similar measures in some of the states—has as its aim, "the reporting of significant data by pressure groups, and not . . . their regulation." It would seem to reflect a belief by Congress, that that body "and the people can evaluate group pressures properly, provided they know the identity and financial participation of those who support such operations." [31] The statute, however, is the product of tough negotiation: in terms it contains many exemptions, and the Supreme Court has had to interpret it narrowly to sustain its constitutionality.[32] Thus, the information filed fails utterly to give an accurate picture of the extent of lobbying or of labor's relative share.

The second and more important statute, because it is an attempt at regulation and control rather than merely at disclosure, deals with corporate and union money in national elections. This is section 304 of the Labor-Management Relations Act. Section 304, an amendment to the Corrupt Practices Act, may be considered an elaboration and development of the 1907 statute and some of the subsequent legislative efforts, including the Smith-Connally Act. In its present form it reads:

It is unlawful for any national bank, or any corporation organized by authority of any law of Congress, to make a contribution or expenditure in connection with any election to any political office, or in connection with any primary election or political convention or caucus held to select candidates for any political office, or for any corporation whatever, or any labor organization to make a contribution or expenditure in connection with any election at which Presidential and Vice Presidential electors or a Senator or Representative in, or a Delegate or Resident Commissioner to Congress are to be voted for, or in connection with any primary election or political convention or caucus held to select candidates for any of the foregoing offices, for any candidate, political committee, or other person to accept or receive any contribution prohibited by this section. . . . Every corporation or labor organization which makes any contribution or expenditure in violation of this section shall be fined not more than $5,000; and every officer or director of any corporation, or officer of any labor organization, who consents to any contribution or expenditure by the corporation or labor organization, as the case may be, and any person who accepts or receives any contribution, in violation of this section, shall be fined not more than $1,000 or imprisoned not more than one year, or both; and if the violation was willful, shall be fined not more than $10,000 or imprisoned not more than two years, or both. . . . For the purposes of this section "labor organization" means any organization of any kind, or any agency or employee representation committee or plan, in which employees participate and which exists for the purpose, in whole or in part, of dealing with employers concerning grievances, labor disputes, wages, rates of pay, hours of employment, or conditions of work.[33]

The Supreme Court majority, in the second of the Court's two encounters with the statute, tells us that the purpose of the 1907 ancestor of the present statute "was not merely to prevent the subversion of the integrity of the electoral process. Its underlying philosophy was to sustain the active, alert responsibility of the individual citizen in a democracy for the wise conduct of government." [34] And in a concurring opinion in the earlier case, Mr. Justice Rutledge, speaking of the statute's application to unions, found the principal purposes of the legislation to be:

> (1) To reduce what had come to be regarded in the light of recent experience as the undue and disproportionate influence of labor unions upon federal elections; (2) to preserve the purity of such elections and of official conduct ensuing from the choices made in them against the use of aggregated wealth by union as well as corporate entities; and (3) to protect union members holding political views contrary to those supported by the union from use of funds contributed by them to promote acceptance of those opposing views.[35]

Each of these purposes perhaps can be extracted from the statute's legislative history if not from the statute's language; but language and history also reveal an understandable ambivalence and restraint on the part of the legislators. To a great extent this manifests concern with the constitutionality of restrictions on the political activities of a group and indirectly, but inescapably, on the majority of the members of the group. The first amendment protects speech and association of all kind, but surely none more vigorously than that having to do with the election of public officials. In part the restraint and ambivalence seem to reflect doubt as to the very wisdom of legal interference with this aspect of union political activity.

First the language of the statute, while seemingly broad in scope, does not regulate political activity apart from the federal election process. Union money in state elections is not—perhaps could not be—covered, although some few states have legislation.[36] Union money used to fight legislation or to sponsor its passage is not a target of the enactment, although lobbying statutes, either state or federal, may require disclosure. Nor does it seem that section 304 purports to prohibit election activities of political action groups established by organized labor such as the A.F.L.-C.I.O.'s Committee on Political Education (C.O.P.E.) or similar organizations established by international unions.[37] C.O.P.E. is not a labor organization within the statutory definition, and the money it receives and spends in support of candidates is collected voluntarily from union members.[38]

Second, the legislative history of section 304 is, as Mr. Justice Rutledge has said, "a veritable fog of contradictions relating to specific possible applications, contradictions necessarily bred among both proponents and opponents of the amendment from the breadth and indefiniteness of the literal scope of the language used." [39] Particularly troublesome in this regard is the meaning to be given to the word "expenditure." Mr. Justice Reed, writing for the majority in the first case, observed:

> The reach of its meaning raised questions during Congressional consideration of the bill when it contained the present text of the section. Did it cover comments upon political personages and events in a corporately owned newspaper? . . . Could unincorporated trade associations make expenditures? . . . Could a union-

owned radio station give time for a political speech?
. . . What of comments of a radio commentator? . . .
Is it an expenditure only when A is running against
B or is free, favorable publicity for prospective candidates illegal? . . . What of corporately owned re-
ligious papers supporting a candidate on moral
grounds? The Anti-Saloon League? [40]

The combination of these legislative problems has
made the task of the courts difficult, and the result of the
judicial struggles has been to limit sharply the importance
of the statute.

United States v. Congress of Industrial Organizations[41]
was the first section 304 case to reach the Supreme Court.
It was planned by the c.i.o. to test the constitutionality of
the statute.

In July 1947, Philip Murray, the President of the
Federation, spoke out in the *C.I.O.-News,* his organization's
weekly paper, in support of a candidate for Congress
running in a special Maryland election. Said Mr. Murray:

I take opportunity to urge that all members of c.i.o.
residing and voting in the Congressional District in
which this election is scheduled to take place cast
their votes for Judge Garmatz, and make every effort
to bring their neighbors and friends and to all persons
eligible to vote in this election a full understanding
of the issues involved and of the importance of voting
for Judge Garmatz.[42]

And Mr. Murray invited the Justice Department to indict
him and his organization under the statute he took to be
unconstitutional: "I firmly believe that the action which
I now take is fully legal under the law of our land. It is my
understanding that the issue as to whether proper respect

will be paid to the fundamental guarantees and principles of our Constitution must now rest in the hands of the law enforcement agencies of the federal government." [43]

The Justice Department did indict the c.i.o. and Mr. Murray, but Mr. Murray failed to obtain a constitutional decision from the Court. Five of the Justices found that what Mr. Murray and the c.i.o. were charged with having done was perfectly legal under the statute, and thus they saw no need to reach ultimate constitutional questions. The minority of four, on the other hand, thought the indictment did allege facts falling squarely within the statute's prohibition; they attended, therefore, to the constitutional question and found the statute in violation of that great document.

The Court majority read the indictment as alleging "only that the c.i.o. and its president published with union funds a regular periodical for the furtherance of its aims, [and] that President Murray authorized the use of those funds for distribution of this issue in regular course to those accustomed to receive copies of the periodical." [44]

"It would require explicit words in an act," said the Court, "to convince us that Congress intended to bar a trade journal, a house organ or a newspaper, published by a corporation, from expressing views on candidates or political proposals in the regular course of its publication." [45] One could not say that "stockholders are unwilling participants in such normal organizational activities." [46] So too unions and their members.

There can be no question whatever that the majority was strongly influenced in the gloss it thus placed upon the statute, and perhaps in its reading of the indictment as well, by the constitutional difficulties that totally occupied the background of the litigation. The Court said as much.

If [the statute] were construed to prohibit the publication, by corporations and unions in the regular course of conducting their affairs, of periodicals advising their members, stockholders or customers of danger or advantage to their interests from the adoption of measures, or the election to office of men espousing such measures, the gravest doubt would arise in our minds as to its constitutionality.[47]

In the second and latest Supreme Court decision to consider section 304, *United States v. United Automobile Workers*,[48] the indictment was found to charge a union with conduct covered by the statute. Specifically, the Court read the indictment to charge the U.A.W. "with having used union dues to sponsor commercial television broadcasts designed to influence the electorate to select certain candidates for Congress in connection with the 1954 elections." [49] This, said the Court, was very different from the *C.I.O.* case. Mr. Murray's statement in the *C.I.O.-News* "was neither directed nor delivered to the public at large. The organization merely distributed its house organ to its own people." But what the U.A.W. was charged with is what Congress has struck at in the statute: "the use of . . . union funds to influence the public at large to vote for a particular candidate or a particular party." [50]

The case had come to the Court on the indictment alone, that is, the government's allegations had not been put to a trial. The lower court had held—erroneously, as it was to learn—that the facts in the indictment, even if proved, did not constitute an offense. In this posture, and given its disposition of the case, the Supreme Court majority found it unnecessary, once again, to consider the constitutionality of section 304. The Court said:

Matter now buried under abstract constitutional issues may, by the elucidation of a trial, be brought to the surface, and in the outcome constitutional questions may disappear. Allegations of the indictment hypothetically framed to elicit a ruling from this Court or based upon misunderstanding of the facts may not survive the test of proof. For example, was the broadcast paid for out of the general dues of the union membership or may the funds be fairly said to have been obtained on a voluntary basis? Did the broadcast reach the public at large or only those affiliated with appellee? Did it constitute active electioneering or simply state the record of particular candidates on economic issues? Did the union sponsor the broadcast with the intent to affect the results of the election? [51]

The case went back to the lower court for trial and, after the evidence was in, the judge in instructing the jury dwelt upon the source of the money the u.a.w. had spent on the political broadcast.

"Was the broadcast paid for out of the general dues of the union membership?"

If the question had ended there, the answer would be unquestionably "Yes" because the plaintiff charges and the defendant admits that the broadcasts were paid for out of the general dues of the union membership. But in arriving at what it thought Congress must have meant by passing this Act, the Supreme Court question doesn't end there. It goes on to ask you to determine not only was the broadcast paid for out of the general dues of the union membership, but

"—may the funds used be fairly said to have been obtained on a voluntary basis?"

If—that last part—if by that is meant passing of the hat for voluntary contributions by individual members approached by some committee or otherwise, then this, what happened here, was not voluntary, because it came out of the dues. There was no passing of the hat or anything like that. But I believe that the word "fairly" was put in there for some reason. The Supreme Court does not usually use words recklessly. It said—and here I quote from part of the question— "—or may the funds be fairly said to have been obtained on a voluntary basis?"

So in deciding whether or not the funds used may be fairly said to have been obtained on a voluntary basis, you have a right to take into consideration the fact that these men, in 1954, were delegates to a convention just like any other convention and just like any other delegates. They represented others. The whole membership couldn't go to the convention any more than the whole membership of some fraternal organization can go to a convention. They send delegates. And at the convention in 1953 these delegates, acting for the UAW membership, voted as they had on previous conventions, authority for their governing board to use part of the dues for this educational program that the governing board had used and was preparing to use in the future.[52]

The u.a.w. was acquitted by the jury.

The result in the *U.A.W.* case on remand is characteristic. Indeed, there have been few cases and no convictions. In *U.S. v. Painters Local 481*,[53] the Court of Appeals for the Second Circuit, elaborating upon the interpretation developed in the *C.I.O.* case, upheld the legality of a union political advertisement in a general newspaper. The court also emphasized the fact that the expenditures had been authorized by a majority of the union membership. The voluntary character of expenditures has been important in at least two other lower court decisions,[54] and in the *Construction & General Laborers* case,[55] the court held that the union had not made expenditures within the meaning of the statute when it paid its employees while they engaged in political activities.

The decisions, narrowing as they do section 304, represent an appropriate response by the judiciary to a statute heavy with constitutional difficulties and reflecting generations of legislative doubt and uncertainty. It would have been wrong—for reasons that I shall examine, in another context, in the next chapter—for the Court to have moved directly to the constitutional questions in the *C.I.O.* case. Nor would it have been proper for the Court to have restrained union activity to any significant extent under circumstances where it was so unclear what the legislative will really was. The wisdom of restraints on unions involves considerations plainly fundamental to the working of the political process yet basically unsusceptible to intelligent testing by the abstract constitutional propositions available to the Court.

But that the Court was right does not answer the question whether the political role of organized labor is "mischief" in need of legislative reform.[56]

UNIONS, POLITICS, AND THE PLURAL SOCIETY

America is a republic with a Constitution that does not provide for its elected or appointed officials to serve as the representatives of the labor unions, or the business corporations, or the organized farmers, veterans, doctors, or lawyers. The Constitution simply does not speak of such groups. And what is true of the nation's Constitution is true of the states' as well. But people cannot act effectively as individuals to obtain most of the things they want to obtain from government. To put it in its simplest form, an individual is not likely to be able to save the park near his home from ruin by the construction of an eight-lane superhighway; a "Save the Park Committee" might. No matter how eloquent the lone Negro may be, he needs organization to force civil rights legislation on a sometimes guilty but often apathetic white majority. It takes more than one oil man to get an oil depletion allowance. In large measure every branch of government acts because some group, or several groups, either ad hoc or permanent, have spent money and energy to make it act.

And while from the beginning this was seen as dangerous, almost from the beginning the right of the people freely to associate for the purposes of political action was seen too as insurance against tyranny. Writing in 1835, Alexis de Tocqueville said of America what might, with but slight amendment, be said today:

> In our own day freedom of association has become a necessary guarantee against the tyranny of the majority . . . no countries need associations more—to prevent either despotism of parties or the arbitrary rule of a prince—than those with a democratic social state. In aristocratic nations secondary bodies form natural associations which hold abuses of power in check. In countries where such associations do not exist, if private people did not artificially and temporarily create something like them, I see no other dike to hold back tyranny of whatever sort, and a great nation might with impunity be oppressed by some tiny faction or by a single man.[57]

And today it is the received learning of political sociology that the participation of individuals in organizations which are an active part of a state's existing political structure gives the individual a stake in the status quo that otherwise he might not have. If he is able to see his interests at least partially respected, his attachment to authority is likely to be deepened; his susceptibility to revolution diminished.

The felt danger today is that any one organization or interest group may achieve an excess of power and, if not again make politics into a Punch and Judy show, at least upset what Robert A. Dahl has called the " 'normal' American political process": "one in which there is a high probability that an active and legitimate group in the population can make itself heard effectively at some crucial stage in the process of decision." [58] Accordingly, if any one interest group can block other legitimate groups from being "heard effectively," it would seem that it has excess political power.

There are several forces at work apart from legal regulation of group activity that make attainment of excess power by any group unlikely. Madison was not wholly wrong in placing his faith in the formal structure of the American republic, in its federalism, its separation of powers, and the checks and balances that this creates. For groups to accomplish their purposes they must have access to formal governmental decision-makers, and where there are many decision-makers, some with the power of review, the potential for undue influence must be reduced.

Safety resides too in the very multiplicity of groups and the countervailing power they exert on the institutions of government and on each other. The members of one group are members of many. This "overlapping membership" tends to narrow the range of conflict among groups. David B. Truman argues that it "is the competing claims of other groups *within* a given interest group that threaten its cohesion and force it to reconcile its claims with those of other groups active on the political scene." [59]

Mr. Truman also suggests that important functions are performed by what he calls the "rules of the game," and what, as he tells us, others have called "systems of belief," "general ideological consensus," and "a broad body of attitudes and understandings regarding the nature and limits of authority." He includes in the "rules" such widely shared and deeply held community values as "the dignity of the individual human being," "mass participation in the designation of leaders and in the selection of policies in all social groups and institutions," and "certain semi-egalitarian notions of material welfare." [60] The "rules" are important because they sharply restrict the freedom of a group. They are a natural restraint on group political action even as the market is a natural restraint on group economic action. They are "interests [perhaps principles would be better] the serious disturbance of which will result in organized interaction and the assertion of fairly explicit claims for conformity." [61]

There is no reason to suppose that organized labor's political power is too great, or, to put it another way, that it is not properly held in check by the structure of American government, the overlapping of group membership, and the "rules of the game." Thus, for example, while the top three spenders among the organizations filing reports under the Federal Regulation of Lobbying Act in 1966 were labor organizations,[62] the labor lobby in Washington has not in recent years been notoriously successful. It did not stop the Labor-Management Reporting and Disclosure Act, or obtain the repeal of the right-to-work section of the Labor-Management Relations Act. And this is at least some evidence that it did not interfere with the normal American political process; that it did not block the hearing that other legitimate groups in the population are entitled to.[63] The assertion that organized labor has achieved excessive political power can be supported only by resorting to what Alexander Heard has termed a "hot political stereotype." [64] Mr. Parker's speech quoted earlier is a good example. Stereotypes badly misdescribe the complex picture of labor's involvement in politics at the present time. Aspects of that complex picture also suggest that labor's political power is well within legitimate bounds.

Organized labor includes within it unions that reflect the general indifference of most citizens to the political process. The fundamental change that may be said to have occurred since the New Deal with regard to labor's political involvement is a phenomenon that is descriptive mainly of the behavior of the large unions of the former c.i.o. It is unrealistic to expect craft unions, with a small membership, to become extensively involved in politics.[65] Nor are all active unions necessarily always united in their political positions. Moreover, union involvement in the political process is limited by the distribution of union membership throughout the nation. Unions are well established only in the large industrial areas of the northeast, midwest, and west. In no state is union membership (as a percentage of employees in nonagricultural establishments) as high as 45 percent. And in Connecticut, for example, it was slightly under 25 percent in 1964. Indeed, in that year only about 22 percent of the nation's total labor force was in unions.[66]

The major evidence, however, that labor's political power need not cause anxiety is to be found in studies of labor's influence and expenditures during elections: that aspect of the political process which, as Mr. Dahl insists, performs "the critical role . . . in maximizing political equality and popular sovereignty." [67] In the first place, while it is difficult to classify union activity as political or nonpolitical (at the margin how is political activity to be separated from collective bargaining, educational, or informational activities?), we do have a rough idea of what organized labor spends on compaign-connected activities in an election year. Mr. Heard has estimated that:

The total UAW international's campaign-connected expenditures in 1956 would have come to less than $1,500,000. If an equal amount was spent by the UAW locals—also nothing but a guess—the total for this union would have been about $3,000,000, or less than $2.50 per member. This represents an outside figure for one of the most aggressive of all unions; for the 17,385,000 members of the labor movement resident in the United States, the per capita average would be a small fraction of it.

Crude though all of this is, the conclusion seems inescapable that labor money in politics from all sources pays a much smaller share of the nation's campaign-connected costs than union members constitute of the population of voting age. The voting-age population was estimated to be 102,743,000 in 1956. Union members made up around 17 per cent of it. Total cash campaign expenditures were estimated as $155,000,000, with at least 5 per cent additional in contributions in kind. Other campaign-connected expenditures, comparable to those included in the UAW tabulation (e.g., editorial and voter-registration costs), would push the total to many tens of millions of dollars more. Seventeen per cent of whatever total might be reached would far exceed any reasonable guess at the total of labor money in politics.[68]

Second, union members often are independent. They do not always vote the way they are urged by their union to vote, and a large percentage do not vote at all. Of course, in some parts of the country where the dominant union is especially active politically—the Detroit area has been the subject of important studies—the percentage of apathetic members is less and the persuasive power of the union perhaps greater;[69] but apathy and opposition remain.[70] Labor's monumental failure to defeat Senator Taft in 1950 is the classic example.[71]

If one attends to the variety of factors that influence the way a man votes, one is not surprised by organized labor's inability to deliver its members in an election. The candidate's personality and charm, his religion, ancestry, color, his position on a variety of issues which may be of only secondary importance to the union, are all factors that compete with the economic positions of a candidate, the positions which are of central importance to the union and which usually determine endorsement. Moreover, the member's inclination to follow a union endorsement may vary with his economic well-being, educational background, and age.[72]

Labor's failure to deliver its members as a block must dilute labor's political power no matter how much money labor contributes or spends in support of candidates and causes. While money may talk, and while votes may not be the sole currency of political power, they are, in the American system, the principal standard of exchange.

Chapter 7

Politics and the
Dissenting Employee

I have argued that the political activities of unions are not a threat to our democratic system; that rather they support the system and help to make it work. Thus, the apocalyptic vision of those judges in the conspiracy cases who saw tragic political consequences flowing from concerted employee action was badly skewed. There is, however, a problem of unions in politics that does not vanish upon inspection: the problem of the individual worker who disagrees with the political position of the union representing him in collective bargaining.

We have seen that the worker who dissents over economic matters is, in a sense, sacrificed to the majority; it rules. The law makes an effort to protect the dissenter from abuse and, to the extent that law is able, to protect his efforts to make the majority change its views.[1] Surely in political matters the dissenter is entitled to at least this much protection; and contemporary law probably affords it. For both at common law and under the Bill of Rights of the Labor-Management Reporting and Disclosure Act, the dissenter is protected from union discipline should he speak out or participate actively in national, state, or local politics in a fashion contrary to the received position of the union. Participation in the Communist Party is probably an exception, but even here one can discern change.[2]

Moreover, while the Civil Rights Act of 1964 does not address the question of membership bars based upon political activity, and while traditionally at common law courts would not order admission to a union, there is

growing indication that the common law is evolving.[3]
One may make the not very bold prediction that at least
some courts will hold that where a union may not discipline a member for political activity, it also may not decline to admit an otherwise qualified applicant to membership.

The truly difficult question, however, is the legitimacy
of the union using dues money collected from the dissenter for political purposes. And of course, this question
is presented most sharply where there is a union shop;
that is, where the dissenting employee must contribute
to the union treasury. Under the union shop, the economic
dissenter has no recourse: to work, he must pay. But what
of the conscientious political dissenter? This question
was posed to the Supreme Court in the celebrated case
of *Machinists v. Street*.[4]

Street had little choice. If he wanted to keep his job,
he had to pay dues to the International Association of
Machinists, the union that represented him in collective
bargaining. His employer was a carrier in the Southern
Railway System. Southern and the Machinists had negotiated a union shop contract, which is permitted by section 2, eleventh of the Railway Labor Act.[5] That section
is similar to section 8(a)(3) of the Labor-Management
Relations Act, except that it applies "notwithstanding
any [right to work] law . . . of any State." Street probably
did not want to join the Machinists at all, and he clearly
objected to the union using his dues to support legislation
and legislators he opposed. He complained to the union;
then he went to court to stop the practice.

It is doubtful that many informed observers, no matter
what their view of the union's practice, thought that
Street's chances in court were promising.[6] In the first
place, there was no express language in the collective
agreement or the Railway Labor Act prohibiting the
union from using dues to engage in politics. Moreover,

neither agreement nor statute was readily susceptible to an interpretation prohibiting such a use.[7] In the second place, unions, as we have seen, have been in politics for a long time, spending money to support legislators and legislation deemed favorable to labor's cause.[8] Perhaps most important, however, was the earlier unanimous decision of the Supreme Court in *Railway Employees' Dep't v. Hanson*.[9] Hanson too had worked for a railroad and had been represented by a union with a contract calling for membership. He had resisted joining the union, arguing that the requirement of "compulsory membership" (which means the compulsory payment of dues) contravened the first and fifth amendments of the Constitution. His theory was that the union shop interfered with "the right to work, which the court has frequently included in the concept of 'liberty' within the meaning of the Due Process Clauses," [10] and that it "forces men into ideological and political associations which violate their right to freedom of conscience, freedom of association, and freedom of thought protected by the Bill of Rights." [11] Hanson had been generally unsuccessful, and Street's arguments were formulated in much the same constitutional terms as his predecessor's.

STATE ACTION

At the threshold in *Street*, as earlier it had been in *Hanson*, was the question whether the first and fifth amendments to the United States Constitution had a direct bearing upon the case. In terms, these amendments are a limitation on the actions of the federal government. Certainly the actions of a labor union ordinarily are not considered those of the government in Washington. Ostensibly private actions, however, may have a sufficient nexus with governmental action to require use of the Constitution as an instrument of control.[12] The question is closely related to the great constitutional issue of "state action," which has figured so importantly in recent civil rights cases before the Supreme Court.[13] There the background question has been the nexus between ostensibly private action (which discriminates against Negroes) and the states which are specifically limited in their conduct by the equal protection clause of the fourteenth amendment.

In the *Hanson* case, the governmental action issue took an odd twist. *Hanson* arose in Nebraska which by constitution and statute forbids the union shop; but, as noted, the Railway Labor Act, unlike the Labor-Management Relations Act, permits the negotiation of a union shop contract "notwithstanding any . . . law . . . of any State." Mr. Justice Douglas, speaking for the Court, seemed to make the governmental action issue turn on this conflict and the inescapable supremacy of the federal law.

> The union shop provision of the Railway Labor Act is only permissive. Congress has not compelled nor required carriers and employees to enter into union shop agreements. The Supreme Court of Nebraska nevertheless took the view that justiciable questions under the First and Fifth Amendments were presented since Congress, by the union shop provision of the Railway Labor Act, sought to strike down inconsistent laws in 17 states. . . . The Supreme Court of Nebraska said, "Such action on the part of Congress is a necessary part of every union shop contract entered into on the railroads as far as these 17 States are concerned for without it such contracts could not be enforced therein." . . . We agree with that view. If private rights are being invaded, it is by force of an agreement made pursuant to federal law which expressly declares that state law is superseded. . . . In other words, the federal statute is the source of the

power and authority by which any private rights are lost or sacrificed. . . . The enactment of the federal statute authorizing union shop agreements is the governmental action on which the Constitution operates, though it takes a private agreement to invoke the federal sanction.

As already noted, the 1951 amendment, permitting the negotiation of union shop agreements, expressly allows those agreements notwithstanding any law "of any State." . . . A union agreement made pursuant to the Railway Labor Act has, therefore, the imprimatur of the federal law upon it and, by force of the Supremacy Clause of Article VI of the Constitution, could not be made illegal nor vitiated by any provision of the laws of a State.[14]

If the Court means what it seems to say, *Hanson* leads to incongruous results. In any given case state law determines whether there is sufficient federal involvement to hold the private agreement to first and fifth amendment standards. Thus, where state law permits the negotiation of a union shop, the federal law is not "a necessary part" of the union shop contract, except in the negative sense that Congress has not exercised its power to prohibit such a contract.[15] Involvement of this negative sort would not seem to be the kind that the Court in *Hanson* was talking about when it sustained a finding of governmental action. If this is so, *Hanson* means that the Constitution applies to railroad union shop agreements only in those states that have right-to-work laws. So bizarre a result casts doubt upon the interpretation, and perhaps the Court, therefore, should be taken to mean that state law, as such, is irrelevant in determining whether there has been governmental action. It is a matter of indifference what the state law was before the federal statute was passed, because the state is now no longer free by changing its laws to

grant rights to someone like Hanson through the enactment of a right-to-work statute.

The case for governmental action, however, might have
been made more persuasively if more broadly. Consider
that the union shop provision of the Railway Labor Act
is but one section of a comprehensive regulatory statute, a
statute establishing a federal program for the railroads
designed to encourage collective bargaining. And collective bargaining "generally has been considered to ab-
sorb and give statutory approval to the philosophy of
bargaining as worked out in the labor movement in the
United States." [16] This is a philosophy in which union
security on the railroad is today a central tenet. Thus,
the statute's union shop provision read in context, as
statutes must be read, embodies a federal policy which
encourages the formation of union security agreements.
The statute says to the unions, go ahead and do what
your philosophy tells you to do. This encouragement
might be thought to provide sufficient governmental involvement to make the first and fifth amendments applicable. Indeed, perhaps the extent to which federal
statutes have given unions control over the economic
well-being of the bulk of employees in an enterprise may
be considered a delegation to the union of governmental
power.[17] For purposes of finding the Constitution applicable, the situation may be analogized to the company
town in the landmark state action case of *Marsh v. Alabama*.[18] While the town was owned by a single private
corporation, it had all the attributes of an ordinary
municipality, and the Supreme Court held that its affairs
had to be conducted in accordance with the dictates of
the fourteenth amendment.

What is troublesome about these lines of analysis—the
Court's as well as the ones I have suggested—is that they
encompass a great variety of activity which in ordinary
language we speak of as private. Most private activity is

infused with the governmental in much the way that the union shop is. And in this conceptual framework there simply is no division between private ordering and public regulation. Enacted and decisional law everywhere conditions and shapes the nature of private arrangements in our society. This is true with the commercial contract—regulated as it is by comprehensive uniform statutes—no less than with the collective bargaining agreement; with the business corporation—chartered and regulated as it is by government, exercising as it does delegated governmental authority—no less than with the labor union. The doctrine of state or governmental action as so viewed, then, seems flexible enough to embrace all that constitutionally can be touched by authoritative regulation.[19] Let us see what such an understanding of governmental action would mean in the labor field.

Responsibility and power over federal labor policy would shift from Congress to the Court were union conduct to be judged by the Constitution. This is not to say that Congress would ever relinquish its role as initiator-in-chief of such policy. It would not. Nor would the Court's principal lawmaking role of interpreter of congressional purpose be affected. But should union conduct be judged by constitutional standards Congress would share, and the Court would assume, responsibility for fashioning afresh federal policy. This is only to say that the Court would take on a new role. It would have the responsibility for deciding without direct congressional guidance whether unregulated union conduct squared with the Constitution. For this purpose, and in this sense, the Court would become the initiator of federal labor policy. How well suited is the Court to assume this new role in the problem which has engaged our attention?

The Court in *Hanson* is suggestive. It held against the

plaintiff on his substantive constitutional arguments, but it advised future litigants, of whom *Street* was one, that if under a union shop assessments "are in fact imposed for purposes not germane to collective bargaining, a different problem would be presented." [20] This dictum seems to mean that the fifth amendment may be violated when union funds are not used for collective bargaining purposes; that is, for what the Court holds are not collective bargaining purposes. If this approach were followed, judicial review of union action would involve the Court in second-guessing the union. The Court would be bound to decide whether money spent in support of proposed state or federal legislation, or for the election of a particular candidate for public office, is or is not germane to the union's role as bargaining agent.

The approach invites the establishment of one of two standards: a "reasonableness" test, which will probably come close to giving the unions *carte blanche;* or a test which translates into constitutional law the same sorts of arbitrary distinctions between legal and illegal union objectives that were inserted into the common law of labor by the judges in the conspiracy and injunction cases.[21] The former is hurtful for it surrounds conduct which should be regulated by Congress with a halo of constitutionality—with the quality of legitimacy, which may make subsequent congressional action difficult[22]—while the latter, as the history of labor and the law reveals, is intolerable.

In *Hanson* the Court also advised future litigants that if they could demonstrate that "the exaction of dues, initiation fees, or assessments is used as a cover for forcing ideological conformity or other action in contravention of the First Amendment, this judgment will not prejudice the decision in that case." [23] If the Court, within the analytical framework of union activity as governmental action, were to decide whether the use of funds by the union contravenes the first amendment, it would seem that the Justices must consider several factors: on the one hand are to be weighed the uses and purposes to which the money is to be put, the importance of the objectives in question to the labor organization, and the extent to which they are supported by the majority within the organization; and on the other hand there is to be assessed the effect of the union's action on the dissenting employee. This requires immersion in the history, structure, and aspirations of the union movement, and of the particular union; it requires immersion in collective bargaining, and an understanding of the relationship between economic power and political action.

The economic position of both labor and management —their power at the bargaining table—is dependent upon many variables, not the least of which (at least in the short run) is ever changing federal and state law. The impact upon economic power of federal legislation which makes certain employer and union practices illegal is obvious. A union, for example, may not apply secondary pressures to bring its adversary to terms. And its freedom to engage in organizational picketing is limited.[24] Less obvious, but also important to the power of a union at the bargaining table, are minimum wage legislation, social security legislation, legislation dealing with unemployment and workmen's compensation, and the many other forms of welfare legislation which provide a foundation upon which unions may build in bargaining with management. Another factor that may be equally important to the union's economic position at the bargaining table is tariff legislation or other types of industry protecting or subsidizing enactments. More attenuated perhaps, but still important, are the general economic policies of an administration. (Is it then any wonder that business-minded unions are interested in politics and politicians?)

Thus the task of the Court would be complicated. And

little could be gained from past judicial experience in determining the importance of any particular union-supported legislative program, and in balancing it with the effect of the union's action on the dissenting employee. Each case would present the Court with a discrete problem. And even with respect to any one union the problem would change from time to time with shifts in union economic power—shifts caused by such factors as changed economic conditions or changed federal and state law. Furthermore, because unions are very different institutions from states, municipalities, or the federal government for that matter, it would be hard for the Court to transfer the wisdom contained in traditional first amendment decisions to its review of union conduct.

But, of course, constitutional litigation is always complicated and difficult. Judicial review of congressional action often pushes the Court to the limits of its institutional capacities, and it frequently involves issues of great weight and moment, issues that make the one we have been discussing seem inconsequential. There is, however, an important difference between most types of constitutional litigation and the type of judicial review involved in *Hanson* and *Street*. The difference turns on the nature of the congressional action under review. The distinction in its gross form—and it needs some refinement—is between legislation that commands someone to do something and legislation that permits someone to do what he pleases.

Consider that Congress might have passed a statute making union membership a condition precedent to employment on the railroads. The Court, under traditional doctrines of judicial review, then would have the inescapable obligation in a case posing the first amendment question of deciding that question. Congressional passage of such a "command-type" statute, however, would have entailed a fact-finding and deliberative process which would have focused congressional attention on the alleged use of union funds to compel ideological conformity within the membership. Two consequences would have attended congressional passage of such a "command-type" statute: first, in all likelihood Congress would have recognized the first amendment problems, and would have accommodated individual rights within the statutory framework; second, if a case requiring judicial review were to arise, the Court would have the benefit of a full congressional history, a history which would assist the Court in performing its judicial task. A specific example will aid an understanding of the differences between "command-type" and "permissive" legislation.

If Congress itself were directly to establish wages, hours, and terms and conditions of employment for railroad workers the deliberative process in the legislature would be very different from what it was when Congress decided that collective bargaining between unions and employers over these matters should be encouraged by federal legislation. For legislators are far likelier to focus hard on the impact their actions will have on individuals when new "commanding" legislation is in issue than when they contemplate simply permitting or encouraging private organizations to go their traditional ways and to assume initial, principal responsibility for decisions affecting the interests of those whom they represent.

Sometimes, as in some of the cases involving state action and racial discrimination, this distinction is blurred. The form of the statute is permissive; however, its purpose is to authorize discrimination against Negroes. In such a case, the permissive statute must be treated as if it were a command.[25] But when Congress provided that union shop agreements were a proper subject for collective bargaining, Congress was involved in the sort of process in which it had engaged when it decided that negotiations between unions and employers over wages, hours, and terms and conditions of employment were to be encouraged. Congressional purpose was not to achieve the ideological conformity of workers. Its purpose was to allow the institution of collective bargaining to go its own free way. The legislative process involved in this decision was not one calculated to develop or clarify the full panoply of problems. This is a crucial difference between legislation which commands and legislation which truly does no more than permit. It follows that for the Court to review the constitutionality of private action taken under a permissive congressional enactment, the Court must perform a difficult legislative task as well as an extraordinary judicial one.

Should not these factors which distinguish "truly permissive" from "command" legislation influence the Court to resist extending the Constitution to private action taken in response to a truly permissive statute? Should not the Court be reluctant to develop a doctrine which requires it without the proper congressional history to regulate with so crude an instrument as the Constitution? Is this not especially the case where the issues involve political and economic complexities and where the Court's isolation and institutional disabilities make an informed judgment unusually difficult? And under these circumstances is not the course of restraint plainly correct when extension of judicial doctrine necessary to justify use of the Constitution will have implications in areas unrelated to the particular substantive problems before the Court? This latter consideration is present whenever the doctrine of governmental action is extended. To apply the Constitution to unions makes it appropriate to bring the great document to bear upon the business corporation. And to make most law ultimately constitutional is to give to the most powerful court in the world more power than even it can long endure.

While the Court in *Hanson* did speak—albeit incon-
clusively, opaquely, and unwisely—to the governmental
action question, it did not decide the substantive constitutional questions Hanson tried to raise, because it did
not think the record properly posed the questions. The
Court in *Street* was later to say that "all that was held in
Hanson was that § 2, Eleventh was constitutional in its
bare authorization of union-shop contracts requiring
workers to give 'financial support' to unions legally authorized to act as their collective bargaining agents. We
sustained this requirement—and only this requirement—
embodied in the statutory authorization of agreements
under which 'all employees shall become members of the
labor organization representing their craft or class.' We
clearly passed neither upon forced association in any other
aspect nor upon the issue of the use of exacted money for
political causes which were opposed by the employees." [26]

It is difficult to understand what the *Street* record dis-
closed that the *Hanson* record did not, for as Mr. Justice
Frankfurter said in dissent:

> The record before the Court in *Hanson* clearly in-
> dicated that dues would be used to further what are
> normally described as political and legislative ends.
> And it surely can be said that the Court was not
> ignorant of a fact that everyone else knew. Union
> constitutions were in evidence which authorized the
> use of union funds for political magazines, for sup-
> port of lobbying groups, and for urging union mem-
> bers to vote for union approved candidates. The con-
> tention now raised by [Street] was succinctly stated
> by the *Hanson* plaintiffs in their brief. We indicated
> that we were deciding the merits of the complaint on
> all the allegations and proofs before us. "On the
> present record, there is no more an infringement or

impairment of First Amendment rights than there would be in the case of a lawyer who by state law is required to be a member of an integrated bar."

One would suppose that *Hanson's* reasoning disposed of the present suit.[27]

The Court, nevertheless, took the view that "the record in [*Street*] is adequate squarely to present the constitutional questions reserved in *Hanson*." [28] These are substantive first and fifth amendment questions: has due process or free speech and assembly been violated by the union spending a portion of the compelled dues of a dissenting member for political purposes? It must be concluded, therefore, that the Court in *Street*, without attending to the question, assumed that there was a sufficient nexus between the union and the United States government to bring the Constitution to bear on the private ordering of the union and railroad.

Yet the Court did not decide the substantive first or fifth amendment questions; rather the majority avoided these constitutional issues through some rather fancy statutory interpretation. The Court held that: "§ 2, Eleventh is to be construed to deny the unions, over an employee's objection, the power to use his exacted funds to support political causes which he opposes." [29]

STATUTORY INTERPRETATION AND
CONSTITUTIONAL AVOIDANCE

Section 2, eleventh, of the Railway Labor Act was enacted by Congress in 1951. It is similar in language, and seemingly in purpose, to its counterpart in the Labor-Management Relations Act. The major difference, which we have remarked, is that union shops in the railroad industry are permitted "notwithstanding any . . . law

. . . of any State." Union and carrier may negotiate an agreement

> requiring as a condition of continued employment, that within sixty days following the beginning of [their] employment . . . all employees shall become members of the labor organization. . . . *Provided,* That no such agreement shall require such condition of employment with respect to employees to whom membership is not available upon the same terms and conditions as are generally applicable to any other member or with respect to employees to whom membership was denied or terminated for any reason other than the failure of the employee to tender the periodic dues, initiation fees, and assessments (not including fines and penalties) uniformly required as a condition of acquiring or retaining membership.

The task the majority set for itself in *Street* was to construe this language to deny "the authority to a union, over the employee's objection, to spend his money for political causes which he opposes." [30] It set about performing this seemingly difficult task by a selective reading of "the legislative history of § 2, Eleventh in the context of the development of unionism in the railroad industry under the regulatory scheme created by the Railway Labor Act." [31] In examining this history, the majority was impressed by several phenomena. First, it noted that railroad unions traditionally had not been especially interested, for philosophical and economic reasons, in union security. Accordingly, these unions had not insisted upon the union or closed-shop contract in negotiating with carriers. Second, the Court observed that Congress in 1934 had prohibited union security contracts on the railroads and that this flat prohibition had continued until the passage of section 2, eleventh, in 1951. These facts afforded the Court its point of departure for assessing what Congress had done and what it had not done when it reversed its 1934 position. As the Court put it:

> The appellant unions, in insisting that § 2, Eleventh contemplates their use of exacted funds to support political causes objected to by the employee, would have us hold that Congress sanctioned an expansion of historical practices in the political area by the rail unions. . . . Both by tradition and, from 1934 to 1951, by force of law, the rail unions did not rely upon the compulsion of union security agreements to exact money to support the political activities in which they engage.[32]

The Court discovered that in 1950–51 the unions had called to the attention of Congress: (1) that the union's obligation under the Railway Labor Act was to represent all employees, non-union as well as union; (2) that under the Railway Labor Act and in the railroad industry this was an expensive business; and (3) that this expense should be shared by all employees. The Court said:

> The conclusion to which this history clearly points is that § 2, Eleventh contemplated compulsory unionism to force employees to share the costs of negotiating and administering collective agreements, and the costs of adjustment and settlement of disputes. One looks in vain for any suggestion that Congress also meant in § 2, Eleventh to provide the unions with a means for forcing employees, over their objection, to support political causes which they oppose.[33]

This may be true. It is also true that "one looks in vain" for language in section 2, eleventh, prohibiting unions from forcing employees "to support political causes which they oppose." And in 1950–51, even as today, it was not a secret, or at least not a well-kept secret, that unions used money obtained from employees for political as well as economic activities. The Court took notice of this:

> We may assume that Congress was . . . fully conversant with the long history of intensive involvement of the railroad unions in political activities. But it does not follow that § 2, Eleventh places no restriction on the use of an employee's money, over his objection, to support political causes he opposes merely because Congress did not enact a comprehensive regulatory scheme covering expenditures. For it is abundantly clear that Congress did not completely abandon the policy of full freedom of choice embodied in the 1934 Act, but rather made inroads on it for the limited purpose of eliminating the problems created by the "free-rider." That policy survives in § 2, Eleventh in the safeguards intended to protect freedom of dissent. Congress was aware of the conflicting interests involved in the question of the union shop and sought to achieve their accommodation.[34]

The difficulty with this conclusion is that an examination of the language of section 2, eleventh indicates that, although a congressional accommodation of the "conflicting interests involved in the question of the union shop" was indeed achieved, the resulting accommodation imposed no restrictions on union expenditures. Rather, it appears that Congress followed closely the accommodations worked out in 1947 after an extensive review of the union security problems that had emerged subsequent to enactment of the Wagner Act. The background of these accommodations is legislative history that the Court chose to ignore.

In the Wagner Act, Congress had placed no prohibitions on the negotiation and enforcement of union security agreements.[35] Unions and employers could make a closed-shop contract,[36] and where such a contract was made an applicant for work had to be a member of the union to qualify for employment. Furthermore, under a closed shop, or a "common law" union shop, an employee had to remain in good standing in his union in order to keep his job. Expulsion from the union for any reason, such as a disagreement with the leadership, meant loss of employment.[37]

The unions that were regulated by the Wagner Act, unlike the railroad unions, were intensely interested in union security. They bargained for the closed shop, frequently with success.[38] Sometimes their success meant that the dissenting employee lost his job. This penalty placed upon dissent led to the changes embodied in the Labor-Management Relations Act. As we have seen in an earlier chapter, that statute goes very far to separate job security from union membership. Under a statutory union shop all an employee need do to protect his job is tender the periodic dues and initiation fees uniformly required as a condition of acquiring or retaining union membership. The employee need not maintain good standing in the union, and, of course, he need not be a member of the union at the time of his employment.[39]

The congressional hearings that led to the changes in the Labor-Management Relations Act focused on these job control problems.[40] While there was discussion in Congress about the use of funds obtained under a union shop for political purposes, it was neither extensive nor systematic.[41] The question of the use of funds for political purposes received almost no attention when Congress in 1951 reversed itself and permitted the union shop on the railroads.[42] Congress accomplished this by employing in section 2, eleventh the same language that it earlier had employed when dealing with the union shop in the Labor-Management Relations Act. The statutes, in those portions relevant to our concern, are twins. Is it not fair then to surmise that Congress, when it enacted section 2, eleventh, was attempting no more than roughly to conform the law of union security in the railroad industry to the law in industries regulated by the Labor-Management Relations Act? This was possible in 1950–51, if not earlier, because of the disappearance on the railroad of the company union. As the Senate Report recognized:

> The present prohibitions against all forms of union security agreements . . . were made part of the Railway Labor Act in 1934. They were enacted into law against the background of employer use of these agreements as devices for establishing and maintaining company unions, thus effectively depriving a substantial number of employees of their right to bargain collectively. . . . Since the enactment of the 1934 Amendments company unions have practically disappeared.[43]

When the text of section 2, eleventh and its particular history is projected against this background of the language and history of the Labor-Management Relations Act's union security provisions, it is not easy to read section 2, eleventh the way the *Street* majority did. It is not, however, impossible to do so. And, for reasons now to be discussed, it might be thought that the canon of statutory interpretation, which counsels that a statute be read to avoid a serious constitutional question,[44] required just the reading that the *Street* majority settled upon.

No matter what the reasons for the 1934 congressional prohibition upon railroad union-shop contracts, there seems to be little question that such contracts were in fact effectively prohibited until 1951.[45] This absence of the union shop afforded maximum freedom to the dissenting railroad employee. When Congress changed the law in 1951 and removed the legal restrictions it earlier had placed upon the union shop, one could have predicted that the result would be a diminution of the dissenting employee's freedom. In determining how much of a diminution Congress meant to allow, should not the presumption be: not one bit more than it clearly provided for in the statute?

It is to be remembered that, in the absence of escape through statutory interpretation, the Court believed that its duty lay in deciding the constitutionality under the first and fifth amendments of the union's use, for political purposes, of dues obtained from protesting employees. This constitutional decision would have to be made in a situation where it was fairly clear that Congress itself had not confronted the question whether it was necessary to restrict individual freedom to this extent. Recall that Congress had not enacted a "command-type" statute, but rather a permissive statute; and that the experience under the Wagner Act had not sufficiently focused congressional attention on the political dissenter. Congress in section 2, eleventh, had not said unequivocally: We, the people's representatives, believe that restriction on the individual's political freedom is necessary in this situation. Congress should have a chance to do this—or to decline to do this —before it is taken to have done it. How can the Court defer to Congress on the first or fifth amendment issue when it is not clear that Congress has made a judgment to be deferred to? In the alternative, how can the Court justify the exercise of its extraordinary and ultimate power to make a declaration of unconstitutionality, when it is not clear that congressional action has compelled a decision on the first and fifth amendment issues?

The question of when the Court should construe a statute to avoid deciding a constitutional issue is a difficult one, and one that we have examined earlier in relation to the *Steele* case and the doctrine of fair representation, and the C.I.O. case and section 304 of L.M.R.A.[46]

It may be helpful to take another example from a different field of law. *Kent v. Dulles*[47] involved an exercise in statutory interpretation which was dictated by the Court's desire to avoid a constitutional confrontation. The Court there limited the seemingly unrestricted power over passports delegated to the Secretary of State by Congress. The Secretary, in denying a passport to a citizen because of his alleged beliefs and associations, had acted as if the delegation were in fact an unrestricted one. To be sure, Congress had not specifically said that the Secretary could deny passports and restrict travel to the extent that he had. But just as surely the Secretary was not unreasonable in interpreting the delegation as an authorization of his actions. Yet, if the Court had read the enabling statute to cover the Secretary's actions, it would have had to subject those actions to close scrutiny in order to ascertain whether they transgressed the fifth amendment's protection of the right to travel. The Court would have had to hold either that the Secretary had been authorized to act and indeed had acted unconstitutionally or that authorized governmental action, drastically restricting an individual's freedom to travel, was constitutional, even though Congress had not itself clearly determined that such restriction was necessary.[48]

The Court's holding that the Secretary's actions were unauthorized was preferable to either of these alternatives.[49] Before governmental restriction upon individual freedom is held to be either unconstitutional or constitutional, it should be absolutely clear to a majority of the Supreme Court that Congress has faced the issue squarely and determined clearly that in its judgment it was necessary to impose the restriction.[50] It is one thing for the Court, largely in deference to a clear determination of necessity by the governmental institution closest to the people, to hold constitutional a previously questionable action. It is quite another thing for the Court to hold action con-

stitutional where the people's representatives have not
themselves declared in clear language that individual
freedom must be curtailed because of an overriding national need. Is not this canon of statutory interpretation
really a corollary of the doctrine of judicial self-restraint
in constitutional adjudication? [51] And is it not closely related in its theoretical underpinnings to the distinction
between "command-type" and permissive legislation?

The trouble with the application of this canon of
statutory interpretation in the *Street* case is that it either
leads the Court to too narrow a reading of section 2,
eleventh, or imposes upon the Court a task that it is not
likely to do well. Consider the following suggestive ex-
cerpt from the brief of the United States filed with the
Supreme Court in the case.

> Numerous union activities and expenditures of dif-
> ferent kinds [were] drawn in question. They range
> from testimony by union officials before legislative
> committees, and solicitation at union meetings of
> voluntary contributions to political organizations, to
> the use of union funds for political campaigns; from
> the endorsement of political candidates by unions and
> their periodicals, to "interpretive" and "non-objec-
> tive" news articles by such journals; from union sup-
> port of legislation concerning wages, hours, and work-
> ing conditions to support of legislation pertaining to
> housing, farm programs and foreign aid; and from
> legislative activities and expenditures by the local
> lodge, to legislative and political activities and ex-
> penditures by the AFL-CIO. . . . These different kinds
> of expenditures and activities . . . may well involve
> differing considerations. For instance, support of leg-
> islation concerning wages and hours might be con-

sidered more "germane" to collective bargaining than support of legislation involving farm programs; and the majority of the union members may have an interest in associating together to publish their views in a newspaper, which interest may be entitled to greater protection than their interest in having the union render financial support to the campaign of a particular political candidate.[52]

What this suggests is that it is quite possible that the Court, by avoiding the first and fifth amendment issues, has prohibited unions from using money obtained from dissenting employees for purposes that realistically cannot be said to raise serious first or fifth amendment difficulties. No matter how economically strong the union, its expenditures in connection with legislation dealing directly with the subject matter of collective bargaining would seem to present such a situation. After all, it must be remembered that in collective bargaining matters the union, by law long deemed constitutional, represents dissenting employees as well as consenting employees; and that "the individual [union] member may express his views in any public or private forum as freely as he could before the union collected his dues. Federal taxes also may diminish the vigor with which a citizen can give partisan support to a political belief, but as yet no one would place such an impediment to making one's views effective within the reach of constitutionally protected 'free speech.' " [53]

If the majority's interpretation of section 2, eleventh does in fact bar the union from using funds in ways that clearly invoke no first or fifth amendment barrier, the justification for such restrictive interpretation of section 2, eleventh, is not compelling. An interpretation of the statute that forces the Court to face up to insubstantial first or fifth amendment questions does not pose the many difficulties discussed earlier. They exist only where those constitutional questions are substantial. For where the constitutional question is insubstantial, its confrontation will not force the Court to exercise its ultimate power of striking down enacted law. And while the Court may be called upon to validate a restriction on individual freedom, that restriction, by hypothesis, fails even to begin to offend a constitutional standard. Constitutional law which is this clear is a part of the background against which Congress enacted section 2, eleventh. One might well argue that the natural implication of what Congress has said and done in such a case should prevail. Looking at this another way, one can say that the Court's interpretation of section 2, eleventh, to the extent that it is more restrictive of union power than is properly called for by serious constitutional doubt, is better characterized as the regulation of collective bargaining than as protection of individual freedom. And it need not be argued again in these pages that the role of the Court in dealing with the regulation of collective bargaining should be as limited as possible.

It is not altogether clear, however, that the Court did construe section 2, eleventh, to avoid insubstantial first and fifth amendment questions, as well as to avoid substantial ones such as direct support of candidates for political office. The Court tells us only:

> We respect . . . congressional purpose when we construe § 2, Eleventh as not vesting the unions with unlimited power to spend exacted money. We are not called upon to delineate the precise limits of that power in this case. We have before us only the question whether the power is restricted to the extent of denying the unions the right, over the employee's objection, to use his money to support political causes which he opposes. Its use to support candidates for public office, and advance political programs, is not a

use which helps defray the expenses of the negotiation or administration of collective agreements, or the expenses entailed in the adjustment of grievances and disputes. In other words, it is a use which falls clearly outside the reasons advanced by the unions and accepted by Congress why authority to make union-shop agreements was justified.[54]

But, of course, money spent in support of some legislation —for example, full crew laws—may make it unnecessary for the union to strike or spend money in support of a bargaining demand. One might think of the monetary expenditures as a collective bargaining activity by means of political action, even as one might think of picketing as a collective bargaining activity by means of "a form of speech." [55]

The point is that the Court's language is ambiguous. Nowhere did it undertake the task—perhaps because it is impossible except in an arbitrary way—of distinguishing between political and collective bargaining activities. Nor has it since attempted to do so. Thus, while it seems probable that the Court meant by "political" anything that has a political element in it, it is not absolutely clear that the Court went this far. Notice, however, that if the Court did not go so far, it has assumed the task of deciding whether the expenditure of money by a union is for political or collective bargaining purposes. It has in the language of *Hanson,* undertaken to determine whether dues money is used for purposes "germane to collective bargaining." As I suggested earlier, this is likely to lead to distinctions that rest on fiat alone.

The Court, in *Street,* one way or another unhappily contrived to entangle itself in legislating about collective bargaining; and to what end? One is forced to wonder

whether the Court will escape the confrontation with the
first and fifth amendments that it so strenuously worked
to avoid. For all of the issues the Court thought it was
avoiding will be before it again if a dissenting employee
asserts that the Labor-Management Relations Act's union
shop is unconstitutional. Should that happen, it will be
difficult for the Court to read that statute in the way in
which it has read the Railway Labor Act. As we have
seen, it cannot be said that in 1947 Congress was cutting
back on a freedom it had earlier granted dissenting employees. Nor can it be asserted that unions regulated by
the Labor-Management Relations Act had traditionally
been uninterested in union security. These propositions
were made by the *Street* majority about congressional
performance in 1951 and about unions regulated by the
Railway Labor Act. They were advanced by that majority
as weighty reasons for its reading of section 2, eleventh.
They are not available as bases for reaching a like conclusion in a section 8(a)(3) case. The first and fifth
amendment questions left unresolved by *Street* may yet
have to be resolved by the Court.

What the Court should have done in the *Street* case
was to reexamine its reasoning as to governmental action
in *Hanson*. Neither restrictive statutory interpretation nor
first and fifth amendment decisions were appropriate in
Street. The Court should have declined to test union conduct by first or fifth amendment standards. Union action
should not be held to be governmental action within the
meaning of the United States Constitution.

THE NEED FOR LEGISLATION

This conclusion is not intended to suggest that the
Court has seen a problem where none exists; rather to suggest that its heroic efforts at statutory interpretation and

its constitutional adjudication—explicit in *Hanson,* implicit in *Street*—were unfortunate.

The underlying problem is there, visible to anyone interested in preserving the individual nonconformist. And because in this area the value of dissent is so much greater than the cost to the majority, unions should not be permitted to use dissenting members' money for certain kinds of political activities. This is true for employees under the Labor-Management Relations Act as well as those under the Railway Labor Act. Moreover, organized employees who are not by contract required to join a union are entitled to the same protection. They should not have to choose between abstention from membership in their legal representative body (even though it does not cost them their jobs) and monetary support of all union political activities. The courts, however, are inappropriate institutions for distinguishing permissible political activities from impermissible activities. For reasons canvassed, distinctions are not amenable to judicial elaboration, and, accordingly, guidelines should be provided by Congress. The give and take of the legislative process is the appropriate process for separating the unions' practice of collective bargaining from their practice of political action. Once the separation is made, the employee who wishes should be free monetarily to opt out from those activities designated as political, and have his dues reduced accordingly.

In *Brotherhood of Railway Clerks v. Allen,*[56] the Court itself, borrowing from British experience, suggested the opting-out approach as a method the unions might employ to comply with *Street.*[57] But, in the first place, the mandate of *Street* does not protect the bulk of organized workers; and in the second place, under *Allen,* the unions, on their peril, must decide the political from the nonpolitical, for as the Court tells us: "It would be impracticable to require a dissenting employee to allege and prove each distinct union political expenditure to which he objects; it is enough that he manifests his opposition to *any* political expenditures by the union." [58]

It is to be hoped that Congress will rescue the unions and the courts from this entanglement; that the political process will separate, as only it can, the political from the economic; and that in so doing it will protect the dissenting worker from the majority union.

Part V

Union Power and
the Economy

Chapter 8

Major Work
Stoppages

Of the four problems that disturbed the judges in the conspiracy cases and are rehearsed in the rhetoric of those early opinions, none is more difficult for modern law or more a present threat to the future of existing labor-management relations than the problem that I have called the economic consequences of collective bargaining. The problem as we know it today is not single, but a variety of complex problems, and at least one of these—efficiency in industrial organization—has been touched upon in an earlier chapter. The effect of collective bargaining on unorganized workers is another problem in this complex that has troubled economists in particular for many years, and not a few members of that profession believe the benefits enjoyed by organized labor are paid for, at least in part, by the unorganized.[1]

Unquestionably, however, the principal concern today is the effect of union policy on the general public; the efficiency question is one aspect of this. Another is the misallocation of labor that may result from the power of unions to raise the wages of organized workers relative to the wages earned by comparable unorganized workers.[2] A third concern is labor-management restrictive practices that may violate the Sherman Anti-Trust Act.[3] These phenomena may result in prices higher than they would be in a more classically competitive system; yet none, as such threatens the survival of collective bargaining as a viable institution.

It is the work stoppage that sometimes accompanies the periodic establishment of the terms and conditions of em-

ployment through collective bargaining, and the totality
of inflationary pressures thought to be generated by bargaining settlements that today attract the lion's share of
attention, and that have precipitated collective bargaining's most important modern crisis.

This chapter addresses the work stoppage problem; the
next the terms of settlement. Neither problem is exclusively economic in nature and this is especially true of
work stoppages. Both chapters are concerned centrally
with a search for the appropriate response of law and
both proceed from the assumption that it is desirable to
preserve as much of the present system as possible.

In the summer of 1966, the International Association of
Machinists struck five major airlines. The results were
massive inconvenience for many people, extensive intervention by the administration to achieve settlement—indeed, one proposed solution was voted down by the union
membership after President Johnson had given it his blessing—a seemingly serious move by Congress to enact legislation ending the strike,[4] and widespread insistence by the
news media that no nation could long endure such labor-
management irresponsibility.

It is hard to imagine a more exaggerated response to a
strike than that which attended this airline dispute. Air
traffic had not stopped and most people found that they
could get where they wanted to go and ship what they
wished to send.[5] Life was more difficult for many, but
not that much more for most. Nor were the consequences
of the strike to the economic health of the country significant, as perhaps they had been in the prolonged 1959 steel
dispute. But the attitudes generated by the strike were not
really surprising. Since World War II the major work
stoppage has tried the patience of the country. Labor

Secretary Wirtz reflected his sensitivity to this when he said, "Neither the traditional collective bargaining procedures nor present labor dispute laws are working to the public's satisfaction, at least so far as major controversies are concerned." [6]

Public impatience with major labor disputes is understandable. A basic premise of an economic system marked by great interdependence and a high division of labor is that production in a particular sector or industry will not be deliberately terminated. People who produce goods for purposes other than their own consumption assume their needs will be met by the production of others. Any strike, therefore, may appear to be a frontal attack upon the system itself. This is particularly true when habitual patterns of reliance are disrupted. The commuter who must find other transportation because of a railroad strike and the housewife whose shopping habits must change for lack of a daily newspaper understandably become intolerant of strikes, and of collective bargaining. It is difficult during a work stoppage to persuade affected individuals that the values of private ordering, achieved through collective bargaining, are worth this public cost.

Government must respond to widespread or intensely held public discontent. But a governmental policy designed to reduce the work stoppages that accompany the periodic renegotiations of collective agreements should not lose sight of the commitment to private ordering contained in our national labor relations law; a commitment often remarked in these pages. The institution of collective bargaining reflects a dual faith in the concept of private ordering. There is faith in the proposition that labor and management—the parties most directly involved—know better than any potential regulator what constitutes the best labor contract for them. And there is faith in the proposition that private determination of wages, hours, and terms and conditions of employment is consonant with our larger commitment to pluralism as an essential ingredient of political democracy.

The effect of a work stoppage is a cost traditionally paid by the public for the benefits of private ordering in labor-management relations. It is a cost that must be paid. For while a collective bargaining agreement usually can be reached without a strike, its threat is the major force moving an employer toward settlement. And it is the occasional strike that legitimates the strike threat. So important is the strike to collective bargaining that the public cost must be exceedingly high before a strike is interdicted. The alternative literally is to abandon, in this area, the pursuit of our dual faith in private ordering.

One way in which government might respond to the work stoppage problem while preserving its commitment to private ordering is to limit intervention to a small group of labor disputes, those thought to have the character of an emergency. This is a traditional approach, and considerable attention has been directed to it. But the study of emergency labor disputes has right along been bedeviled by definitional problems; and understandably so. In the first place, the word "emergency" unlike "major" or "important," makes powerful demands upon its user to demonstrate the need for its use. The question, "Why do you say a steel strike is an emergency dispute?" is to be expected. The question, "Why do you say a steel strike is a major dispute?" is not. Second, students of emergency labor disputes also are apt to be students of labor relations generally. They therefore rightly view the labor dispute as a normal, often an essential, part of collective bargaining. Restraints upon normal procedures are understandably suspect and must be justified by extraordinary countervailing considerations. The existence of an emergency is such a consideration, but care must be taken with definition if the extraordinary is not to lose its special quality and undermine the collective bargaining system itself.[7]

Thus, for example, one student of the work stoppage problem has proffered the following as a definition of a national emergency dispute: "1. The impacts of the dispute must be national rather than purely local. 2. The product or service must be essential, in the sense that its use cannot be dispensed with or postponed without quickly and seriously impairing the safety or health of the whole nation. 3. The dispute must embrace all or a substantial part of the industry. 4. The emergency must be imminent or actual, rather than an ultimate prospect if the stoppage were to last an indefinitely long period." [8]

The trouble is that while a definition of this sort may satisfy one's conception of an emergency, it fails to satisfy the political pressures generated by a public that is inconvenienced by work stoppages falling short of an emergency. This is one hard lesson of the 1966 airline strike, and it suggests that there is little utility in attempting to limit government's role to emergency situations, however an emergency is defined. The word simply will not bear a definition that is politically acceptable.

Public opinion is merely one source of the pressure on government to intervene in labor disputes. While the effects of the airline strike were quickly and intensively felt by a vocal segment of the public, the impact on the public of a steel strike at first may be negligible, yet its potential economic significance may make it advisable for government to act quickly. And, of course, the needs of the defense establishment call for intervention long before public opinion has crystallized. These obvious facts, it seems to me, strengthen the claim that it is not useful to attempt to define "emergency," if the object of the exercise is to produce an operational definition—a definition that triggers the use of special governmental intervention.

Nor is it necessary to speak of emergency disputes rather
than major disputes if the question is when government
should be alerted to a potential need for ultimate intervention. Moreover, while intervention may take many
forms, ranging from mediation to a temporary but nevertheless outright substitute for collective bargaining, the
employment of even the most extreme form may be politically necessary in a non-emergency situation. Such probably would have been the case if the 1966 airline strike
had lasted much longer. This may be regrettable; but
there it is.

The quest, then, cannot be for a definition limiting
drastic intervention. The political responsibility of the
governmental decision-makers is the only realistic protection available. For the enduring values nourished by collective bargaining and the immediate demands made by
public opinion, economic, and defense requirements can
be accommodated through the political process and
through that process alone.

Accordingly, it would seem that: (1) The attention of
the executive branch of government must be engaged by
the existence of any actual or potential major labor dispute. (2) The techniques of governmental intervention
must be authorized by Congress; timing and method must
be within the discretion of the executive. (3) The exercise of this discretion must be informed by economic and
political considerations. And (4) the government, when
intervening, must continue to preserve whenever possible
the values associated with free labor-management relations
and our present labor relations laws.[9]

THE EXISTING LEGAL FRAMEWORK

The law of labor-management relations at present not
only purports to rely upon private ordering, but, as earlier
chapters have stressed, reflects commitment to the propo-

sition that free collective bargaining—including the right to strike—is the preferred method for achieving industrial peace. This faith, however, has not prevented Congress from enacting legislation that, in limited areas, restricts the union's employment of economic force. Some of this legislation applies irrespective of the economic or political effects of a labor dispute (that is, regardless of whether a strike, if allowed, would be of major dimensions); some only in disputes affecting the national health and welfare (a major strike of the first magnitude); some to major disputes on the railroads and airlines.

Limitation on the legality of the secondary boycott is regulation of the first type which may tend to reduce the number of major strikes by imposing restrictions on their scope. Section 8(b) (4) of the Labor-Management Relations Act makes most secondary boycotts unfair labor practices, and section 10 (l) provides mandatory injunctive relief. The former section is complicated, but its central purpose is to protect neutral employers—those not directly involved in a labor dispute—from direct union sanctions. Since strikes cannot fan out in the way they otherwise might, their economic effect may be contained. But the section does not interdict the primary strike or its attendant consequences.[10] These may impose a substantial hardship upon the neutral employer who does business with the primary employer. A national steel strike is always a major strike for this reason among others.

The so-called national emergency provisions of the Labor-Management Relations Act work in the following way.[11] When the President determines that a threatened or actual strike or lockout in an entire or substantial part of an industry will endanger the national health or safety, he may appoint an emergency fact-finding board to report on the situation. The jurisdiction of the fact-finders is strictly limited by statute to information gathering and dispensing. No recommendations for settlement are to be submitted.

After the fact-finding board makes its report, the President may direct the Attorney General to petition a district court for an injunction halting the strike for 80 days. "The statute imposes upon the Courts the duty of finding, upon the evidence adduced, whether a strike . . . meets the statutory conditions of breadth of involvement and peril to the national health or safety." [12] But, as Mr. Justice Frankfurter and Mr. Justice Harlan (concurring in the case that upheld the constitutionality of this portion of the statute) have said, "in the discharge of its duty a District Court would disregard reason not to give due weight to determinations previously made by the President, who is, after all, the ultimate constitutional executive repository for assuring the safety of the Nation, and upon whose judgment the invocation of the emergency provisions depends." [13] Thus, the President has broad discretion indeed in deciding when to invoke the statute.

During the 80-day "cooling-off" period, the parties are under a duty to bargain. If, however, the dispute is unsettled after 60 of the 80 days, the emergency fact-finding board is required to make a public report on the current positions of the parties and the settlement efforts made, and to present "a statement by each party of its position and a statement of the employer's last offer of settlement." The National Labor Relations Board then conducts, within 15 days, a "last offer ballot" to determine if the striking employees wish to accept this offer. If the employees reject the offer and no settlement has been reached within the 80-day life of the injunction, the parties concerned are completely free to resume the strike. The President, however, has an additional statutory obligation. He must submit to Congress a full report of the strike proceedings and whatever recommendations he may see fit to make "for consideration and appropriate action."

Experience with the statute[14] plus rumination about its problems have led many disinterested observers to suggest that the statute, while it functions reasonably well, is unfortunate in several respects. First, because the statute equips the government with a single, rigidly defined procedure, the parties to a dispute can calculate with fair accuracy the timing and consequence of the government's intervention. Accordingly, that intervention may be relied upon in the bargaining by one side or the other, and for this reason is likely to forestall settlement until governmental action runs its course. Second, a predictable strike injunction may be relied upon by the parties as a time for getting their second wind and reassessing the situation. Consequently, pre-injunction settlement is hindered. Third, the fact-finding board often does not have time to perform its task properly. Moreover, because it does not have the option to make recommendations, the force of public opinion cannot be encouraged to cluster around one party or the other and hence to pressure for settlement. And in some situations this might be helpful. Fourth, the publicized last offer ballot tends to harden the position of the parties and makes it difficult for them to retreat. In sum, the major difficulty with the national emergency provisions is that they sometimes tend to impede rather than to facilitate collective bargaining. And yet—aside from instant legislation—collective bargaining is the only method provided in the statute for resolving the dispute.[15]

Labor disputes in the railroad and airline industries are governed by the provisions of the Railway Labor Act. The act, as construed, distinguishes between "major" and "minor" disputes and provides separate procedures for each. Minor disputes are those that relate either to the meaning or proper application of a particular provision of an existing collective agreement or to an omitted case. Major disputes are those which arise over the formation of collective agreements or efforts to secure them. They look to the acquisition of rights for the future rather than to the assertion of rights claimed to have vested in the past.[16]

As a first step toward settlement of a controversy under both kinds of disputes, the Act requires the parties to negotiate. If negotiations fail in a minor dispute, either party may submit the matter to the National Railroad Adjustment Board whose award is final and binding upon the parties.

Major disputes are treated differently. If negotiations fail, the dispute becomes the subject of mediation by the National Mediation Board, either by request of either party or offer by the Board. If mediation fails, the parties may accept or reject arbitration. If arbitration is rejected, and in the opinion of the Board the dispute threatens to deprive the country of essential transportation service, the Board is required to certify this fact to the President, who may then appoint an emergency board to study the dispute, report to the President, and make recommendations which are not binding upon the parties. Section 10 of the act provides that from the time an emergency board is created until 30 days after the board makes its report to the President "no change, except by agreement, shall be made by the parties to the controversy in the conditions out of which the dispute arose." There are several other status quo or "freeze" provisions in the Act, which read together cover the entire duration of the dispute proceedings from the time notice of intended change is given by either party.[17] Until the major dispute procedures are exhausted the union may not legally strike and the Norris-La Guardia Act does not bar the courts from enjoining an illegal strike in such a situation. Where the provisions of the Railway Labor Act have been exhausted, however, the Supreme Court has held that Norris-La Guardia does bar a district court from enjoining a strike.[18] Thus a Court of Appeals could rightly say: "When the cooling-off procedures of the Act . . . are exhausted and the final thirty day period has elapsed it is quite clear that the Act contemplates that further progress toward the determination of the controversy will be left entirely to the interplay of economic forces without further governmental intervention." [19] Governmental tolerance for strikes on the railroads, however, is very low, and where the statutory procedures have failed, ad hoc executive or congressional intervention has been employed. Thus, Congress has ordered compulsory arbitration and it has imposed extra statutory freeze periods on the parties.[20]

The Railway Labor Act procedures seem more rigid than the corresponding provisions of the Labor-Management Relations Act in that the President may have less flexibility as to timing in creating a railroad emergency board. This is because a national railroad strike approaches the unthinkable. It is clear, moreover, that the rigidity of the statutory provisions allows the parties to calculate with more certainty the impact of their use. Thus, creation of emergency boards is habitual rather than extraordinary, and it has been fairly claimed that: "The appointment of an 'emergency board,' when a strike or lock-out is threatened, has become an almost automatic part of the process of settling the terms of contracts." [21] As a result, the Railway Labor Act's dispute settlement procedures may reasonably be said to deter and delay, rather than encourage, serious bargaining by the parties. Moreover, the case for having dispute settlement procedures for the railroad and airline industries that are separate from the procedures in other industries seems untenable.

Finally, in reviewing the present state of the law, it should be remarked that governmental intervention of a much less drastic character is contemplated by the Labor-Management Relations Act which creates the Federal Mediation and Conciliation Service.[22] (Its counterpart under the Railway Labor Act is the National Mediation Board.) Conciliation or mediation—the terms are interchangeable —is sharply different from arbitration. It relies upon negotiation as the method for achieving agreement rather than upon third party decision-making. The mediator, of course, is a third party, but his function is not to decide. It is to aid the parties in reaching their own decision. He may help in many ways. For example, a mediator through private conversations may discover that the parties are really closer together than they thought. It may be that there is a misunderstanding that he can point out. He may suggest techniques for resolving difficult issues. It is obvious, therefore, that conciliation represents a mild form of outside intervention.

The statute insists hard upon this. Section 203(c) provides that if conciliation does not work the mediator shall "seek to induce the parties voluntarily to seek other means of settling the dispute without resort to strike." But the section goes on to provide: "The failure or refusal of either party to agree to any procedure suggested . . . shall not be deemed a violation of any duty or obligation imposed by this Act."

Section 203(c) applies to all disputes with which the Service becomes involved whether of major dimensions or not. And the Service has responsibility over labor-management relations covered by the act, except that it is "directed to avoid attempting to mediate disputes which would have only a minor effect on interstate commerce if State or other conciliation services are available to the parties."

AD HOC INTERVENTION

Ad hoc intervention to achieve the settlement of major labor disputes is a traditional function of the executive branch of government. It takes many forms ranging from a statement by the Secretary of Labor at a news conference that the nation is counting on the parties quickly to reach accord, through the appointment of special, non-statutory boards of inquiry, to the massive intervention of President Johnson in the April 1964 railroad dispute, when the President contrived, with vast political skill and the full prestige of office, to obtain a collective agreement.[23]

The reasons for ad hoc intervention are in one sense as broad as the reasons for governmental intervention generally; namely, the pressures of economics, politics, and international affairs, independently and as translated through public opinion. But in another sense the reasons for extensive ad hoc intervention may root in the inadequacy of existing statutory solutions. Consider the great advantage of the ad hoc approach, and contrast it with the statutory approaches under which we now function. The great advantage of the former is flexibility. Executive moves can be tailored to the special needs of the particular situation. The striking fact about our existing statutory structure, as we have seen, is its lack of flexibility. Hence, while some ad hoc intervention by the executive branch of government is inevitable, its extent (other things being equal) is very likely to vary with the flexibility of the statutory scheme.

There are difficulties with any sort of extensive governmental intervention in labor disputes, but there are special additional difficulties with frequent executive ad hoc intervention. Without the sanction or obvious legitimacy of enacted law, ad hoc intervention imposes demands upon labor and management officials which they may justly believe are inconsistent with their legal and institutional obligations to union or corporation. For example, it seems unfair to expect union leaders to seek to maximize the interests of their members and, at the same time, to demand that these leaders respond to interests other than, and often conflicting with, those of their members. Substitute shareholder, and the same may be said of management officials. This does not mean, however, that the sanctions of public opinion perform no role. Neither union nor management officials represent their constituents well when they ceaselessly and flagrantly act in a manner contrary to the felt requirements of the community, even if their actions are entirely legal. But it is one thing to say that these private parties must take public opinion into account in their decisions and quite another to ask that every private decision be governed by the public interest as defined by the administration then in office.

Moreover, ad hoc intervention invites, indeed compels, overextension of the prestige of the President and high officers in his administration. Prestige is an important weapon of the executive branch in labor disputes, but it can be exhausted through use; and once prestige is exhausted, subsequent intervention may be ineffective. Mr. Johnson became acutely aware of this phenomenon when, during the airline strike of 1966, he appeared on national television to place his weight behind a negotiated settlement reached by the airlines and the officers of the Machinists' union. Subsequently the members of the union, in perhaps a foolish but surely a forthright display of internal democracy, rejected the settlement and inescapably—and for the President more regrettably—Mr. Johnson as well.[24]

Ad hoc intervention by Congress—a not common but seemingly an increasing method of control—has drawbacks of a different character. Legislation which responds to a specific crisis may be ill-considered, for Congress cannot effectively undertake to deal with the work stoppage problem at retail. Such a course is too consuming of the time of busy men. It would be no small undertaking to crank up the legislative process each time the nation faced a major work stoppage. And the picture of an adjourned Congress during an election campaign being called into special session to cope with a national railroad strike, must suggest that it would be better to be properly forearmed on this domestic front.[25]

TOWARD LEGAL CONTROL OF MAJOR DISPUTES

Two conclusions seem justified by the foregoing discussion. First, the political, economic, and national security effects of major labor disputes make governmental intervention inevitable. Second, the existing methods of intervention are unsatisfactory. Therefore, the quest must be for new methods of legal control; one must assess proposed methods, however, not only in terms of their effectiveness but also by the changes they work upon the existing order. The goal of industrial peace must be purchased at as small a cost to private ordering—to free collective bargaining— as possible because the existence of private ordering is both a major promise and a principal condition of political democracy. It is in these terms that a variety of techniques will be evaluated. The list is not exhaustive, and some of the techniques are currently employed.

Mediation. Mediation has the great virtue of not interfering to any substantial degree with private ordering. Mediators do not make collective bargaining any less free. It has other virtues too: it is often very useful indeed in the prevention and settlement of disputes. But mediation cannot provide a substitute for collective bargaining that will eliminate work stoppages when bargaining breaks down. It can, and often does, make it less likely that a substitute will be required, by reducing the frequency or duration of breakdowns. There is reason to suppose, however, that the mediation services presently available could be improved if the Federal Service would more frequently enlist the assistance "in important or unusually obstinate cases" of private citizens "with the proper attributes of temperament and skill." [26]

Fact Finding. The use of boards of inquiry, or fact-finding boards, in major labor disputes is common, and the statutes, as we have seen, empower the President under certain conditions to appoint such boards. Moreover, nonstatutory boards often have been established.

Recall that the Labor-Management Relations Act in section 206 provides that boards shall "inquire into the issues involved in the dispute and . . . make a written report to [the President . . . which] shall include a statement of the facts with respect to the dispute, including each party's statement of its position but shall not contain any recommendations." As noted, it would seem that fact-finding boards ought to have power to recommend the terms of settlement where the fact-finders judge that recommendations would facilitate settlement. Recommendations —although they have no binding effect—in some cases may serve as a focus for settlement,[27] or they may tend to crystallize public opinion and concentrate governmental pressure on one side or the other. Thus, the recommendations once made may help resolve the dispute. Moreover, anticipation of this before recommendations are made creates some unpredictability as to the external pressure that might be generated by settlement delay. The parties may thereby be encouraged to reach agreement prior to the issuance of the recommendations.

Fact-finding, when contrasted with, say, compulsory arbitration, is a minor intrusion on private ordering. It has been suggested, however, that once recommendations are made they are "intended to carry a significant moral force, if not a moral obligation." [28] Neil Chamberlain has suggested, in turn, that if this is so—or were to become so—recommendations by a fact-finding board would have to be considered a substantial interference with private ordering (though, under such circumstances, an effective means of settling a dispute). "The findings of boards would become binding upon the parties to a dispute, morally if not legally, so that the terms of settlement would pass from those obliged to live under them." [29] Such fear perhaps explains in part the prohibition upon recommendations in the Labor-Management Relations Act; but if there must be intervention, moral pressure, in some cases, is to be preferred to legal compulsion.

Injunction. The injunction obtained by government or a legal freeze period provided by statute has the great virtue of getting men back to work or of preventing them from striking—at least it usually does. It has several disadvantages as well. First, since it preserves the status quo, it may not work evenhandedly. Generally, one party is pressing for a more favorable collective agreement; the other, for as little change as possible. Moreover, in such a situation—both before and during the injunction—there may not be any serious collective bargaining by the party resisting change. Since this is usually the employer, it helps explain labor's stated hostility to the national emergency provisions.[30]

Second, while the injunction is an effective method of maintaining the status quo, it does not resolve the underlying dispute; it relies on collective bargaining. But an injunction is employed only where the collective bargaining process is working badly; and, as suggested, the injunction itself may aggravate that process.

Third, the role of strike injunctions in American history remains in the minds of labor leaders, for the injunction once was the principal legal instrument used to forestall collective bargaining. This misuse has injured its present utility.[31]

Fourth, the injunction has its limits even as a preserver of the status quo. It cannot prevent individuals from not working. The use of the injunction in some situations may be ill-advised because its effect is considered by workers or union to be so unfair that large numbers of workers will disregard the court's order. This has happened.[32] It is not, however, common, and it should not be taken as a suggestion that resort to the injunction is generally ill-advised.

Seizure. Government seizure of an enterprise can theoretically at least take many forms.[33] Writing in 1955, Archibald Cox sketched the form that seizures in fact had taken in labor disputes during and subsequent to World War II.

> The semantics and trappings of seizure are those of government possession and operation of property taken for public use. The military march in. The flag is raised. Orders are issued in the name of the United States. Below the surface the arrangement usually looks quite different. The same executives run the business as before. Production is not limited to articles required by the government. Business is transacted as if by a private concern rather than public authority; indeed there is often an agreement by which the company undertakes to operate the properties as the government's agent for its own risk and account. To the best of my knowledge, no important business decision has ever been made by the government rather than the management. Workers are treated as employees in private industry under statutes clearly inapplicable to government employees save that they may be prohibited from striking.[34]

What can be said for this method of governmental intervention? The case for seizure must be made in terms of its effectiveness in keeping or getting employees back to work and in aiding in the settlement of the underlying dispute. Seizure may prevent or end a strike if the union or employer is looking for a way to back down from a difficult position it has assumed during bargaining. Moreover, seizure is a symbolic event that may deter an employer or a union from acting rashly, particularly in a time of national crisis. It may be difficult, for example, to strike against the government—against the flag itself—even in a setting where a strike injunction would be ignored. There is some evidence, however, that when seizure becomes a common method of intervention this no longer holds.[35]

Apart from the problem of the work stoppage, how much can be expected in the way of settlement pressure from seizure of the type usually proposed; that is, where the seized business is run for the account of its owners? First of all, seizure, like an injunction, may tend to forestall collective bargaining if its effects are foreseeable. Moreover, and again like an injunction, seizure contemplates that the underlying dispute will be resolved by collective bargaining. But while an injunction is generally disproportionately painful to the union, seizure may impose a countervailing pressure on the employer. He may desire to get the government out of his plant, even though the government may not really be in his plant to any marked extent. And, of course, if wages can be revised upward during seizure, as some have proposed, pressure on the employer would be further increased.[36]

Mr. Cox has suggested that one of the advantages of seizure as an occasional method of governmental intervention is that its legal consequences are unclear. The questions of governmental versus private liability, employees' rights under social welfare legislation, and so forth, are so cloudy that they generate legal fears which in turn may spur agreement.[37] These burdens would seem to fall mainly on the employer, and thus seizure may be rather more weighted against him than the union. If so, this would explain management's general opposition to the method and labor's rather more favorable view.[38] But unless seizure is combined with some other form of pain-inflicting technique (for example, a tax on one or both parties based on the length of the seizure), it is mainly a symbolic gesture; but one that can be useful in some cases.

Compulsory Arbitration. No other method of governmental intervention is as far-reaching as compulsory arbitration. It substitutes third party decision-making for private ordering, and it does so without the consent of the parties.

Compulsory arbitration is to be sharply distinguished from grievance arbitration which not only is more or less voluntary, but in which the decision-maker is more or less supplied with preexisting standards formulated by the parties.[39] In compulsory arbitration decision-makers themselves must formulate the standards that will govern the parties' relationship in the future. Compulsory arbitration of a new contract, therefore, is explicitly legislation, not adjudication—although it may follow procedures ordinarily employed in adjudication—and for these reasons it is contrary to the basic philosophy of our national labor policy. Indeed, it may be thought to be contrary to our basic method of economic organization. There is, after all, some reason to see a link between third party wage determination and governmental price control.

Three questions are important to an evaluation of compulsory arbitration.[40] First, how does an arbitrator go about his business? Second, how effective is this method of intervention? Third, what is its effect on collective bargaining? First, the arbitrator's task in its most fundamental sense is to render a fair decision. In any given dispute insight into fairness between the parties may be provided by such factors as the prior history of the dispute and the bargaining positions assumed by the parties; prior settlements, that is, the history of collective bargaining between the parties; other settlements in the same industry or in comparable industries; areas of agreement in the present negotiation; and the arbitrator's best estimate of the form a negotiated settlement would have taken. If, for example, the issue is wages, assistance may be found in such factors as comparable wage rates, productivity, cost of living figures, or ability to pay. Sometimes the arbitrator's task is very difficult, sometimes less so, but under any circumstances his task is difficult indeed. How could it not be when there is no agreement on the relevant factors for determining fairness or on their mix?

Second, the question of arbitration's effectiveness may be closely linked to the question of fairness. An arbitration award purports to resolve the underlying dispute. During and after the arbitration proceeding resort to economic force presumably will be barred. The legal status of the award, together with our habit of obeying the law (as well as the sanctions available to law) go far to insure arbitration's effectiveness; but not all the way. Paul Jacobs, in what may be an overstatement, is suggestive when he writes:

> All experience in this country indicates that compulsory arbitration succeeds only when the parties to the dispute would be disposed to agree without it. Union members can always find other ways than the formal, legal strike for achieving their purposes even over the opposition of their leaders. If they are sufficiently ingenious, they can always slow down operations legally, and if this is done by enough employees it will have the same effect as an actual strike. Compulsory arbitration of industrial disputes does not *resolve* disputes; it merely seeks to impose a truce upon the combatants. But either the need for such truces must be understood and accepted, or the state

must have the police power to enforce them. A society that forces men to work by use of police power cannot be called free.[41]

If the arbitration award is accepted by the parties as fair, it will settle the underlying dispute. It will be more than a truce, and there is absolutely no reason to suppose that this will happen only when "the parties to the dispute would be disposed to agree without it." But if the award is taken by one or both parties to be unfair then perhaps the best that can be hoped for is a truce until the negotiation of the next agreement. The worst that must be expected is an open defiance of law. And if it is correct to suggest that arbitration can be effective only if the parties judge the award fair, the ultimate question is when and how often this is likely to occur. We simply do not know. We do know that in some situations the quest for fairness is easier than in others, but we need much more study of this problem before we can reach confident conclusions.

Third, the possibility of eventual arbitration may result in the elimination of present collective bargaining. This is apt to occur when one of the parties concludes that it will gain more through arbitration than it will through negotiation. Moreover, even where this is not the situation, the fact that arbitration is a possibility may undermine the bargaining process. The parties may engage in making a record for arbitration if it occurs, rather than in attempting to resolve their underlying dispute through good faith negotiation.[42]

One type of compulsory arbitration has been suggested which might eliminate arbitration's inhibiting effect on prior collective bargaining, make the arbitrator's task manageable, and perhaps enhance the chances of compliance with an award. If the arbitrator were empowered to adopt the final negotiating position of either the employer or the union, some pressure might be generated on the parties to

narrow their differences. Clearly, pressure would be felt by
each to make objectively reasonable proposals, proposals
that would win acceptance by the arbitrator. This "one-or-
the-other" arbitration—as Carl M. Stevens has called it—
has risks, however.[43] The parties may be substantially
apart, each honestly thinking its position reasonable; in a
complicated arbitration the decision-maker may have trouble knowing which proposals—particularly the nonfinan-
cial ones—are fair; and each party's package may have
reasonable and unreasonable proposals. In each of these
potential situations the prospect for compliance with an
arbitration award is none too bright.

Thus, there are dangers that have made many close students of labor-management affairs wary, and often hostile,
to the suggestion of compulsory arbitration, whatever its
form.[44]

The Nonstoppage Strike. Perhaps the most interesting
idea for the prevention of major work stoppages is the nonstoppage strike, which, since 1949, has engaged the attention of those concerned with these problems.[45] Here is a
description of a version by one of its first advocates.

> If the function of the strike is to make disagreement
> on one party's terms costly to the other party, this ob-
> jective can be achieved by alternative means. A strike
> is a contest of endurance, and it is possible to invoke
> such a contest without ceasing production.
>
> The operation of such a substitute strike procedure
> can be simply outlined. At the time when negotiations
> between the parties have broken down and a stoppage
> of work would normally occur, in those cases in which
> a governmental authority determines that public hard-
> ship would result . . . the private strike is converted
> into a statutory strike, or—to use other terminology—
> the work-stoppage strike is transformed into a non-
> stoppage strike. The governmental order which effects

such a conversion directs the employees to remain on their jobs, unless as individuals they choose to resign their employment and all attaching rights. It directs management to continue production to fill all incoming orders, maintaining the schedule of prices then in effect. The interests of the public, both as consumers and producers, are thus protected.

In order to permit a subsequent voluntary agreement between the parties, each must have the power to impose penalties on the other by precipitating such a statutory strike, whether it is the union or management which initiates it by making or refusing demands. This means that although production continues each party must receive less during the period of the statutory strike than it would had no dispute arisen. By resorting to the statutory strike, the initiating party willingly subjects itself to some loss in order to impose a loss on the other party. It thereby invokes a contest of economic power, as it now does through the stoppage strike.

If workers and management are to continue production, *some* return must be earned by them. Continuing production must have some advantage over not producing. Each of the parties, then, must secure some advantage which it would not have in a stoppage strike, but at the same time each must incur some loss in consequence of the statutory strike. The gains to each party over the present strike method must be relatively equal, that is, the proportion under the present method must be relatively equal, if the same relative bargaining powers are to be preserved. This result will probably be achieved if—while production continues during the nonstoppage strike period—the wages of workers are reduced by 50 percent and the returns of the company are reduced to actual out-ofpocket or variable expenses plus one half of fixed costs.

With operations continuing and with these losses bearing on the parties, the contest of endurance would be on. It would continue until one or the other or both of the parties agreed to concessions that made settlement possible. At this point the statutory strike would be ended, and the parties would revert to full payment for services under a new collective bargaining agreement. The plan thus appears to satisfy both the requisites for a satisfactory system of controlling public-affecting strikes. Public rights of expectancy are honored. Voluntarism in union-management relations is preserved.[46]

The advantages of a statute permitting the appropriate governmental official to substitute a nonstoppage strike for a major work stoppage are obvious: the public consequences of the work stoppage are eliminated; the economic pressures of a strike are retained and, thus, the chances of a negotiated settlement held high.

The disadvantages, while less apparent, have been thought by some astute observers to make the nonstoppage strike virtually unacceptable.[47] First, where should the money—employees' wages, employers' revenue—go? Perhaps to the U. S. Treasury, but there may be legal and there certainly are political difficulties with a tax on strikes. Second, workers sometimes may not obey a compulsory arbitration award or an injunction. They also may decline to work for a fraction of their regular pay. At least until the idea became an accustomed one, this would be a predictable response in those cases where the use of the nonstoppage strike was thought to be unfair. Third, it is not easy to fix in legislation the actual cost to each party of a work stoppage. The effect of a strike on an employer varies substantially from firm to firm, industry to industry, and time to time. For some employers, for example, the potential loss of customers rather than the immediate loss of revenue is the major reason for averting a work stoppage. Employees, too, vary in their ability to withstand the economic discomfort of a strike. The point is, that as with the injunction or compulsory arbitration, the statutorily imposed nonstoppage strike, if it is predictable, may forestall collective bargaining. One party or the other may stand to gain from its employment and know that this is the case.

A Choice of Procedures. As the name implies, a choice of procedures, or, as it is sometimes called, an arsenal of weapons, envisions giving the President, perhaps after advice from a special board, the statutory authority to choose among a variety of techniques—fact-finding, injunction, seizure, arbitration—and to pick the one most appropriate for the settlement of a particular major labor dispute.[48]

The case for a choice of procedures may be approached by reexamining the shortcomings of some of the other techniques we have discussed. What is wrong, for example, with compulsory arbitration? The immediate answer may be that it substitutes governmental dictation for private ordering. It abandons collective bargaining. But its advocates would reply that it does so only when collective bargaining fails because public cost of agreement is too high. No one proposes that labor contracts be made through arbitration if they can be made by peaceful negotiation. At this point in the dialogue, however, the following conclusions seem persuasive: First, the existence of a compulsory arbitration statute or of the injunction procedure contained in the Labor-Management Relations Act sometimes has a significant and deleterious impact upon the collective bargaining process. Such methods of control will chill collective bargaining if one of the parties anticipates that at a relatively predictable point in time an injunction will issue for a completely predictable period of time, and if he reasons that this event is advantageous to him. For he will then refrain from bargaining with a sincere desire to reach agreement in order to insure an injunction. In the arbitration situation one party may believe that arbitration is more advantageous than negotiation. He may, therefore, bargain in a fashion calculated to bring about arbitration.

This speculation about behavior has support in experience. For example, there is reason to suppose that in the railroad work rules dispute that led to governmentally sponsored compulsory arbitration, the preference of the carriers for arbitration contributed to the collapse of collective bargaining. And Willard Wirtz argues strongly that the Labor-Management Relations Act procedures caused collective bargaining to fail in a bituminous coal strike with which he is particularly familiar.[49]

Second, the burden of the argument above is that collective bargaining may be chilled by a rigid, single method of intervention. It suggests another argument against a number of the methods of governmental intervention that we have explored. The injunction can, in certain disputes, be an example of overkill; in others, grossly unfair. Each dispute is unique. Why should one assume that a pre-determined remedy will work?

The key then to the choice of procedures approach is flexibility. A statute that allows the employment of any one of the several methods of intervention permits intervention—when necessary—that is tailored to the particular dispute in which it is employed. It also eliminates the predictability that invites the parties to rely upon intervention as a negotiating stratagem.

But more may be claimed for the choice-of-procedures approach. It may actually improve the chances of settlement through collective bargaining (that is, make it better than it would have been in the absence of potential governmental intervention). Where there is a choice-of-procedures statute, the range of alternatives available to government is numerous enough, and the effects sufficiently diverse, to make it too chancy for the parties to allow intervention. Prudence dictates that they negotiate an agreement for the alternative may be costly.[50]

The arguments against a choice of procedures are first, that some of the procedures intrude too much upon private ordering, and second, that the President is given too much discretion and is bound to exercise it in response to irrelevant political considerations. But if the public cost of some work stoppages is too high, the government must have means to cope. The hope is that extreme means will not often be employed because their availability will make their use unnecessary. As to presidential discretion, the objection misses the point. A choice-of-procedures statute eliminates the difficulties associated with ad hoc intervention (the risk to presidential prestige; inconsistent duties on union and management officials); and predictably it would reduce such intervention by building flexibility into law. While presidential action would indeed be based on political considerations, those considerations are not irrelevant at all. They alone must be the standard for decision. The right to strike is too important to surrender on any other basis.

Consider again the disadvantage of a choice-of-procedures approach: some of the procedures are too great an intrusion on private ordering. Consider again the disadvantages of the statutory nonstoppage strike: where does the money go; will the employees work; how can employee-employer contributions fail to affect the bargaining balance and thereby forestall collective bargaining?

If the parties were free to opt out of a choice-of-procedures statute, the objection to such a statute would lose much of its force. And if the parties themselves negotiated a nonstoppage strike agreement—which is one way to opt out—they could decide where the money would go and how much money each should contribute to approximate the effects on each of a work stoppage. Moreover, if the parties negotiated the agreement, the employees would be more likely to think it fair and work under it when collective bargaining tactics persuaded one party or the other to invoke it.

To my knowledge, there has been only one collective agreement that has contained a nonstoppage strike provision,[51] but the situation might change in industries with a major work stoppage potential if the alternative were governmental control through a choice-of-procedures statute. Thus, such a statute, with procedures sufficiently disagreeable to both parties, could lead in this way to at least a partial collective bargaining solution to the major work stoppage problem. That would be an important beginning, indeed.

Chapter 9

Bargaining Settlements
and Economic Policy

The Sunday after President Johnson announced settlement of the 1966 airline strike, the same Sunday that the union rank and file was to reject the announced settlement, their leaders' recommendations, and Mr. Johnson himself, the *New York Times* reported:

> Since 1962 the Government has sought to avert inflation partly through a mechanism known as wage-price guideposts. They are based on the proposition that even though general supply and demand conditions in the economy may be in balance, prices can still be pushed up by unions obtaining excessive wage increases or large industries with "pricing power" seeking excessive profits. The Johnson Administration has sought to keep wages and prices within a 3.2 per cent range. . . . Last week the most widely felt strike of the year—the walkout by the International Association of Machinists against five major airlines—was settled after intervention by President Johnson. There were indications that the Administration's wage guideposts had been breached in the agreement. The full effect of the settlement will not be known until after a vote by the union today, but informed sources reported that it would cost about 4.5 per cent a year over a three-year term. It could have a sharp impact on the anti-inflationary wage guideposts.[1]

What is most interesting about the *Times'* story, when viewed as a document of labor history, is its central concern with the terms of settlement rather than with the fact of what seemed to be a settlement and the dynamics of its achievement. This concern reflects the state of modern capitalism here and abroad. In all the developed western nations the terms of collective bargaining settlements and their allegedly inflationary effects have become an obsession.[2]

It is critically important to understand the implications for our national labor policy that inescapably follow from this growing concern, a concern of government, the press, and the public with the financial terms of collective bargaining agreements. I have insisted that labor policy, embodied in federal statutes, supported by a legal theory of collective bargaining and by the rhetoric of the labor movement, reflects the commitment of our legal order to freedom of contract. While the collective agreement is not the traditionally free contract, many of the policies that support it pull in that direction. A major objective of policy and a central quest of law have been to create an environment that would produce agreements which are fair as between the parties; that is, fair enough to permit government to rely upon contract, upon private ordering to establish the terms and conditions of employment. This was made possible by law helping labor organize and bargain collectively.

Concern with the terms of settlement is not evidence that this policy and its implementing legal institutions have failed. Although it is true that a changing concept of public fairness influences one's judgment of what is fair between the parties, there are no independent reasons to believe that, as between the parties, collective agreements now are less fair than once they were. Concern with the terms of settlement rather is evidence of the emergence of a new goal, one requiring new policy. No longer can one merely ask: is the settlement fair between the parties? The new goal demands an answer to the question: is the settlement fair to the public? [3] Once it was thought that fairness to the public would take care of itself, that what the parties agreed upon was what was best for the nation, economically as well as politically and socially. Some, to be sure, still believe this.

Observe that the political and social desirability of free collective bargaining is not challenged by the deepening concern over the terms of settlement. Accordingly, here, as with the problem of peaceful settlement discussed in the last chapter, the aim of policy-makers should be to solve a perceived problem with as little disruption to existing institutions as possible. For while those institutions are far from perfect, they do continue to serve their now traditional and important roles. Labor unions are much more than economic entities.

The initial question, however, is the source of concern with the terms of settlement. Why the emphasis on the goal of fairness to the public? Second, how is fairness to be defined, and finally, if it can be defined, how is the defined goal to be achieved?

INFLATION, EMPLOYMENT, AND GROWTH

An important reason for increased concern over the terms of collective bargaining settlements is increased concern over the performance of the economy. It is widely believed that economic growth is essential if the nation is to fight a war in Vietnam, maintain its other international commitments and carry forward programs of domestic reform. Moreover, the maintenance of a high level of employment is itself firmly established as a federal responsibility. The Employment Act of 1946, making the federal government responsible for preventing unemployment, is but one example;[4] the rhetoric of both political parties, another. Thus, growth and full employment are economic goals about which a political consensus seems well formed. There is, to be sure, considerable disagreement about the appropriate policies required to achieve these goals, but here too there does seem to be political—if not professional —agreement emerging that one important policy is to induce unions to exercise restraint in collective bargaining.[5]

The fear of inflation connects the goals of full employment and economic growth with the policy of governmentally induced restraint in collective bargaining.[6] As traditionally understood, inflation is an excess of aggregate money demand over the productive capacity of the economy at existing prices. The result, of course, is a rising price level. This phenomenon has numerous consequences. Rising prices mean that the dollar is worth less in terms of what it can buy; and accordingly, people with relatively fixed incomes are faced with a declining standard of living. Moreover, rising prices at home may have an adverse effect on our international balance of payments.[7]

These are serious consequences, indeed, and of grave concern. But it is helpful to consider moderate inflation within the context that James Tobin has provided.

> Inflation is only one of many sources of the redistribution of income and wealth, some anticipated and some not, continually occurring in a dynamic economy. Technological, social and political events are always moving prices and property values up and down in relation to each other, making and destroying fortunes in their wake.[8]

And, as to our international balance of payments, Mr. Tobin has said:

> The seemingly perennial U.S. balance-of-payments deficit is commonly cited as a special reason for avoiding inflation at this time. U.S. goods will be more attractive, for Americans and foreigners alike, the lower our prices and costs relative to prices and costs abroad. This makes sense. But the fact is that the U.S. has been

improving its competitive position for eight years, thanks to inflation in Europe and elsewhere, yet the payments deficit is still with us. Our trouble is not our trade account, which is probably about as favorable as the mercantilistic interests and policies of other countries will permit. Our trouble is the outflow of capital, and here Europe's relatively faster inflation may very well have hurt rather than helped. An American could gain by buying European properties, watching them appreciate in terms of francs or marks or lire, along with the general inflations in those countries, then later selling and converting the proceeds into dollars to spend at home. The U.S. boom, with heavy demands and high yields for investment funds at home, may help the capital account as much as it hurts the trade balance.[9]

But if inflation gallops rather than creeps—to use the traditional terminology—we must concern ourselves with the new poor and worry both about the capital account and the trade balance. And inflation may gallop because people anticipate that it will and act accordingly.

Monetary and fiscal policies—policies relating to interest rates, taxation, and public expenditures—are tools the government may employ to deal with too much inflation. Ideally, these economic tools will be used to increase output and to reduce aggregate money demand to that point where it corresponds to the productive capacity of the economy, thereby creating a condition of full employment with a stable price level. The trouble with the ideal is that these tools are not that finely calibrated. It is easy to go too far and shrink aggregate money demand below the chosen equilibrium point, thereby causing unemployment and depressing growth. Moreover, adjustment is made difficult by such factors as the resistance of union negotiated wages to downward market pressures; market pressures must be substantial indeed before a union will accept an agreement for lower wages.[10] If product demand is down and wages constant, unemployment is likely.

In addition to the economic phenomena described above, there is the widely held—and as widely disputed— theory that inflation can be caused by the push of increasing costs as well as by the pull of excess demand. "Cost push" purports to explain rising prices in an economy where there is unemployment and excess capacity, although it also has relevance to a full employment economy. The models employed by economists to demonstrate the theory can be quite elaborate, but they all seem to assume —to the extent that the cost push is a wage push—that inflation results from some degree of unliquidated monopoly power in the unions. It is argued that the unions have power to raise wage levels above the point that they are justified by increases in average productivity, that is, those levels which, it is assumed, free factor markets would establish in the absence of collective bargaining.[11]

The wage-push process can be a complex one. Some employers may not raise prices when wages rise because they are producing more efficiently—their increase in productivity is higher than the national average. But, because some unions set collective bargaining patterns for others, other employers, with average or less than average productivity increases, will respond to wage increases by raising prices, some from necessity, some, with unliquidated monopoly power, from choice. (Indeed, it may be that these employers feel that only after a wage increase can they raise prices without fear of antitrust or consumer reprisals.) Thus, unless aggregate money demand increases, increased unemployment can be expected, for it is generally true that producers can sell less at higher prices than at lower ones.

Where prices are rising as a result of cost push, the government may attempt through expansionary monetary and fiscal policies to stimulate demand and thereby deter further unemployment. If such measures are successful, they will validate or in a sense legitimate the inflation in terms of the newly increased demand. Or the government may be more concerned with price stability than with employment, and sacrifice the latter to the former by using monetary and fiscal policies to depress the economy.[12]

While these descriptions of demand-pull and cost-push inflation vastly simplify matters as seen by the economic theorist, they do suggest the reason for the deep concern with the terms of collective bargaining settlements. The relationship between wage increases and cost-push inflation is one of cause and effect. Hold down wages and you may deter price increases. Much more sophisticated, however, is the reasoning with respect to collective bargaining settlements and demand-pull inflation. Causation runs from demand to cost; wages rise because prices have risen, not vice-versa. It should also be noted that at times, perhaps much of the time, it is the operation of the product market and ineffective monetary and fiscal policy, not union monopoly power, that forces up prices.[13] And we should also recognize that monopoly power itself may be turned to advantage in stopping demand inflation.

Consider the following paragraph from the 1962 Report of the Council of Economic Advisers:

> There are important segments of the economy where firms are large or employees well-organized, or both. In these sectors, private parties may exercise considerable discretion over the terms of wage bargains and price decisions. Thus, at least in the short run, there is considerable room for the exercise of private power and a parallel need for the assumption of private responsibility.[14]

The recommendation for policy that flows from this premise about monopoly power is union restraint in wage negotiations, management restraint in price setting—giving rise to the so-called guideposts of the Council of Economic Advisers. The premise and the policy recommendations are plainly consistent with cost push. Also they are consistent, and plainly so, with demand pull according to Robert Solow, who had a hand in the 1962 Report. In an exchange with Milton Friedman, a firm critic of the theory of cost push and of guidepost policy, Mr. Solow was emphatic.

> I want to make this very clear, I am not resting my case on a theory of cost-push inflation. That's an issue by itself and one on which I have, as on most things, a little more uncertainty than Milton. The case it seems to me rests only on the *degree of tightness in the economy at which the price level begins to rise unacceptably rapidly.*[15]

The proposition suggested appears to be this: Demand pull permits—indeed in a competitive market would seem to require—wage and price increases greater than the average increase in productivity. Many unions and employers, however, have at least some short-run discretion in their pricing policies, because they have some monopoly power. This monopoly power permits them to resist inflationary increases, resist the pull of demand, refrain for a while from maximizing; and this they should do for the good of the economy.

The desired pause in the spiral may be time enough to close the inflationary gap, time to bring aggregate money demand into equilibrium with productive capacity at a level of full employment. This might result for example, from the end of the Vietnam war which, after all, could happen. It might result from the wise employment of monetary and fiscal policies, freed to stimulate growth rather than to fight inflation.

In sum, a considerable number of economists believe that collective bargaining decisions can have an adverse

effect on the economic goals to which the nation now is
dedicated. While some economists deny cost push and some
reject the counsel of private restraint advocated by the
President's economic advisers their voices seem unable to
stem the growing political endorsement of the position
which asks, "is that collective bargaining settlement fair
to society?" Our task must be to ask what "fair" means in
this context.

FAIRNESS AS THE TREND RATE
OF OVERALL PRODUCTIVITY INCREASE

Implicit in the description of inflation and its possible
relationship to collective bargaining is the standard by
which one may judge whether aggregate wage settlements
are publicly fair, that is, consonant with the goals of full
employment and growth. The following is from the
January 1960 Report of the Council of Economic Advisers:

> [Labor-management disputes] should be settled . . .
> on terms that are fair to the public at large as well as
> to the parties directly involved. . . . Labor-manage-
> ment negotiations in all industries offer opportunities
> to help promote sound growth by avoiding settle-
> ments that contribute to inflation. Settlements should
> not be such as to cause the national average of wage
> rate increases to exceed sustainable rates of improve-
> ment in national productivity. A national wage pat-
> tern that fails to meet this criterion would put an up-
> ward pressure on the price level. Hourly rates of
> pay and related labor benefits can, of course, be in-
> creased without jeopardizing price stability. Indeed,
> such increases are the major means in our free econ-
> omy by which labor shares in the fruits of industrial
> progress. But improvements in compensation rates
> must, on the average, remain within the limits of gen-

eral productivity gains if reasonable stability of prices is to be achieved and maintained. Furthermore, price reductions warranted by especially rapid productivity gains must be a normal and frequent feature of our economy. Without such reductions we shall not be able to keep the price level as a whole from advancing.[16]

Observe that the standard—"national average of wage rate increases" should not exceed "sustainable rates of improvement in national productivity"—does not purport to furnish a test for judging individual collective bargaining agreements. It is addressed to aggregate wage settlements. But even here the proposed standard is far from clear. What is meant by "sustainable rates of improvement in national productivity"? Productivity itself is simply the relationship between inputs—physical inputs of all factors of production including capital and labor—and output. Thus, it measures efficiency. National productivity is an average of the productivity of individual units, and "rates of improvement in national productivity" is an average of unit productivity gains. If, for example, this figure is 3 percent, and if labor's "national average of wage rate increases" is 3 percent, the return to other factors of production, including owners, also may increase by 3 percent without generating inflationary pressures.[17]

Measurement of the "rate of improvement in national productivity" is a complicated matter that invites disagreement among those qualified to have a view.[18] The difficulty and the disagreement are compounded when the test is partially converted into a forward looking standard by modifying it with the word "sustainable."

The language employed in the 1962 Report, which is the most significant of the reports for our purposes, did not ease the problem. It substituted "trend rate of overall productivity increase" for the earlier formulation. The

Council in 1962 was candid about the difficulties of measurement. It said:

> If the rate of growth of productivity over time is to serve as a useful benchmark for wage and price behavior, there must be some meeting of minds about the appropriate methods of measuring the trend rate of increase in productivity, both for industry as a whole and for individual industries. This is a large and complex subject and there is much still to be learned. The most that can be done at present is to give some indication of orders of magnitude, and of the range within which most plausible measures are likely to fall.
>
> There are a number of conceptual problems in connection with productivity measurement which can give rise to differences in estimates of its rate of growth. Three important conceptual problems are the following:
>
> (1) Over what time interval should productivity trends be measured? Very short intervals may give excessive weight to business-cycle movements in productivity, which are not the relevant standards for wage behavior. . . . Very long intervals may hide significant breaks in trends; indeed in the United States— and in other countries as well—productivity appears to have risen more rapidly since the end of the Second World War than before. It would be wholly inappropriate for wage behavior in the 1960s to be governed by events long in the past. On the other hand, productivity in the total private economy appears to have advanced less rapidly in the second half of the postwar period than in the first.
>
> (2) Even for periods of intermediate length, it is desirable to segregate the trend movements in productivity from those that reflect business-cycle forces.

Where the basic statistical materials are available, this problem can be handled by an analytical separation of trend effects and the effects of changes in the rate of capacity utilization.

(3) Even apart from such difficulties, there often exist alternative statistical measures of output and labor input. The alternatives may differ conceptually or may simply be derived from different statistical sources. A difficult problem of choice may emerge, unless the alternative measures happen to give similar results.[19]

In the 1966 Report the Council talked about "sustainable trend of productivity" as the standard, and then went on as follows:

The original formulation of the guideposts did not specify any particular trend productivity figure, but rather listed various historical averages, covering different time spans and various segments of the economy. Since the economy was just recovering from the second of two recessions in a very short interval, it was difficult to identify the trend productivity rate from the immediately preceding experience. This difficulty was compounded by speculation that the trend rate might be accelerating as a result of faster technological change, particularly the spread of automation.

In the Report of 1964, no single figure for trend productivity was specified, but in a related table the now well-known 3.2 percent appeared as the latest figure in a column labeled "Trend productivity." The figures in that column were described as the "annual average percentage change in output per man-hour during the latest 5 years." A 5-year period was chosen because, at that time, it was sufficiently long to include both the extraordinarily high produc-

tivity gains of a year of recovery (1962) and the extraordinarily low productivity gains of a year of recession (1960). Under the conditions of 1964, a 5-year
average gave a good approximation of the trend productivity, because, in effect, it averaged out the ups
and downs of cyclical productivity swings. These
same conditions prevailed in 1964, and the 3.2 percent
figure appeared for that year in a similar table in the
1965 Report. Subsequent revisions of GNP data would
have made the 5-year average 3.4 percent in both
1964 and 1965.

Now that the economy is at the end of its fifth year
of uninterrupted expansion, a 5-year average no longer
gives a reasonable approximation of the true productivity trend. The last recession year drops out of the
average, yet the unsustainable productivity gains of
a year of recovery and 4 years of improving utilization
are retained. If use of the 5-year average were continued this year and in coming years, the figure
yielded by the 5-year moving average would rise at
this time to 3.6 percent and would undoubtedly fall
substantially thereafter.

An analysis of recent productivity movements was
presented earlier in this chapter. It is clear from this
analysis that 3.6 percent would not be an accurate
measure of the true trend of productivity. Rather, it
appears that the long-term trend, independent of
cyclical swings, is slightly over 3 percent.[20]

Under these circumstances, some are likely to be doubtful about the utility of "trend rate of overall productivity
increase" as a standard. Yet the intensity of this doubt may
depend upon the use to which the standard is to be put.
Is it the rule for judgment? Is it a principle among others?
Whatever the answer may be when the question is the
fairness of aggregate wage increases (has Labor behaved

itself during the year), it has not usually been suggested authoritatively that trend rate productivity increase is the rule to employ in judging the fairness of particular collective bargaining settlements. It has been suggested authoritatively, however, that it is a principle among others and indeed the principle of first importance. This was the great innovation of the 1962 Report: utilization of average productivity increase as one important criterion in judging the fairness of particular collective bargaining settlements. It was in 1962 that the Council first published the wage (and price) guideposts. The heart of that proposal follows:

> *Prices and wages in individual industries.* What are the guideposts which may be used in judging whether a particular price or wage decision may be inflationary? The desired objective is a stable price level, within which particular prices rise, fall, or remain stable in response to economic pressures. Hence, price stability within any particular industry is not necessarily a correct guide to price and wage decisions in that industry. It is possible, however, to describe in broad outline a set of guides which, if followed, would preserve over-all price stability while still allowing sufficient flexibility to accommodate objectives of efficiency and equity. These are not arbitrary guides. They describe—briefly and no doubt incompletely— how prices and wage rates would behave in a smoothly functioning competitive economy operating near full employment. Nor do they constitute a mechanical formula for determining whether a particular price or wage decision is inflationary. They will serve their purpose if they suggest to the interested public a useful way of approaching the appraisal of such a decision.

> If, as a point of departure, we assume no change

in the relative shares of labor and nonlabor incomes in a particular industry, then a general guide may be advanced for noninflationary wage behavior, and another for noninflationary price behavior. Both guides, as will be seen, are only first approximations.

The general guide for noninflationary wage behavior is that the rate of increase in wage rates (including fringe benefits) in each industry be equal to the trend rate of over-all productivity increase. General acceptance of this guide would maintain stability of labor cost per unit of output for the economy as a whole—though not of course for individual industries.

The general guide for noninflationary price behavior calls for price reduction if the industry's rate of productivity increase exceeds the over-all rate—for this would mean declining unit labor costs; it calls for an appropriate increase in price if the opposite relationship prevails; and it calls for stable prices if the two rates of productivity increase are equal.

These are advanced as general guideposts. To reconcile them with objectives of equity and efficiency, specific modifications must be made to adapt them to the circumstances of particular industries. If all of these modifications are made, each in the specific circumstances to which it applies, they are consistent with stability of the general price level. Public judgments about the effects on the price level of particular wage or price decisions should take into account the modifications as well as the general guides. The most important modifications are the following:

(1) Wage rate increases would exceed the general guide rate in an industry which would otherwise be unable to attract sufficient labor; or in which wage rates are exceptionally low compared with the range of wages earned elsewhere by similar labor, because

the bargaining position of workers has been weak in particular local labor markets.

(2) Wage rate increases would fall short of the general guide rate in an industry which could not provide jobs for its entire labor force even in times of generally full employment; or in which wage rates are exceptionally high compared with the range of wages earned elsewhere by similar labor, because the bargaining position of workers has been especially strong.

(3) Prices would rise more rapidly, or fall more slowly, than indicated by the general guide rate in an industry in which the level of profits was insufficient to attract the capital required to finance a needed expansion in capacity; or in which costs other than labor costs had risen.

(4) Prices would rise more slowly, or fall more rapidly, than indicated by the general guide in an industry in which the relation of productive capacity to full employment demand shows the desirability of an outflow of capital from the industry; or in which costs other than labor costs have fallen; or in which excessive market power has resulted in rates of profit substantially higher than those earned elsewhere on investments of comparable risk.

It is a measure of the difficulty of the problem that even these complex guideposts leave out of account several important considerations. Although output per man-hour rises mainly in response to improvements in the quantity and quality of capital goods with which employees are equipped, employees are often able to improve their performance by means within their own control. It is obviously in the public interest that incentives be preserved which would reward employees for such efforts.

Also, in connection with the use of measures of

over-all productivity gain as benchmarks for wage increases, it must be borne in mind that average hourly
labor costs often change through the process of up- or
down-grading, shifts between wage and salaried employment, and other forces. Such changes may either
add to or subtract from the increment which is available for wage increases under the over-all productivity
guide.

Finally, it must be reiterated that collective bargaining within an industry over the division of the
proceeds between labor and nonlabor income is not
necessarily disruptive of over-all price stability. The
relative shares can change within the bounds of noninflationary price behavior. But when a disagreement
between management and labor is resolved by passing
the bill to the rest of the economy, the bill is paid
in depreciated currency to the ultimate advantage of
no one.[21]

This flexible and sensitive approach to the job of artic-
ulating a standard of public fairness lost favor in subsequent reports of the Council, and was replaced by an increasingly rigid formulation. The stress was exclusively on
the trend rate of overall productivity increase, which the
Council figured at 3.2 percent.[22] Then, in the 1967 Report, this development was sharply reversed. Responding
perhaps to a realistic expectation of how organized labor
would behave in 1967, the Council noted that a 3.3 percent increase in consumer prices during 1966, plus the
fact that "corporate profits have increased considerably
more than aggregate labor income," raised serious questions for guidepost policy. The Council's answer was to
put emphasis on the price guideposts, move back to the
flexibility of the 1962 wage guideposts and to observe that
"the recent rise in living costs makes it unlikely that most
collective bargaining settlements in 1967 will fully conform

to the trend increase of productivity." [23] The Council
went on to say:

No useful purpose [is] served by suggesting some
higher standard for wage increases, even on a temporary basis. . . . In 1967, the national interest continues to require restraint in wage settlements; indeed,
it is more essential than ever that restraint be practiced in order to turn the trend of prices back toward
stability. If restraint cannot mean an average wage advance only equal to the rise in productivity, it surely
must mean wage advances which are substantially less
than the productivity trend plus the recent rise in
consumer prices. [24]

It would be wrong, I think, to conclude that this 1967
Report marked an official abandonment of the guideposts
as the standard for judging the public fairness of collective
bargaining settlements. What it and the 1968 Report,
which follows much the same approach, did mark was a
present abandonment of any serious attempt to implement
the standard. Both were a bow to political reality not a
rejection of economic principle. This administration like
its Democratic and Republican predecessors continues, as
best one can tell, to believe in the theory that supports all
of the excerpts I have quoted from the Council's reports.
Nor is there reason to suppose that the underlying long
run economic problems have changed or will change. And
this means that in the future, as in the recent past, government again must actively concern itself with implementing
the standard of public fairness. How it might proceed is
informed by how it has performed.

IMPLEMENTATION OF THE STANDARD

The guideposts, both those dealing with wages and with
prices, are not designed to impose legal duties upon labor

or management. Indeed, the principles in the 1962 Report
are written as much to educate and channel public opinion
as directly to educate and influence private decision-makers. Nevertheless, the administration from time to time
has acted—most notoriously with respect to the price
guideposts—as if the guideposts were at least quasi-legal
obligations, the breech of which required vigorous governmental action. The sanctions that have been invoked
were not merely namecalling, although there has been
plenty of that; there were sticks and stones that must have
hurt, and hurt badly. Of these episodes, the most highly
visible occurred in April 1962.

Following hard upon the March 1962 collective bargaining settlement in big steel—a settlement in which the
Kennedy administration took an active hand, and one
which may well have restrained the wage demands of the
Steelworkers—most major companies, led by U. S. Steel,
raised the price of their product by six dollars a ton. This
the administration saw as contrary to the price guideposts
and, because of the governmental efforts in the collective
bargaining settlement, as perhaps a personal affront as
well as a rejection of the administration's economic policies.[25]

President Kennedy's reaction was swift and rather fright-
ening. He termed the price increases a "ruthless disregard of . . . public responsibility," [26] and he turned that
great and powerful bulldozer whose care was in his charge,
pointed it throttle open at the steel industry, and let go.

The press reported that among other things: the Department of Defense and other agencies were reviewing the effect of the price rise on their procurement policies; the
Federal Trade Commission had begun an informal inquiry
that could lead to penalties up to $5,000 a day for viola-
tion of its consent order of June 15, 1961; the antitrust
division of the Justice Department was taking "an immediate and close look" to see if the price increases violated

the Clayton or Sherman Acts; House and Senate committees made plans to investigate; the Attorney General ordered a grand jury investigation of the price increases; documents in the possession of U. S. Steel were subpoenaed and newspaper reporters were awakened before sunrise by the F.B.I. and questioned about statements reportedly made by a Bethlehem Steel executive.[27] The *New York Times* summarized three days of governmental effort:

> For three days the great forces at the command of the President of the United States had been brought to bear on the steel industry. . . . Some of the effort was exerted in the open—the President's open denunciation of the companies, calculated to arouse public opinion against them; the opening of grand jury proceedings leading to possible antitrust action, and the threat to divert orders to companies that had not raised prices. . . . But privately as well, the President and his advisers were bringing every form of persuasion to bear on the industry, trying to hold back the companies that had not yet raised prices and induce the others to roll back the price increase.[28]

It worked. The steel executives seeing how "wrong" they had been rescinded the price rises.[29]

Ad hoc enforcement and attempted enforcement of the guideposts—here, there, and wherever it seemed useful, with big guns and little, with talk, public and private, and action tough and moderate—had been the stock approach of both the Kennedy and Johnson administrations through 1966. Thus, for example, the threat to dispose of government stockpiles was effective in persuading aluminum and copper companies to rescind price increases in 1965.[30]

As with ad hoc intervention in major disputes—intervention designed to stop or prevent a strike—discussed in the last chapter, the intervention to protect the guideposts raises serious questions. The activity of the government may not be fully visible; neither law nor public opinion may be able to guard against abuse. And some have suggested that some governmental techniques of intervention are illegal, perhaps unconstitutional.[31] Moreover, the executive is overextended, his prestige too often put on the line; and the legal duties of labor and corporate leaders—duties to act in the best interest of members or stockholders—may conflict rather directly with the demands made upon them by guidepost policy. Furthermore, ad hoc intervention is possible only where the private decision-making units are large enough to invite attention, and the policing of the guideposts, therefore, poses troublesome problems of evenhanded administration.[32]

Nor is it clear that the guideposts and their implementation have been especially successful. This is difficult to judge, and opinions differ. The Council's opinion is that "in the areas in which the guideposts were expected to apply—among strongly organized groups of workers and in firms which have appreciable discretion with regard to their prices—the guideposts were reasonably well observed at least until mid-1966."[33] In John Dunlop's judgment:

> The guideposts have probably played a role, on the price side anyway, in mitigating the psychological and speculative elements of inflationary pressures in recent years.
>
> On the wage side, it is my considered judgment that the guideposts probably have had no independent restraining influence on wage changes in private industry. They have been used to insist upon smaller increases for federal government employees than might otherwise have been enacted by Congress; but even here the independent effect of the guideposts is unclear. I know of no person actually involved in wage setting on the side of industry, labor organizations, or

as a government or private mediator or arbitrator
who thinks that the guideposts have had on balance
a constrictive influence; and I have discussed the issue
in detail with scores of such persons in the past six
months.[34]

If Mr. Dunlop is correct about the impact of the wage
guideposts, the explanation may be both the difficulties
with the guideposts and their implementation already
noted, and the uneasy fit between the new standard of
public fairness and the collective bargaining process. No
effort has been made to integrate guidepost policy into
the collective bargaining process, or to achieve an institutionalized accommodation. Collective bargaining and
the guideposts coexist in a state of cold war that has from
time to time become very hot. This is because the guideposts seem to ignore many of the traditional determinants
of collective bargaining settlements; most importantly, the
relative economic strength of the parties. Indeed, rigid adherence to the guideposts, as they developed *after* 1962,
would appear to leave relatively little scope for bargaining.
Moreover, the guideposts, and the way in which they were
presented *after* 1962 and before 1967, seemed to ask the
parties to freeze relationships and distortions which were
the results of past settlements either above or below productivity increases. Thus, all too often, the guideposts invited the parties to agree to settlements that one or the
other was bound to think unrealistic. Education and admo-
nition in time may help here, but more seems necessary in
the way of an integrating policy if the widely shared goal
of publicly fair collective bargaining settlements is to be
realized.

THE QUEST FOR POLICY

Theoretical alternatives to the present system are numerous. Wage and price control, after the wartime models,

are one. Another extreme measure is compulsory arbitration of wages and other conditions of employment. The
guideposts would serve as the principal standard for the
arbitrators legislative judgments. Hand in glove with arbitration would go some form of price control. Both of
these approaches are objectionable because they abandon
existing institutions and reject the values they support.

Very different is an approach (abandoning entirely the
guideposts) that would remove from the unions whatever
monopoly power they may have. This might be accomplished by attempting to limit the size of the de facto bargaining unit: to break the unions themselves into smaller
units, to tighten the bans on secondary pressure, and to
bar sympathetic action by co-unionists. This approach
too is extreme in that it brings the axe to existing institutions, and with uncertain consequences.[35] In the first place
it does not assure that management will not use the
monopoly power it may have to raise prices in a publicly
inappropriate fashion. Perhaps more vigorous antitrust
policy could be employed here. In the absence of such
policy, the alternative again is price control. Second, the
approach is most relevant as a response to cost-push inflation which depends upon the existence of unliquidated
monopoly wage-setting power; demand pull does not. Indeed, the guideposts attempt to turn monopoly power to
public benefit in the demand-pull situation, but to neu-
tralize it where cost push is the problem.

Breaking up the unions, however, might lead to more
efficient production, thus increasing productivity. It might
stimulate growth by freeing employers from "make-work"
practices imposed by too powerful unions. But it is a
chancy business at best, and history suggests that the cost
could be extensive industrial unrest, for the proposal envisions a role for law reminiscent of pre-Wagner Act days.

Some think that efficiency can be accomplished by less
radical surgery. Why not outlaw inefficient union-induced

work practices—featherbedding is a usual term? This would allow unions to push harder in wage negotiations without causing inflation because average productivity increases would be greater. The trouble with such suggestions—as earlier chapters should have made clear—is that law cannot draw principled distinctions between permissible bargaining subjects and impermissible ones.[36] Nor, if the law intervenes, can collective bargaining be an effective instrument for the achievement of industrial democracy or industrial peace. This is the burden of the argument advanced in the chapter dealing with the duty to bargain. It was there suggested, however, that government through law could, and plainly should, play an important role in the quest for industrial efficiency through such techniques as retraining and job placement programs.[37]

Many other suggestions have been made for dealing with collective bargaining and inflation. Too few, however, attempt to turn the existing legal and institutional structure to advantage. In what follows, I shall make this attempt. I shall suggest—tentatively, and more with the hope of stimulating further discussion of this enormously difficult problem than anything else—some means by which government intervention in collective bargaining may be directed to the end of channeling the parties into settlements that are consistent with public fairness, with national economic policy.[38] Some devices to be suggested, such as the modification of the duty to bargain, will have an effect on collective bargaining generally. Others, such as the permanent commissions, might be employed in a selective fashion. An attempt will also be made to suggest means by which the legal controls employed to prevent and to settle major disputes, discussed in the last chapter, may be meshed with devices designed to channel bargaining in the interest of national economic policy.

First, however, it may be useful to recall some earlier

discussion dealing with existing federal regulation of collective bargaining, for it is important, in evaluating new
techniques of control, to have in mind the extent of present controls. Under the law, an agency of the government
is empowered to decide the appropriate employee unit
for representational purposes.[39] This is often a critical factor—there are others—in determining whether there will
be collective bargaining at all; whether there will be a
craft or industrial union; and whether bargaining will
involve a small group within a single plant, all the employees of one employer, or the employees of several employers.
The exercise of such power can affect the substance of collective agreements. Bargaining along craft lines, for example, may produce results quite different from bargaining
along industry lines. It should be remembered, however,
that the unit appropriate for representation is not necessarily the de facto bargaining unit. And thus one does not
want to overemphasize the effect of this important governmental decision.

Another instance of present-day governmental control
is the regulation of economic coercion in collective bargaining. Under present law unions may not use economic
force for every purpose they deem desirable, and some
weapons are denied them entirely. The use of economic
force to disrupt a recognized bargaining relationship is prohibited.[40] Secondary boycotts[41] and organizational picketing are limited.[42] And in a dispute affecting the health and
welfare of the nation, the use of all force by union and
employer can be prohibited for 80 days.[43] Such regulation
—and there is much more dealing with such matters as the
employer's right to replace strikers and to lock out[44]—
affects the bargaining power of the parties and, therefore,
the bargains they make.

The duty to bargain in good faith is another and, for
our purposes, a more suggestive control that shapes the
substance of collective agreements. As spelled out in Chap-

ter 2, the employer under present law must bargain in good faith with the union over "terms and conditions of employment." The content of this phrase is determined by the Labor Board and the courts. This power in turn shapes the content of the bargain by barring the parties from taking the very important negotiating position of refusing to discuss an issue, and this in turn makes agreement on that issue more likely. The Board decision that the subjects of pension and welfare funds are terms and conditions of employment, and accordingly have to be discussed, was significant in the widespread establishment of such funds. This decision proved to be a dramatic example of the impact of governmental power on the content of private bargains.[45] It will be recalled, moreover, that the end results of negotiations are influenced not only by what the parties must discuss, but also by the informational base from which discussion proceeds. Good faith bargaining is a process of mutual persuasion as well as a contest of power. Its rational elements depend on knowledge of the underlying facts. Other things being equal, the more shared knowledge of the facts, the more rational the bargain is likely to be. This judgment is reflected in the cases holding that employer reliance in negotiations upon an alleged inability to pay increased wages carries a corresponding employer duty to furnish substantiating financial data to the union.[46] These decisions have had an effect on the process of mutual persuasion, and thereby on the content of bargains.

Since they lack the necessary selectivity and purpose, however, these existing governmental controls are not directed toward the effectuation of national economic policy. Some of this regulation, for instance the outlawing of certain of labor's economic weapons, is notorious for its greater impact on the weak than on the strong. Yet generally it is only the strong that can upset national economic policy.

Working within this existing framework, might it not be possible to make governmental control more selective and purposeful? I have argued throughout this book that freedom of contract is a desirable policy, one that all too often has been sacrificed for no good reason by Board and Court. But the quest for bargaining settlements in the public interest—if it is earnestly to be pursued—demands a change in the policy goals of the Labor-Management Relations Act. Without significantly increasing the total quantum of regulation, might it not be possible to modify some of our present legal controls in ways that will facilitate, to some extent at least, an accommodation between collective bargaining and economic policy? Can we not take a weakness of collective bargaining law—its all too extensive intrusion on private ordering—and turn it to strength by purposefully relating it to the nation's economic goals? Thus, if bargaining settlements are to follow the guideposts more closely, might not existing law be modified so as to channel private bargains in a direction that will help accomplish this result?

The law could compel the parties, as part of the duty to bargain, to discuss in good faith the application to the particular firm of the several flexible guideposts promulgated in the 1962 Report. The union would be required to bargain over the proper influence of the "trend rate of overall productivity increase" on wage rates, and the bearing, in the particular context, of such factors mentioned in the 1962 Report as an industry's labor supply and "wages earned elsewhere by similar labor." Discussion would force the particular union involved to take a position on the appropriate relation of wages to productivity and to other factors deemed relevant in the Council's Report, and thus it would channel the negotiations into courses directly concerned with national economic goals. It would create pressures tending to make union wage demands more consistent with economic policy. Employers also would have to define their positions on these subjects in a way which might well affect subsequent behavior as to prices. Indeed, the employer would be required to bargain over the relationship between his projected pricing policies, the guideposts' criteria for pricing behavior, and his proposals as to wages.

To legally require the parties to bargain in good faith about the application to them of guidepost policy is not the same, of course, as the parties in fact bargaining in good faith. But the requirement often will be to the advantage of one of the parties, who may be expected here as elsewhere to push his advantage to the point of enforcement if necessary. Our experience, it will be recalled, with the duty to bargain in good faith has on the whole been successful.[47] Moreover, in some situations enforcement might be initiated by government itself; enforcement, that is, of the duty to bargain, not of a duty to comply with the policy recommendations of the Council of Economic Advisers.

Integrating guidepost policy with collective bargaining in the suggested fashion entitles one to expect that the context in which the demands of the private parties are framed will be altered. Bargaining should assume a direction that is at least somewhat more in line with national economic policy. And the sanction of public opinion behind national policy should itself be strengthened, for it will now be endowed with the prestige associated with law. Yet the ultimate decisions will still be made by the private parties, and the government will not have to undertake detailed regulation of wages and prices.

This proposal, since it makes guidepost policy an integral part of the collective bargaining process, should avoid some of the more difficult problems that have been associated with guideposts and collective bargaining. While the guideposts in their more rigid formulation seem to ignore the relative bargaining strength of the parties and other factors traditionally deemed relevant to collective bargaining, the present proposal envisions the guideposts in their 1962 formulation and does not insist that even as so formulated they necessarily exhaust the relevant criteria for decision or constitute the sole measure of the parties' "responsibility." By integrating the guideposts into the collective bargaining process, bargaining power and the peculiar and often unique problems of the parties will be reflected in the settlement. This avoids the complaint that the parties are being asked to accept what seems to them to be an unrealistic settlement. Moreover, the proposal draws the sting from the charge that the guideposts perpetuate distortions which are the result of previous bargains that have either exceeded or been less than the trend rate of overall productivity increases. Since the issue to be discussed is the appropriate influence of the various guideposts, any factor which seems to differentiate the particular relationship from others generally may be legitimately taken into account. In short, the proposal to integrate the guideposts into collective bargaining through the legal duty to bargain seeks, on the one hand, to mold guidepost policy in a fashion which takes into account the nature of the collective bargaining system and, on the other hand, to change that system so as to effect a viable accommodation between the parties' responsibilities to their respective constituencies and to the public.

To be sure, the proposal will not produce the same results as rigid adherence to even the flexible 1962 guideposts. And, for this reason, it may seem to some far too weak. But, there is no evidence that enforcement of the guideposts through ad hoc intervention will have a significant impact in the long run, and the guideposts' educational role will, if anything, be strengthened under the duty to bargain approach. Use of the duty to bargain in the purposeful fashion suggested, moreover, retains the essentials of collective bargaining and may produce some results which are not only relatively consistent with the public interest but also palatable to the parties. It must be remembered, that the strongest advocates of the guidepost approach do not claim for it what many of its critics seem to suggest. This is a statement of Gardner Ackley when he was Chairman of the Council of Economic Advisers:

> You will not hear from me any extravagant claims for the effectiveness of the guideposts. I think that they have made and can make a modest but significant contribution to price stability. . . . For five years we have been hammering home some fairly simple arithmetic about the relations among wages, productivity, and costs; and between individual actions and overall results. Leaders of labor, I think, increasingly understand that wage increases in excess of productivity gains raise costs and therefore prices, and in the end do labor no good. And they know that what one powerful union gets away with influences what other unions try to achieve. As a result of this educational effort, the labor unions, at least in many cases, are bringing a different attitude to the bargaining table. And the public, too, has learned about this arithmetic, and a somewhat different public attitude surrounds the negotiations.[48]

In addition to the suggested change in the duty to bargain, other approaches which seek to channel bargaining settlements along public interest lines are also available should they be necessary; that is, should the duty to bargain approach prove too weak. Because it would be desirable to bring management, labor, and neutrals knowledgeable about collective bargaining into the process at an early stage, a tribunal of labor, management, and public members under the jurisdiction of the Secretaries

of Labor and Commerce might be established with responsibility to define, in conjunction with the Council
of Economic Advisers, standards of public fairness that
related national economic policy to collective bargaining.
In this fashion, the flexible guideposts of the 1962 Report
perhaps could be given even greater flexibility. Subordi-
nate to this tribunal, permanent commissions composed
of public members might be created on geographical and
industry lines with power to intervene in selected negotiations, the results of which were thought to be especially
important to the economy. A commission's function would
be to make a continuing study of, and to relate the parent
tribunal's guides to, the collective bargaining relationships within its jurisdiction. It would be expected that a
commission would give advance notice of the government's
interest and general position in particular negotiations.
This might increase the pressure of public opinion upon
the private parties and itself obviate the necessity of more
extensive intervention. If it did not, then the commission
would itself become involved in the negotiations and,
where it deemed desirable, state, in terms of varying
specificity depending on the situation, the government's
position and indeed, in some cases, openly recommend
alternative settlement terms within the developed standards of public fairness.

    Under the commission device selectivity as to the in-
dustries in which intervention seems appropriate would
be possible. If pattern setting were found to exist and to
exert a substantial influence on wage rates generally, governmental intervention through commissions might be
restricted to those industries which set the pattern. Or,
establishment of commissions might be restricted to bargaining relationships with a major work stoppage potential, either because such relationships are thought to be of
crucial importance to the economy or because it is believed
that intervention to settle the dispute may create excessive

pressure for a bargain inconsistent with national economic policy.

The commission approach has advantages over both ad hoc intervention (which hopefully it would replace) and modification of the duty to bargain (which it would supplement where necessary). Ad hoc intervention, relying as it does upon the office of the Chairman of the Council, or the Secretary of Labor, Commerce, or Defense, and the prestige of the Presidency, is not well suited to intervention in local bargaining relationships that, cumulatively, may have substantial effect on the economy. The construction industry is such an example. The commissions, however, because they can be established on geographical as well as industry lines, can overcome this difficulty. Modification of the duty to bargain, on the other hand, relies principally upon each party's desire to limit the gains of the other. But some collective bargaining relationships may not involve a sufficient conflict of interest to insure invocation of the law by the parties. It may be possible, for instance, to pass on to the public by one means or another, without any serious effect on profits, the costs of whatever settlement is reached. In those circumstances, the parties may well find cooperation rather than conflict to be to their mutual advantage and forego whatever legal advantages the suggested modification of the duty to bargain offers. Nor can one expect too much in such a case from governmental enforcement of the duty. The commission approach does not depend upon a preexisting conflict of interest between the parties. It depends upon the authority of government and the force of public opinion.

There are difficulties, of course, with the commission approach. First, unless flexibility is built into all levels of governmental participation, one party or the other in any relationship might believe that commission action would be beneficial to it, and might, therefore, make intervention a strategic objective of its bargaining. This in turn could reduce the importance of private bargaining and perhaps the diminished responsibility of the parties for their own agreements would aggravate bargaining relationships. This is a risk, but the proposal envisions sufficient flexibility to reduce it substantially, and it is less of a risk than most equally purposeful alternatives.

Second, the proposal represents rather substantial governmental intervention into the collective bargaining process: more perhaps than modification of the duty to bargain, but perhaps no more than ad hoc intervention. Government's role, however, under the commission approach would remain devoted to integrating national policy and the collective bargaining process. This is in keeping with our institutional arrangements in a way that, for instance, governmental review of private decision-making by a prices and incomes board, as in Britain, is not.[49] It is in keeping because government today, through our labor laws, integrates national policies with collective bargaining. The goal of industrial peace, for example, reflects a policy to which government has attempted to accommodate collective bargaining. As the political process changes governmental policies—and it so clearly is today in this area—so, too, must collective bargaining change. That has been the traditional nature of the relationship between collective bargaining and the law.

Procedures designed to achieve settlements consistent with economic policy might be meshed with those (discussed in Chapter 8) intended to avoid major work stoppages. In many major work stoppage situations, the public interest is thought to demand both the avoidance of the stoppage and a settlement consistent with national economic policy. The steel strike of 1952 and the 1962 controversy in the same industry will serve to illustrate the complexities created by this dual demand. In 1952, in the midst of the Korean war, the Steelworkers pressed for higher wages. The companies were apparently willing to make concessions but only if they got price relief. Otherwise, they wanted to take the strike and force the union to temper its demands. The government feared that a strike would hamper military efforts, and that a price increase would destroy the stabilization program. The result of governmental intervention was failure on all fronts.[50] In the 1962 controversy, recounted earlier, the administration apparently succeeded in persuading the Steelworkers to accept what was widely publicized as a noninflationary settlement. Almost immediately after the agreements were signed, however, the companies raised their prices, and although the increases were rescinded as a result of massive government pressure the administration's victory may well have been Pyrrhic. The prestige of the President became deeply involved in a controversy thought by many to have implications transcending the immediate results achieved. In the absence of a legislatively established process, no administration long can continue intervention on such a scale.

Rather than such ad hoc intervention, the procedures and devices discussed above may be statutorily meshed with the choice-of-procedures approach to the major work stoppage problem, discussed in the last chapter. This should help to make intervention by the government effective, purposeful, and evenhanded, while leaving scope for private bargaining. If the procedure chosen to settle a major strike is fact-finding with recommendations or compulsory arbitration, a flexible standard related to public fairness could be employed by the dispute settlers to render the intervention purposeful in terms of national economic policy.

While some of the uncertainty as to the nature and effect of governmental intervention—so necessary to the success of a choice-of-procedures statute—may disappear if standards relating to national economic policy are incorporated into a choice-of-procedures approach to major work stoppages, one cannot hope to channel private bargaining by conscious governmental action and still leave the parties totally uncertain as to the role the government will play. The government in fact cannot influence the private decision without defining its range of acceptable solutions. But because acceptable solutions are within a range, some substantive uncertainty would remain. Moreover, the parties could not calculate with any certainty the total effect of governmental intervention since the procedures to be picked, from among a choice of procedures, would not be known ahead of time. Some procedures—seizure is an example—envision that the dispute will be resolved by collective bargaining. If seizure were employed, the commission (if there were one) would function much as it would in the absence of seizure; so too the proposed duty to bargain. And a recommended settlement or compulsory arbitration, even though consciously related to economic goals, would continue to have different consequences for the parties. Uncertainty as to the procedure to be employed by the government in resolving the dispute, therefore, should encourage the parties to reach a private settlement, but the public interest would be a large factor governing their behavior. Similarly, requiring bargaining over the relationship between projected pricing policies, the criteria for pricing behavior, and wages should encourage management to give serious consideration to its position on prices before and after signing the agreement. This should reduce the prospect of another 1969 steel controversy, which many believed, rightly or wrongly, involved questions of good faith.

These proposals grow out of a basic belief, reflected throughout this book, that collective bargaining remains the best way of ordering labor-management relations, and that the unions are institutions of great utility for American democracy. The proposals, or others that root in this basic belief, at some point may be advanced through the political process by people with political authority. Should this happen, the chances are that the unions will fight the suggested changes, and fight as hard and as unconditionally as they know how. This is the way they have responded in the past to needed legislative reform.[51] If the unions win that battle, however, they may be rewarded at some not too distant time with constraints that will make of them much less than they ought to be. The lesson that then will be drawn is that short-run maximization is often not maximization at all. Maybe this is what the guideposts are all about. Let us hope that the unions learn to read the signs.

Notes

Notes

1. See generally Introduction to 3 and 4 *A Documentary History of American Industrial Society* 19 et. seq., ed. John R. Commons and Eugene A. Gilmore (Cleveland, Ohio, Arthur H. Clark, 1910) (cited hereafter as Commons and Gilmore).

2. See, e.g., State v. Glidden, 55 Conn. 46; 8 Atl. 890 (1887) (Use of boycott in order to obtain collective agreements with closed shop clause); State v. Stewart, 59 Vt. 273; 9 Atl. 559 (1887) (Use of threats against employer to prevent his using scab labor). The incidence of criminal conspiracy cases in this second period increased greatly with the passage of time: between 1842 and 1862 there appear to have been only three cases. Between 1863 and 1880, with the general revival of union activity toward the end of the Civil War, the number of prosecutions increased—there seem to have been at least eighteen in this period—reaching a peak between 1885 and 1887. Legislation to outlaw such prosecutions was enacted in a number of states, notably Pennsylvania (1869) and New York (1870); but such legislation, even after amendment, failed substantially to change the law. See Edwin E. Witte, "Early American Labor Cases," 35 *Yale L. J.* 825, 828–32 (1926).

3. 4 Metc. 111 (Mass. 1842). This decision reversed Judge Thatcher. For the report of defendant's trial and conviction see Thatcher's Crim. Cas. 609 (1840). For discussions of the case itself see Walter Nelles, "Commonwealth v. Hunt," 32 *Colum. L. Rev.* 1128 (1932); Leonard W. Levy, *The Law of the Commonwealth and Chief Justice Shaw* 183–206 (New York, Harper Torchbook, 1967) (hereafter cited as Levy).

4. State v. Glidden, 55 Conn. 46, 72, 8 Atl. 890, 894 (1887).

5. The Philadelphia Cordwainers Case, Commonwealth v. Pullis (1806), 3 Commons and Gilmore 59, 229.

6. Id. at 231.

7. The Case of The Twenty Journeymen Tailors, People v. Faulkner, New York (1836), *Courier and Enquirer*, May 31, 1836, reproduced in 4 Commons and Gilmore 315, 322.

8. The Philadelphia Cordwainers Case, supra note 5 at 211.

9. Id. at 229.

10. See generally 3 Commons and Gilmore at 39.

11. Perry Miller, *The Life of the Mind in America from the Revolution to the Civil War* 121 (New York, Harcourt Brace, 1965) (Hereafter cited as Miller).

12. Richard B. Morris, *Government and Labor in Early America* 207 (New York, Harper Torchbooks, 1965). See also, e.g., Morris, "Criminal Conspiracy and Early Labor Combinations In New York," 52 *Pol. Sci. Q.* 51 (1937); Francis B. Sayre, "Criminal Conspiracy," 35 *Harv. L. Rev.* 393 (1922).

That there were no American precedents available to the courts has also been demonstrated by Mr. Morris in his *Government and Labor in Early America;* "The attitude of the colonial and Revolutionary courts toward combinations by . . . journeymen is too obscure to furnish satisfactory precedents from which the judiciary might induce the principle of an American 'common law of criminal conspiracy.' " Id. at 207.

13. Norway Plains Co. v. Boston and Maine R.R., 1 Gray 263, 267 (Mass. 1854). See generally Levy 140–65.

14. Miller 209.

15. Ibid. *The Federalist Papers,* No. 10, 77–84 (Rossiter ed. N.Y., Mentor, 1961).

16. Miller 211–12.

17. Vegelahn v. Guntner, 167 Mass. 92, 107, 44 N.E. 1077, 1081 (1896) (dissenting opinion).

18. See note 2 supra; Marjorie S. Turner, *The Early American Conspiracy Cases, Their Place in Labor Law* (San Diego, San Diego State College Press, 1967).

19. Cf. Devlin, *The Enforcement of Morals* (New York, Oxford University Press, 1959); H. L. A. Hart, *Law, Liberty and Morality* (Stanford, Stanford University Press, 1963); and Ronald M. Dworkin, "Lord Devlin and the Enforcement of Morals," 75 *Yale L. J.* 986 (1966).

20. Walter Nelles, "The First American Labor Case," 41 *Yale L. J.* 165, 168 (1931).

21. Id. at 169–73.

22. See Samuel Eliot Morison and Henry Steele Commager, *The Growth of the American Republic 1,* 331 (5th ed. N.Y., Oxford University Press, 1962).

23. Richard Hofstadter, *The American Political Tradition* 38–39 (New York, Alfred A. Knopf, Vintage Books, 1954).

24. Nelles, supra note 20 at 190.

25. Witte, supra note 2 at 837.

26. See his dissenting opinions in Vegelahn v. Guntner, 167 Mass.

92, 104–09, 44 N.E. 1077, 1079–82 (1896); and in Plant v. Woods, 176 Mass. 492, 504–05, 57 N.E. 1011, 1015–16 (1900).

27. The question of what means were peaceful was itself in issue. See, e.g., the statement of the court in Atchison, T. & S. F. Ry. v. Gee, 139 Fed. 582 at 584 (C.C. Iowa, 1905): "There is and can be no such thing as peaceful picketing, any more than there can be chaste vulgarity, or peaceful mobbing, or lawful lynching."

28. Holmes, "Privilege, Malice and Intent," 8 *Harv. L. Rev.* 1, 8 (1894).

29. "On May 27, 1895, the Supreme Court of the United States for the first time in its history passed on the scope and validity of an injunction in a labor controversy. Yet the very next year this modern application of an ancient procedure was made a party issue, and since then has maintained itself at the forefront of American political problems. 'Government by injunction' was the slogan by which the Democratic platform of 1896 inveighed against the practice of issuing labor injunctions. After 1908, the Republican Party also proposed the correction of abuses due to judicial intervention in labor conflicts. In response to this agitation, important federal legislation was enacted in 1914. But the hopes in which it was conceived soon foundered. Protest revived and grew. And so, in the campaign of 1928 both parties acknowledged the existence of abuses and committed themselves to the need of further legislation. What is true of the nation is true of the states. In 1896, the Chief Justice of Massachusetts remarked that the 'practice of issuing injunctions in cases of this kind is of very recent origin.' . . . Since then the practice has grown widely, giving rise to vigorous counter-agitation. State legislatures have followed Congress in corrective legislation, but proposals for curbing resort to labor injunctions continue to be urged by Democratic and Republican governors alike." Felix Frankfurter and Nathan Greene, *The Labor Injunction* 1 (New York, Macmillan, 1930).

30. See Plant v. Woods, supra note 26. For the classic account and criticism of the drawing of these distinctions, see Frankfurter and Greene, *The Labor Injunction* 24–46, supra note 29.

31. See Loewe v. Lawlor, 208 U.S. 274 (1908); Lawlor v. Loewe, 235 U.S. 522 (1915). The argument against this development is perhaps most fully stated in Edward Berman, *Labor and the Sherman Act* (New York, Harper, 1930). And see generally, Ralph K. Winter, Jr., "Collective Bargaining and Competition: The Application of Antitrust Standards to Union Activities," 73 *Yale L. J.* 14 (1963).

32. See, e.g., Adair v. U.S., 208 U.S. 161 (1908); *Coppage v. Kansas*, 236 U.S. 1 (1915).

33 See, e.g., *Final Report of the Commission on Industrial Relations*, S. Doc. No. 415, 64th Cong., 1st Sess., 1, 38–61 (1916); Frankfurter and Greene, supra note 29 at 52–53, fn. 19.

34. See *Testimony of Louis D. Brandeis before the Commission on Industrial Relations*, Jan. 23, 1915, S. Doc. No. 415, 64th Cong., 1st Sess., 8, 7657–81 (1916).

35. "By the organization of labor, and by no other means, it is possible to introduce an element of democracy into the government of industry. By this means only the workers can effectively take part in determining the conditions under which they work." *Final Report of the Industrial Commission* 805 (Washington, Gov't Printing Office, 1902). See Clyde W. Summers, "American Legislation for Union Democracy," 25 *Mod. L. Rev.* 273, 275 (1962).

36. See generally Chapter 6, infra; and Seymour Martin Lipset, Martin A. Trow, and James S. Coleman, *Union Democracy* 3–16 (Glencoe, The Free Press, 1956). Cf. Milton Derber's discussion of the views of John R. Commons, in "The Idea of Industrial Democracy in America, 1898–1915," 7 *Labor History* 259, 279–80 (1966).

37. See, e.g., *Final Report of the Industrial Commission*, supra note 35 at 844. ("Most strikes and lockouts would not occur if each party understood exactly the position of the other.")

38. See, e.g., *Final Report of the Industrial Commission*, supra note 35 at 800: "It is quite generally recognized that the growth of great aggregations of capital under the control of single groups of men, which is so prominent a feature of the economic development of recent years, necessitates a corresponding aggregation of workingmen into unions, which may be able also to act as units. It is readily perceived that the position of the single workman, face to face with one of our great modern combinations, such as the United States Steel Corporation, is a position of very great weakness. The workman has one thing to sell—his labor. He has perhaps devoted years to the acquirement of a skill which gives his labor power a relatively high value, so long as he is able to put it to use in combination with certain materials and machinery. A single legal person has, to a very great extent, the control of such machinery, and in particular of such materials. Under such conditions there is little competition for the workman's labor. Control of the means of production gives power to dictate to the workingman upon what terms he shall make use of them."

39. The literature on the subject is immense; probably the most illuminating studies are those by Karl N. Llewellyn and Friedrich Kessler. For the former, see, e.g., "What Price Contract—An Essay in Perspective," 40 *Yale L. J.* 704 (1931), and, "On Warranty of Quality

and Society," 36 *Colum. L. Rev.* 699 (1936), 37 *Colum. L. Rev.* 341
(1937); for the latter see e.g., "Contracts of Adhesion—Some Thoughts
About Freedom of Contract," 43 *Colum. L. Rev.* 629 (1943); "Culpa
in Contrahendo, Bargaining in Good Faith and Freedom of Contract:
A Comparative Study," 77 *Harv. L. Rev.* 401 (1964) (with Edith
Fine). Recent notable additions to the material in this field include,
e.g., H. B. Sales, "Standard Form Contracts," 16 *Mod. L. Rev.* 318
(1953), and Cyril Grunfeld, "Reform in the Law of Contract," 24
Mod. L. Rev. 62 (1961).

40. See Kessler, "Contracts of Adhesion," supra note 39 at 629.

41. Cf. Karl N. Llewllyn, *The Common Law Tradition: Deciding
Appeals* 362–71 (Boston, Little Brown, 1960).

42. See, e.g., "Book Review," Karl N. Llewellyn, 52 *Harv. L. Rev.*
700 (1939).

43. Lloyd G. Reynolds, *Labor Economics and Labor Relations* 18–
19 (3rd ed. Englewood Cliffs, N.J., Prentice Hall, 1961).

44. Cf. Guido Calabresi, "The Decision for Accidents: An Approach
to Nonfault Allocation of Costs," 78 *Harv. L. Rev.* 713, 726–29 (1965);
Calabresi, "Fault, Accidents and the Wonderful World of Blum and
Kalvin," 75 *Yale L. J.* 216, 225–31 (1965).

45. See, e.g., "The U.S. Steel Corporation: III," *Fortune*, May
1936, p. 141, quoted in Neil W. Chamberlain, *The Union Challenge
to Management Control* 94 (New York, Harper, 1948): "Although
U.S. Steel established central employment offices in 1919, control of
jobs, the rotation of work, was left in the hands of foremen. In
stable periods this power is relatively unimportant. In a depression-
ridden steel town, where getting a day's work has been as prized
as finding a nugget, it increased in importance a thousandfold. . . .
The power to assign work in such a situation means the difference
between living or being destitute to the man who receives it, and
the reminiscences of steelworkers are filled with stories of money lent
to foremen after a better-than-usual pay, and never repaid or expected, of minor officials who have small business interests that men
patronize in the hope of getting more work."

46. On some of the difficulties with the use of these approaches
to reach results that are unrelated to the sense of the agreement,
see Kessler, "Contracts of Adhesion" 43 *Colum. L. Rev.* 629 (1943).

47. See, e.g., Henningsen v. Bloomfield Motors, Inc., 32 N.J. 358,
161 A.2d 69 (1960). This case is discussed in Chapter 5, infra. See
generally, Arthur A. Leff, "Unconscionability And The Code—The
Emperor's New Clause," 115 *U. of Pa. L. Rev.* 485 (1967).

48. Railroad Co. v. Lockwood, 17 Wall. 357 (84 U.S.) (1873).

49. Id. at 379.

50. Id. at 380. For an interesting discussion of the problems raised by this case see Comment, "Exculpatory Clauses: The Historical Impact of Common-Carrier Law and the Modern Relevance of Insurance," 24 *U. Chi. L. Rev.* 315 (1957).

51. Henry M. Hart, Jr., and Albert M. Sacks, *The Legal Process: Basic Problems in the Making and Application of Law* 265–66 (tentative ed., mimeo., Cambridge, Mass. 1958).

52. See, e.g., among a multitude of enactments, the Fair Labor Standards Act, 52 Stat. 1060 (1938), as amended, 29 U.S.C. §§ 201 et seq. (1964); the Federal Safety Appliance Acts, 27 Stat. 531 (1893), as amended, 45 U.S.C. §§ 1 et seq. (1964).

53. See, e.g., Papers on "The Consequences of Minimum Wages," by Harry Weiss and Fred H. Blum, with discussion, in Industrial Relations Research Association *Proceedings,* 1956, pp. 154–94.

54. Some of the difficulties are suggested by experience with State safety legislation. For example, Mr. George C. Daniels pointed out in 1940 that New York State had a field inspectors force of 105 to police approximately 70,000 factories. And it was often necessary to visit a factory that had violated regulations from 6 to perhaps 15 or 20 times a year. See his statement at the Proceedings of the Twenty-Sixth Convention of the International Association of Governmental Labor Officials, in *The Employment Relation and the Law* 117 (ed. Benjamin Aaron, Boston, Little Brown & Co., 1957).

55. 44 Stat. 577 (1926), as amended, 45 U.S.C. §§ 151–63, 181–88 (1964).

56. 73 Stat. 519 (1959), 29 U.S.C. §§ 401 et. seq. (1964).

57. 47 Stat. 70 (1932), as amended, 29 U.S.C. §§ 101–15 (1964) (Norris-LaGuardia) (cited hereafter by section number and Norris-LaGuardia); 49 Stat. 449 (1935), as amended, 61 Stat. 136 (1947), as amended, 73 Stat. 541 (1959), 28 U.S.C. §§ 151 et seq. (1964) (Labor-Management Relations Act) (cited hereafter by section number and L.M.R.A.).

58. The relevant sections are § 6, 38 Stat. 731 (1914), 15 U.S.C. § 17 (1964); § 20, 38 Stat. 738 (1914), 29 U.S.C. §52 (1964). For the "nullification" of these provisions, see Duplex Printing Press Co. v. Deering, 254 U.S. 443 (1921). On congressional purpose and the Clayton Act, see Frankfurter and Greene, supra note 29, at 141–45; Alexander M. Bickel, *The Unpublished Opinions of Mr. Justice Brandeis* 80–81 (Cambridge, Mass., Harvard University Press, 1957); Dallas L. Jones, "The Enigma of the Clayton Act," 10 *Ind. & Lab. Rel. Rev.* 201 (1957).

59. For a full discussion and enumeration of these measures see

Benjamin Aaron, "Labor Injunctions in State Courts," 50 *Va. L. Rev.* 951 and 1147 (1964).

60. Frankfurter and Greene, supra note 29 at 64.

61. See "Labor Injunctions and Judge-Made Labor Law: The Contemporary Role of Norris-LaGuardia," 70 *Yale L. J.* 70, 71–76 (1960); Harry H. Wellington and Lee A. Albert, "Statutory Interpretation and the Political Process: A Comment on Sinclair v. Atkinson," 72 *Yale L. J.* 1547, 1553–57 (1963).

62. See note 34 supra at 7659–60.

63. § 2, Norris-LaGuardia Act.

64. See generally, Henry Pelling, *American Labor* (Chicago, University of Chicago Press, 1960).

65. The National Industrial Recovery Act, 48 Stat. 195 (1933). For an early appraisal of § 7(a) of the enactment, 48 Stat. 198–99, see Edwin E. Witte, "The Background of the Labor Provisions of the N.I.R.A.", 1 *U. Chi. L. Rev.* 572 (1934). The N.I.R.A. was, of course, held unconstitutional in Schechter Poultry Corporation v. United States, 295 U.S. 495 (1935).

66. N.L.R.A. § 1, 49 Stat. 449 (1935). (The statute now reads: "denial by *some* employers . . . refusal by *some* employers. . . .")

67. §§ 3 and 10, L.M.R.A.

68. For definition of the General Counsel's powers, see, in addition to § 10, L.M.R.A., § 3(d), L.M.R.A. The board also has rule-making powers under § 6 of the statute, but it seems to have made strenuous efforts to avoid acting under this section. For a cogent criticism of this attitude, see Cornelius J. Peck, "The Atrophied Rule-Making Powers of the National Labor Relations Board," 70 *Yale L. J.* 729 (1961).

69. This is reflected, e.g., in § 10(b), L.M.R.A. which, contrary to its original form, requires the proceeding . . . so far as practicable" to follow the rules of evidence prevailing in the federal courts. A trial examiner still participates in the hearings and questions witnesses more fully than the average judge. See Archibald Cox and Derek C. Bok, *Cases and Materials on Labor Law* 172 (5th ed. Brooklyn, The Foundation Press, 1962).

70. § 10(e) and (f), L.M.R.A.

71. § 10(a), (b), and (d), L.M.R.A.

72. § 10(l) and (j), L.M.R.A.

73. See generally Cox and Bok, supra note 69 at 350–61.

74. See J. I. Case Co. v. N.L.R.B., 321 U.S. 332 (1944); Ruth Weyand, "Majority Rule in Collective Bargaining," 45 *Colum. L. Rev.* 556 (1945); Clyde W. Summers, "Exclusive Representation by

344 Notes for Pages 44-54

the Majority Union: A Unique Principle of American Labor Law,"
in Hedendaags Arbeidsrecht, *Essays in Honor of Prof. Marius A.
Levenbach,* (Alphen, N. Samson N.V. AAN Den RIJN, 1966) at 304.

75. See, e.g., Allied Stores of New York and District 65, 150
N.L.R.B. 799 (1965); Note, "The Board and Section 9(c)(5): Multi-
Location and Single Location Bargaining Units in the Insurance and
Retail Industries," 79 *Harv. L. Rev.* 811 (1966).

76. See, e.g., N.L.R.B. v. Virginia Electric & Power Co., 314 U.S.
469 (1941) (freedom of speech); Republic Aviation Corp. v. N.L.R.B.,
324 U.S. 793 (1945) (employer's rights over his own property). See
among many discussions, W. Willard Wirtz, "The New National
Labor Relations Board; Herein of 'Employer Persuasion,'" 49 *Nw.
L. Rev.* 594 (1954); Derek C. Bok, "The Regulation of Campaign
Tactics in Representation Elections under the National Labor Relations Act," 78 *Harv. L. Rev.* 38 (1964).

77. Compare American Federation of Labor v. N.L.R.B., 308 U.S.
401 (1940), with Leedom v. Kyne, 358 U.S. 184 (1958). Cf. N.L.R.B.
v. Metropolitan Life Insurance Co., 380 U.S. 438 1965).

78. See, e.g., San Diego Bldg. Trades Council v. Garmon, 359 U.S.
236 (1959). See generally Bernard D. Meltzer, "The Supreme Court,
Congress, and State Jurisdiction over Labor Relations," 59 *Colum. L.
Rev.* 6 and 269 (1959); Harry H. Wellington, "Labor and the Federal
System," 26 *U. Chi. L. Rev.* 542 (1959).

79. See § 14(c) L.M.R.A. For the background of this provision, see
Guss v. Utah Labor Relations Board, 353 U.S. 1 (1957); Allan H.
McCoid, "Notes on a 'G-String': A Study of the 'No-Man's Land' of
Labor Law," 44 *Minn. L. Rev.* 205 (1959).

CHAPTER 2

1. See §§ 8(a)(3), 8(e), L.M.R.A.; see note 63 infra.

2. See, e.g., J. I. Case v. N.L.R.B., 321 U.S. 332 (1944); N.L.R.B.
v. Crompton-Highland Mills, Inc., 337 U.S. 217 (1949).

3. See, e.g., N.L.R.B. v. Katz, 369 U.S. 736 (1962).

4. §§ 8(a)(5), 8(d), L.M.R.A.

5. § 301, L.M.R.A. See Chapter 3 infra.

6. §§ 8(b)(3), 8(d), L.M.R.A.

7. See notes 2 and 3 supra.

8. Compare what follows with Philip Ross, *The Government as a
Source of Union Power* (Providence, Brown University Press, 1965).
Perhaps the most interesting portion of the Ross book is the section
called "An Empirical Analysis of the Duty to Bargain," Id. at 182-

220. Ross concludes that "broadly speaking, the empirical analysis of refusal-to-bargain charges . . . leads to the conclusion that the impact of the NLRB upon the individual firm induces compliance with public policy in two ways: first, by the imposition of sanctions, and second, by what has been called 'voluntary compliance.'" Id. at 239. Further empirical study has led Mr. Ross to conclude: "The legal standards of bargaining have been extremely pervasive and have influenced employer behavior in a manner that, in general and as a whole, has been consistent with the congressional mandate. Employers, by and large, take their legal obligations in this area seriously and most of them have accepted Board policies and procedures in their dealings with unions. . . . The major shortcoming of the NLRB lies in its failure to adopt adequate and realistic remedies in those cases where the employer has unmistakenly demonstrated a continuing intent to frustrate the Act." Ross, *The Labor Law in Action* 2 (Rep. to N.L.R.B., Sept., 1966). On developing Board remedies in the duty to bargain area, see Frank W. McCulloch, "Past, Present and Future Remedies under Section 8(a)(5) of the NLRA," 19 *Labor L. J.* 131 (1968).

9. S. Rep. No. 573, 74th Cong., 1st Sess. 12 (1935).

10. Final Report of the Industrial Commission 844 (Washington, Gov't Printing Office, 1902).

11. See, e.g., Prudential Ins. Co., 119 N.L.R.B. 768 (1957), order set aside sub nom. Insurance Agents' Union v. N.L.R.B., 260 F.2d 736 (D.C. Cir. 1958) (per curiam), aff'd, 361 U.S. 477 (1960).

12. Russell A. Smith, "The Evolution of the 'Duty to Bargain' Concept in American Law," 39 *Mich. L. Rev.* 1065, 1108 (1941).

13. See notes 16, 17, and 18 infra.

14. The Wagner Act did not use the term "good faith," but the Board and courts did. See, e.g., N.L.R.B. v. Griswold Mfg. Co., 106 F.2d 713 (3d Cir. 1939). § 8(d), L.M.R.A. wrote decisional law into the statute.

15. See, e.g., N.L.R.B. v. Truitt Mfg. Co., 351 U.S. 149 (1956).

16. Terminal R.R. Assoc. v. Brotherhood of R.R. Trainmen, 318 U.S. 1, 6 (1943) (R.L.A.).

17. N.L.R.B. v. American Nat'l. Insurance Co., 343 U.S. 395, 404 (1952).

18. N.L.R.B. v. Insurance Agents' Int'l Union, 361 U.S. 477, 488–89 (1960).

19. N.L.R.B. v. Reed & Prince Mfg. Co., 205 F.2d 131, 134 (1st Cir. 1953), cert. denied, 346 U.S. 887 (1953).

20. See, e.g., N.L.R.B. v. Cummer-Graham Co., 279 F.2d 757 (5th Cir. 1960); White v. N.L.R.B., 255 F.2d 564 (5th Cir. 1958). But see

United Steelworkers (H. K. Porter Co.) v. N.L.R.B., 389 F.2d 295 (D.C. Cir. 1967).

21. General Electric Co., 150 N.L.R.B. 192, 195 (1964).

22. See Archibald Cox, "The Duty to Bargain in Good Faith," 71 *Harv. L. Rev.* 1401, 1425–28 (1958).

23. Truitt Mfg. Co., 110 N.L.R.B. 856 (1954). See note 15 supra.

24. See "Comment," Clyde W. Summers, in *Collective Bargaining and The Law* 51, 53 (Ann Arbor, University of Michigan Law School, 1959).

25. Prudential Ins. Co., 119 N.L.R.B. 768, 770 (1957).

26. N.L.R.B. v. Insurance Agents' Int'l Union, 361 U.S. 477, 490 (1960).

27. See Inland Steel Co. v. N.L.R.B., 170 F.2d 247 (7th Cir. 1948), cert. denied, 336 U.S. 960 (1949).

28. See N.L.R.B. v. Wooster Div. of Borg-Warner Corp., 356 U.S. 342 (1958). And see, e.g., Donald H. Wollett, "The Borg-Warner Case and the Role of the N.L.R.B. in the Bargaining Process," 12 *N.Y.U. Conf. Lab.* 39 (1959).

29. See N.L.R.B. v. American Nat'l Insurance, 343 U.S. 395 (1952).

30. Ibid. Compare Archibald Cox and John T. Dunlop, "Regulation of Collective Bargaining by the National Labor Relations Board," 63 *Harv. L. Rev.* 389 (1950), with David P. Findling and William E. Colby, "Regulation of Collective Bargaining by the National Labor Relations Board—Another View," 51 *Colum. L. Rev.* 170 (1951).

31. See *The Public Interest in National Labor Policy* 82 (N.Y., Committee for Economic Development, 1961).

32. N.L.R.B. v. Wooster Div. of Borg-Warner Corp., 356 U.S. 342, 349–50 (1958).

33. Id. at 350.

34. Id. at 353 (dissenting opinion). See Archibald Cox, "Labor Decisions of the Supreme Court at the October Term, 1957," 44 *Va. L. Rev.* 1057, 1074–86 (1958).

35. Fibreboard Paper Products Corp. v. N.L.R.B., 379 U.S. 203 (1964). For commentary on this case, see, e.g., Clyde W. Summers, "Labor Law in the Supreme Court: 1964 Term," 75 *Yale L. J.* 59 60–67 (1965).

36. Compare 130 N.L.R.B. 1558 (1961), with 138 N.L.R.B. 550 (1962), and cases cited therein, particularly Shamrock Dairy, Inc., 124 N.L.R.B. 494 (1959), enforced, 280 F.2d 665 (D.C. Cir. 1960), cert. denied 364 U.S. 892; and Timken Roller Bearing Co., 70 N.L.R.B. 500 (1947), reversed on other grounds, 161 F.2d 949 (6th Cir. 1947).

37. Supra note 35 at 210–11.

38. Id. at 217–18.

39. Id. at 225.

40. W. Willard Wirtz, *Labor And The Public Interest* 48 (New York, Harper & Row, 1964).

41. Supra note 35 at 225–26.

42. Id. at 220.

43. Id. at 220–21 (footnotes omitted).

44. See, for a discussion of these problems, Margaret K. Chandler, *Management Rights and Union Interests* (New York, McGraw-Hill, 1964).

45. The strike of public school teachers in New York in September 1967 is an example. See Board of Education v. Shanker, 66 L.R.R.M. 2308 (Sup. Ct. N.Y. Oct. 4, 1967).

46. In its original decision in *Fibreboard*—a decision subsequently reconsidered and changed, see note 36 supra—the Board had held that the employer did not have a duty to bargain about his decision to subcontract. But the Board made it clear that he did have a duty to bargain about the effects of that decision: "The statutory obligation imposed upon employers by Section 8(a)(5) is unquestionably broad, and includes the obligation to bargain not only concerning matters affecting employees while they are employed, but also concerning matters as they affect termination and post-termination rights and obligations. None of the obligations heretofore imposed with respect to this latter category concern, however, the question whether, as here, a termination will occur; all rather presuppose that terminations will occur, and are concerned solely with such matters as selection for termination among present employees, and benefits flowing from present employment which employees may be entitled to receive at the time of or following the termination of employment. These matters, therefore, although they look to the future, nevertheless involve matters presently affecting employees within an existing bargaining unit; for that reason they fall within the statutory language as 'conditions of employment.'" 130 N.L.R.B. 1558, 1560 (1961).

47. See, e.g., N.L.R.B. v. Katz, 369 U.S. 736 (1962); J. Gilmer Bowman, Jr., "An Employer's Unilateral Action—An Unfair Labor Practice," 9 *Van. L. Rev.* 487 (1956).

48. See, e.g., the way in which the law had developed with respect to employer lockouts prior to recent Supreme Court decisions. The best introduction is Bernard D. Meltzer, "Single Employer and Multi-Employer Lockouts under the Taft-Hartley Act," 24 *U. Chi. L. Rev.* 70 (1956). See also Meltzer, "Lockouts under the Labor Management Relations Act: New Shadows on an Old Terrain," 28 *U. Chi. L. Rev.* 614 (1961). The recent decisions of the Supreme

Court are: American Shipbuilding Co. v. N.L.R.B., 380 U.S. 300 (1965); and, N.L.R.B. v. Brown, 380 U.S. 278 (1965). See Meltzer, "The Lockout Cases," 1965 *Supreme Court Review* 87 (Chicago, University of Chicago Press, 1965).

49. Comment, "Unilateral Action as a Legitimate Economic Weapon: Power Bargaining by the Employer upon Expiration of the Collective Bargaining Agreement," 37 *N.Y.U. L. Rev.* 666, 674 (1962) (footnotes omitted).

50. See, e.g., Jacobs Mfg. Co. 94 N.L.R.B. 1214 (1951), enforced, 196 F.2d 680 (2d. Cir.); "The Continuing Duty to Bargain During a Collective Agreement," 21 *Record of the Association of the Bar of the City of New York* 653 (1966); Archibald Cox and John T. Dunlop, "The Duty to Bargain Collectively During the Term of an Existing Agreement," 63 *Harv. L. Rev.* 1097 (1950); Note, "The NLRB and Deference to Arbitration," 77 *Yale L. J.* 1191, 1208–18 (1968). See also Ador Corp., 150 N.L.R.B. 1658 (1965).

51. See generally on pension plans in industry, Merton C. Bernstein, *The Future of Private Pensions* (New York, Free Press of Glencoe, 1964).

52. See, e.g., Allied Chemical Corp., 151 N.L.R.B. 718 (1965). The courts of appeals have been more restrictive. See, e.g., N.L.R.B. v. Adams Dairy, 350 F.2d 108 (8th Cir. 1965), cert. denied, 382 U.S. 1011 (1966); N.L.R.B. v. Royal Plating and Polishing Co., 350 F.2d 191 (3d Cir. 1965). See generally Elihu Platt, "The Duty to Bargain as Applied to Management Decisions," 19 *Labor L. J.* 143 (1968).

53. Textile Workers Union v. Darlington Mfg. Co., 380 U.S. 263, 273–74 (1965).

54. Supra note 28 at 349.

55. Id. at 357–58 (emphasis in original).

56. Note, "Union Refusal to Bargain: Section 8(b)(3) of the National Labor Relations Act," 71 *Harv. L. Rev.* 502, 512 (1958).

57. See notes 30 and 31 supra.

58. See, e.g., cases cited in note 52 supra. See generally Robben W. Fleming, "The Obligation to Bargain in Good Faith," in *Public Policy and Collective Bargaining*, eds. Joseph Shister, Benjamin Aaron, and Clyde W. Summers (New York, Harper & Row, 1962), at p. 60.

59. See generally Neil W. Chamberlain and James W. Kuhn, *Collective Bargaining* (2d ed. New York, McGraw-Hill, 1965).

60. Fibreboard Paper Products v. N.L.R.B., 379 U.S. 203, 211 (1964).

61. Holmes, "Privilege, Malice and Intent," 8 *Harv. L. Rev.* 1, 8 (1894).

62. *The Public Interest In National Labor Policy* 82 (N.Y., Committee for Economic Development, 1961).

63. Howard Lesnick, "Job Security and Secondary Boycotts: The Reach of N.L.R.A. Sections 8(b)(4) and 8(e)," 113 *U. of Pa. L. Rev.* 1000 at 1040–41 (1965).

64. See National Woodwork Manufacturers Association v. N.L.R.B., 386 U.S. 612 (1967).

65. Neil W. Chamberlain, *The Labor Sector* 342 (N.Y., McGraw-Hill, 1965).

66. Id. at 343, 345.

67. Id. at 349.

68. 75 *Cong. Rec.* 4918, 72d Cong., 1st Sess. (1932).

69. See Chapter 9 infra.

70. Margaret K. Chandler, *Management Rights and Union Interests* 241, supra note 44.

71. Nor should it be overestimated. See generally Richard R. Nelson, Merton J. Peck, and Edward D. Kalachek, *Technology, Economic Growth and Public Policy* (Washington, Brookings Institution, 1967), particularly pp. 113–33. For a very different view indeed, see Donald M. Michael, *Cybernation: The Silent Conquest* (Santa Barbara, Center for the Study of Democratic Institutions, 1962).

72. Chandler, *Management Rights and Union Interests* 169, supra note 44.

73. See Nelson, Peck, and Kalachek, supra note 71; note 74 infra.

74. See *Technology and the American Economy* (Report to the President and the Congress of the National Commission on Technology Automation, and Economic Progress, 1 (Washington, Gov't. Printing Office, 1966).

75. For a general discussion of these among other problems in advanced capitalist societies, see Andrew Shonfield, *Modern Capitalism* (London, Oxford University Press, 1965).

CHAPTER 3

1. Harry Shulman, *Opinions of the Arbitrator, Ford Motor Co.—U.A.W.,* Section III, preface (Published privately, 1946).

2. This is not to suggest that similar obligations are unknown in the commercial world. Cf. Stewart Macaulay, "Non-Contractual Relations in Business: A Preliminary Study," 28 *Amer. Soc. Rev.* 55 (1963).

3. 2 B.N.A. Collective Bargaining Negotiations & Contract Serv. § 51:6 (Aug. 26, 1965).

4. Textile Workers Union v. Lincoln Mills, 353 U.S. 448 (1957). On labor-management attitudes toward arbitration, see Dallas L. Jones and Russell A. Smith, "Management and Labor Appraisals and Criticisms of the Arbitration Process: A Report with Comments," 62 *Mich. L. Rev.* 1115 (1964).

5. Some state courts termed the collective agreement a "mere gentlemen's agreement, unenforceable at law" and used the analogy of a treaty. Charles O. Gregory, "The Collective Bargaining Agreement: Its Nature and Scope," 1949 *Wash. U. L. Q.* 3, 11. Other courts enforced the agreement under an agency or third-party beneficiary theory. Compare, e.g., Barnes & Co. v. Berry, 169 Fed. 225 (6th Cir. 1909), with Blum & Co. v. Landau, 23 Ohio App. 426, 155 N.E. 154 (1926). "A substantial body of case law . . . dealt with collective agreements according to the traditional pattern of contract litigation." *Labor Relations and the Law* 308 (ed. Robert E. Mathews, Boston, Little Brown & Co., 1953).

While § 301 was enacted in 1947, it was 1955 before the Supreme Court entertained a case involving the section. In that case, however, the Court was unable to give anything remotely approaching an authoritative view of the effect of the section. See Association of Westinghouse Salaried Employees v. Westinghouse Electric Corp., 348 U.S. 437 (1955). See generally Donald H. Wollett and Harry H. Wellington, "Federalism and Breach of the Labor Agreement," 7 *Stan. L. Rev.* 445 (1955).

6. See Association of Westinghouse Salaried Employees v. Westinghouse Electric Corp., 348 U.S. 437, 441–49 (1955).

7. See, e.g., New York Arbitration Act, Article 75, N.Y. Civ. Prac. Act §§ 7501–14 (1964).

8. 9 U.S.C. §§ 1–14 (1964). See Archibald Cox, "Grievance Arbitration in the Federal Courts," 67 *Harv. L. Rev.* 591 (1954).

9. See American Arbitration Association, *Procedural and Substantive Aspects of Labor-Management Arbitration,* 11–12 (1957).

10. Compare Harry Shulman and Neil W. Chamberlain, *Cases on Labor Relations* 2–8 (Brooklyn, Foundation Press, 1949).

11. See note 6 supra.

12. The legislative history is collected as an appendix to the dissenting opinion of Mr. Justice Frankfurter in Textile Workers Union v. Lincoln Mills, 353 U.S. 448, 485–546 (1957).

13. 353 U.S. 448 (1957).

14. See Chapter 1, supra.

15. 353 U.S. at 457–59. The same result had been reached by Judge

Magruder in Local 205, United Elec. Workers v. General Elec. Co., 233 F.2d 85 (1st Cir. 1956), aff'd 353 U.S. 547 (1957) (this case was one of three controlled by the *Lincoln Mills* decision).

16. See, e.g., Rowe v. Williams, 97 Mass. 163 (1867). Cf. Cogswell v. Cogswell, 70 Wash. 178, 126 P. 431 (1912).

17. See generally *Restatement of the Law of Contracts* § 550 (St. Paul, Am. Law. Inst., 1932); Samuel Williston, *A Treatise on the Law of Contracts, 6,* § 1919 (rev. ed. New York, Baker, Voorhis & Co., 1938).

18. See Red Cross Line v. Atlantic Fruit Co., 264 U.S. 109, 120–22 (1924).

19. The statutes are collected in 4 B.N.A. Labor Relations Reporter.

20. See note 8 supra.

21. Compare United Furniture Workers v. Colonial Hardwood Flooring Co., 168 F.2d 33 (4th Cir. 1948), with Mercury Oil Refining Co. v. Oil Workers Int'l Union, 187 F.2d 980 (10th Cir. 1951), and Tenney Engineering Inc. v. United Elec. Workers, 207 F.2d 450 (3d Cir. 1953).

22. See generally Alexander M. Bickel and Harry H. Wellington, "Legislative Purpose and the Judicial Process: The Lincoln Mills Case," 71 *Harv. L. Rev.* 1 (1957).

23. United Steelworkers v. Enterprise Wheel & Car Corp., 363 U.S. 593 (1960); United Steelworkers v. Warrior & Gulf Nav. Co., 363 U.S. 574 (1960); United Steelworkers v. American Mfg. Co., 363 U.S. 564 (1960).

24. 363 U.S. 574 (1960).

25. It is also the approach that was followed by most courts prior to *Warrior.* See, e.g., Local 201, Int'l Ass'n of Elec. Workers v. General Elec. Co., 262 F.2d 265 (1st Cir. 1959); Lodge 12, Int'l Ass'n of Machinists v. Cameron Iron Works, Inc., 257 F.2d 467 (5th Cir.) cert. denied, 358 U.S. 880 (1958).

26. 363 U.S. at 582–85.

27. 363 U.S. at 578.

28. Id. at 579–82.

29. See, e.g., Clyde W. Summers, "Judicial Review of Labor Arbitration or Alice Through the Looking Glass," 2 *Buffalo L. Rev.* 1 (1952); Archibald Cox, "Current Problems in the Law of Grievance Arbitration," 30 *Rocky Mt. L. Rev.* 247 (1958); Cox, "Reflections upon Labor Arbitration," 72 *Harv. L. Rev.* 1482 (1959).

30. Compare, e.g., United Steelworkers v. Caster Mold & Match Co., 345 F.2d 429 (6th Cir. 1965), with Truck Drivers Union v. Ulry-Talbert Co., 330 F.2d 562 (8th Cir. 1964), and H. K. Porter Co. v. United Saw Workers, 333 F.2d 596 (3d Cir. 1964). See also the ma-

jority and dissenting opinions in Textile Workers v. American Thread Co., 291 F.2d 894 (4th Cir. 1961). And see generally Thomas G. S. Christensen, "Labor Arbitration and Judicial Oversight," 19 *Stan. L. Rev.* 671 (1967).

31. 363 U.S. 593 (1960).

32. Id. at 597.

33. Id. at 596–97.

34. Id. at 597.

35. Id. at 598 (footnote omitted).

36. It is common practice for arbitrators to write opinions which often are reasoned.

37. See generally Bernard D. Meltzer, "The Supreme Court, Arbitrability, and Collective Bargaining," 28 *U. Chi. L. Rev.* 464 (1960); Meltzer, "Ruminations about Ideology, Law, and Labor Arbitration," 34 *U. Chi. L. Rev.* 545 (1967).

38. 363 U.S. at 597.

39. "Until today, I had understood it to be the unquestioned law, as this Court has consistently held, that arbitrators are private judges chosen by the parties to decide particular matters specifically submitted; that the contract under which matters are submitted to arbitrators is at once the source and limit of their authority and power." United Steelworkers v. Warrior & Gulf Nav. Co., 363 U.S. 574, 585–86 (1960) (dissenting opinion).

40. Id. at 582.

41. Local 28, Int'l Bhd. of Elec. Workers v. Maryland Chapter, Nat'l Elec. Contractors Ass'n, 194 F. Supp. 494, 497 (D. Md. 1961).

42. United Steelworkers v. Warrior & Gulf Nav. Co., 363 U.S. 574, 582 (1960).

43. 369 U.S. 95 (1962).

44. Id. at 96.

45. Ibid.

46. "The employer . . . brought . . . suit against the union in the Superior Court of King's County, Washington asking damages for business losses caused by the strike. After a trial the court entered a judgment in favor of the employer in the amount of $6,501.60. On appeal the judgment was affirmed by Department One of the Supreme Court of Washington, 57 Wash. 2d 95, 356 P.2d 1. The reviewing court held that the preemption doctrine of *San Diego Building Trades Council,* 359 U.S. 236, did not deprive it of jurisdiction over the controversy. The court further held that § 301 . . . could not reasonably be interpreted as preempting state jurisdiction, or as affecting it by limiting the substantive law to be applied. 57 Wash. 2d at 102, 356 P.2d at 5. Expressly applying the principles

of state law, the court reasoned that the strike was a violation of the collective bargaining contract, because it was an attempt to coerce the employer to forego his contractual right to discharge an employee for unsatisfactory work." Id. at 97–98 (footnotes omitted).

47. The Court also considered the question whether the Washington court was right in holding that the primary rights and liabilities of the parties were governed by state law. The Supreme Court held that the Washington court was wrong for reasons that are adumbrated in Harry H. Wellington, "Labor and the Federal System," 26 *U. Chi. L. Rev.* 542, 556–58 (1959).

48. 369 U.S. at 105.

49. Id. at 105.

50. Ibid.

51. Id. at 108.

52. Id. at 109.

53. "Some form of no-strike clause appears in 94 percent of union contracts." 2 B.N.A. Collective Bargaining Negotiations & Contracts Serv. § 77:1 (Sept. 21, 1964).

54. See Charles O. Gregory, "The Collective Bargaining Agreement: Its Nature and Scope," 1949 *Wash. U. L. Q.* 3, 12.

55. Cf. Clyde W. Summers, "Labor Law Decisions of The Supreme Court: 1961 Term," in A.B.A. Section of *Labor Relations Law, 1962 Proceedings* 51, 57.

56. Lon L. Fuller, *Basic Contract Law* 764 (St. Paul, Minn., West Publishing Co., 1947).

57. It is clear that this would not violate the employer's duty to bargain. Cf. N.L.R.B. v. American Nat'l Ins. Co., 343 U.S. 395 (1952).

58. See Chapter 2 supra.

59. See note 51 supra.

60. See Chapter 2 supra.

61. N.L.R.B. v. Insurance Agents' Union, 361 U.S. 477, 490 (1960).

62. On these questions, there seems to be little empirical evidence. The Bureau of Labor Statistics in its annual analysis of work stoppages unhappily does not attempt to distinguish between strikes over arbitrable grievances and strikes over non-arbitrable grievances. In both 1961 and 1965, however, the percentage of "man-days idle" resulting from all strikes during contract term consisted of only 11.6 percent of the total idle man-days resulting from all strikes. (There were more strikes and a higher percentage of strikes during contract time, relative to all strikes, more workers involved, and a higher percentage of workers in such strikes, relative to all strikes, in 1965 than in 1961.) *Analysis of Work Stoppages 1961* at 9 (Dep. Lab. Bull. No. 1339, 1962); Id. 1965 at 11 (Dep. Lab. Bull. No. 1525, 1966). Prior to

mid-1960, B.L.S. did not classify "strikes according to the status of
the union-management agreement at the start of the stoppage." Id.
1961 at 1, fn. 3. Since mid-1960 was also the time of the Supreme
Court's arbitration decisions, the B.L.S. statistics cast no light on the
effect of those decisions on strikes. *Lucas Flour,* supra note 43, however, was decided in 1962. Accordingly, if the statistics suggest anything as to the effect of that decision on industrial peace, it is that
it has had no effect.

63. Judicial procedures are rarely invoked either to compel arbitration or to confirm or vacate awards. American Arbitration Association, "Procedural and Substantive Aspects of Labor-Management
Arbitration," 12 *Arb. J.* (n.s.) 67, 77 (1957).

64. The extent to which these propositions are true generally in
our society is suggested by Macaulay, supra note 2.

65. See generally Harry Shulman, "Reason, Contract and Law in
Labor Relations," 68 *Harv. L. Rev.* 999 (1955).

66. See, e.g., Neil W. Chamberlain, "Strikes in Contemporary Context," 20 *Ind. & Lab. Rel. Rev.* 602 (1967).

67. See note 62 supra.

68. 370 U.S. 195 (1962). See Harry H. Wellington and Lee A. Albert, "Statutory Interpretation and the Political Process: A Comment
on Sinclair v. Atkinson," 72 *Yale L. J.* 1547 (1963).

69. Compare Board of Education v. Shanker, 66 L.R.R.M. 2308
(Sup. Ct. N.Y., Oct. 4, 1967).

70. See Paul Jacobs, *Old Before Its Time: Collective Bargaining at
28* (Center for the Study of Democratic Institutions, 1963), p. 15.

71. See Paul R. Hays, "The Supreme Court and Labor Law,
October Term, 1959," 60 *Colum. L. Rev.* 901, 925 (1960).

72. 376 U.S. 543 (1964).

73. Id. at 550.

74. Id. at 549, quoting from *Warrior.*

75. Ibid.

76. See Chapter 2, supra.

77. For two quite different views on this subject, compare Paul R.
Hays, *Labor Arbitration: A Dissenting View* (New Haven, Yale Uni-
versity Press, 1966), with Robben W. Fleming, *The Labor Arbitration
Process* (Urbana, University of Illinois Press, 1965).

78. "Reason, Contract and Law in Labor Relations," supra note 65
at 1024.

CHAPTER 4

1. See note 3 infra.

2. See Chapter 2 supra.

3. J. I. Case Co. v. N.L.R.B., 321 U.S. 332, 338–39 (1944). See Order of R.R. Telegraphers v. Railway Express Agency, Inc., 321 U.S. 342 (1944).

4. Id. at 339.

5. See §§ 8(a)(3) and 8(b)(2), L.M.R.A.

6. See, e.g., the testimony of Mr. Walter Reuther, President, C.I.O., *Hearings on Taft-Hartley Act Revisions* 409–18 (Senate Committee on Labor and Public Welfare, 83d Cong. 1st Sess., 1953). In the course of his testimony Mr. Reuther remarked: "Since all the workers in the industrial community get the benefits of these services performed by the union, made possible by the union, we believe that since all the workers share in the services all the workers ought to share in the cost of providing those services." Id. at 409–10. See also Clinton S. Golden and Harold J. Ruttenberg, *The Dynamics of Industrial Democracy* 193–229 (New York, Harper, 1942).

7. See, e.g., S. Rep. No. 105, 80th Cong. 1st Sess. 5–7 (1947).

8. § 8(a)(3), L.M.R.A.

9. See, e.g., Leonard John Turner, "Is the Closed Shop Democratic?", *The Painter and Decorator* (June 1953), reprinted in Neil W. Chamberlain, *Source Book on Labor* 153–54 (rev. ed. New York, McGraw-Hill, 1964). Mr. Turner in part says: "But the rights of an individual do not extend to the right of non-payment of taxes. All workingmen owe it to themselves and to their country to join a Brotherhood or Union and to pay dues willingly. They also owe it to their fellow workers to become self-governed and to obey the Industrial laws which they themselves have set up." Id. at 154.

10. See generally Seymour Martin Lipset, *Political Man* 387–433 (Garden City, N.Y., Anchor Books, 1963); Seymour Martin Lipset, Martin A. Trow, and James S. Coleman, *Union Democracy* (Glencoe, Ill., The Free Press, 1956); Ralph C. James and Estelle D. James, *Hoffa and The Teamsters* (Princeton, N.J., Van Nostrand, 1965); Paul E. Sultan, *The Disenchanted Unionist* (New York, Harper & Row, 1963); Comment, "Judicial Intervention in Revolts Against Labor Union Leaders," 51 *Yale L. J.* 1372 (1942).

11. § 14(b), L.M.R.A.

12. On "Right to Work Laws," see generally Paul Sultan, *Right to Work Laws: A Study in Conflict* (Los Angeles, Institute of Industrial Relations, 1958); Daniel H. Pollitt, "Right to Work Issue: An Evidential Approach," 37 *N.C.L. Rev.* 233 (1959); James R. Grodin and Duane B. Beeson, "State Right-to-Work Laws and Federal Labor Policy," 52 *Calif. L. Rev.* 95 (1964).

13. See Radio Officers' Union v. N.L.R.B., 347 U.S. 17 (1954); Local 357, Teamsters v. N.L.R.B., 365 U.S. 667 (1961). The "dis-

couragement" aspect of § 8(a)(3) is important mainly to protect employees in their organizational activities.

14. Radio Officers' Union v. N.L.R.B., supra note 13 at 42–43.

15. See, e.g., S. Rep. No. 1827, 81st Cong., 2d Sess. (1950); Joseph P. Goldberg, *The Maritime Story* 241–46 (Cambridge, Harvard University Press, 1958); William Haber and Harold M. Levinson, *Labor Relations and Productivity in the Building Trades* 62–65, 71 (Ann Arbor, Bureau of Industrial Relations, University of Michigan, 1956).

16. Testimony of William Glazier, Washington representative, International Longshoremen's and Warehousemen's Union, *Hearings on Hiring Halls in the Maritime Industry* 97, 100–01 (Subcommittee on Labor-Management Relations, Senate Committee on Labor and Public Welfare, 81st Cong., 2d Sess. 1950).

17. See, e.g., Lummus Company, 142 N.L.R.B. 517 (1963), modified 339 F.2d 728 (D.C. Cir. 1964).

18. E.g., Hunkin-Conkey Const. Co., 95 N.L.R.B. 433 (1951), 100 N.L.R.B. 955 (1952). See generally Note, "Unilateral Union Control of Hiring Halls: The Wrong and the Remedy," 70 *Yale L. J.* 661 (1961).

19. Mountain Pac. Chapter of the Associated Gen. Contractors Inc., 119 N.L.R.B. 883, 895 (1957).

20. Id. at 897.

21. Plumbers & Pipefitters (Brown-Olds Plumbing & Heating Co.), 115 N.L.R.B. 594 (1956).

22. Local 60, United Bhd. of Carpenters and Joiners v. N.L.R.B., 365 U.S. 651, 655 (1961).

23. 365 U.S. 667 (1961).

24. Id. at 668.

25. Id. at 679–80 (Harlan, J., concurring); American Ship Bldg. Co. v. N.L.R.B., 380 U.S. 300, 311 (1965). But cf. N.L.R.B. v. Great Dane Trailers, 388 U.S. 26 (1967).

26. 365 U.S. at 675.

27. See, e.g., N.L.R.B. v. Burnup & Sims, Inc., 379 U.S. 21 (1964). But cf. American Ship Bldg. Co. v. N.L.R.B., supra note 25; N.L.R.B. v. Brown, 380 U.S. 278 (1965).

28. Compare Walter E. Oberer, "The Scienter Factor in Sections 8(a) (1) and (3) of the Labor Act: Of Balancing, Hostile Motive, Dogs and Tails," 52 *Cornell L.Q.* 491 (1967).

29. Republic Aviation Corp. v. N.L.R.B., 324 U.S. 793 (1945).

30. Compare Henry J. Friendly, "The Federal Administrative Agencies: The Need for Better Definition of Standards," 75 *Harv. L. Rev.* 863, 891–903 (1962).

31. J. J. Haggerty, 139 N.L.R.B. 633 (1962).

32. Local 138, International Union of Operating Engineers v. N.L.R.B., 321 F.2d 130 (2d Cir. 1963).

33. Majority rule is most clearly stated in § 9(a), L.M.R.A. and § 2, Fourth, R.L.A.

34. 323 U.S. 192 (1944).

35. The Court reversed the Supreme Court of Alabama, Steele v. Louisville & N. R. Co., 245 Ala. 113, 16 So. 2d 416 (1944). As the proceeding was in a state court, there was no problem raised as to whether the Norris-LaGuardia Act barred injunctive relief. In other fair representation cases it has been held that a federal court may issue an injunction. Tunstall v. Brotherhood of Locomotive Firemen, 323 U.S. 210 (1944); Syres v. Local 23, Oil Workers Int'l Union, 350 U.S. 892 (1955), reversing per curiam, 223 F.2d 739 (5th Cir.).

36. 323 U.S. at 200.

37. See id. at 198–99; compare concurring opinion of Mr. Justice Murphy at 208–09.

38. See infra, Chapter 7.

39. 323 U.S. at 202 (footnote omitted).

40. Ibid.

41. This was true under the "separate but equal" doctrine of 1944, see, e.g., Missouri ex rel. Gaines v. Canada, 305 U.S. 337 (1938), and is, of course, true since that doctrine met its demise in Brown v. Board of Education, 347 U.S. 483 (1954).

42. The problem is discussed in some detail in Chapter 7.

43. See Syres v. Oil Workers Int'l Union, supra note 35.

44. Ibid.

45. 355 U.S. 41, 47 (1957).

46. Id. at 46 (footnote omitted).

47. The Board sometimes paid lip service to the principles of *Steele*, See Larus & Bros. Co., 62 N.L.R.B. 1075, 1081 (1945), but it did not go beyond this. Compare Bethlehem–Alameda Shipyard Inc., 53 N.L. R.B. 999 (1943), with Veneer Products, Inc., 81 N.L.R.B. 492 (1949). See generally Benjamin Aaron and Michael I. Komaroff, "Statutory Regulation of Internal Union Affairs—I," 44 Ill. L. Rev. 425, 438–46 (1949).

48. "Every indication is that so long as Negroes are excluded from membership the unions will not represent them fairly. . . . The Court's decision in . . . *Steele* . . . [has] not put an end to racial discrimination by the B.L.F.E. For further instances see Hinton v. Seaboard Air Line R.R., 23 L.R.R.M. 2097 (4th Cir. 1948); Graham v. Southern Ry., 74 F. Supp. 663 (D.D.C. 1947)." Aaron and Komaroff, supra note 47 at 436 and n. 56. See also Graham v. Brotherhood of Locomotive Firemen, 338 U.S. 232 (1949); Brotherhood of R.R.

Trainmen v. Howard, 343 U.S. 768 (1952). Compare U.S. Comm'n on
Civil Rights, *Report on Employment* 128–31 (Washington, D.C.,
Gov't Printing Office, 1961).

49. See generally S. Rep. No. 187, 86th Cong., 1st Sess. (1959).

50. 323 U.S. at 204.

51. Independent Metal Workers Union, Local No. 1 Hughes Tool),
147 N.L.R.B. 1573, 1601 (1964) (footnote omitted).

52. Id. at 1577.

53. See, e.g., Aaron and Komaroff, "Statutory Regulation Of Internal Union Affairs—I," supra note 47; Michael I. Sovern, "The
National Labor Relations Act and Racial Discrimination," 62 *Colum.
L. Rev.* 563 (1962); cf. Archibald Cox, "The Duty of Fair Representation," 2 *Vill. L. Rev.* 151 (1957).

54. 78 Stat. 253 (1964), 42 U.S.C. § 2000e (Supp. I 1965) (cited hereafter, C.R.A. 1964).

55. There is a full discussion of the statute in Michael I. Sovern,
Legal Restraints on Racial Discrimination in Employment (New York,
Twentieth Century Fund, 1966). In 1967 Congress made it illegal for
employers, employment agencies, and labor organizations to discriminate on grounds of age. See *Age Discrimination in Employment Act
of 1967*, P.L. 90–202 (90th Cong. 1st Sess., Dec. 6, 1967).

56. § 706(g), C.R.A. 1964.

57. § 706(a), C.R.A. 1964.

58. Ibid.

59. § 706(g), (k), C.R.A. (1964).

60. Compare Dent v. St. Louis–San Francisco Ry. Co., 265 F. Supp.
56 (N.D. Ala. 1967), and Mickel v. South Carolina State Employment
Service, 377 F.2d 239 (4th Cir. 1967), with Evenson v. Northwest Airlines, Inc., 268 F. Supp. 29 (E.D. Va. 1967).

61. See, e.g., Vogler v. McCarty, Inc., C.C.H. Emp. Pract. Guide,
Para. 9063 (E.D. La., May 31, 1967).

62. Executive Order 11246, 30 Fed. Reg. 12319 (1965); see Sovern,
Legal Restraints on Racial Discrimination in Employment, supra
note 55 at 103–42.

63. The most difficult problem is in the area of seniority. See, e.g.,
Whitfield v. United Steelworkers Local 2708, 263 F.2d 246 (5th Cir.),
cert. denied, 360 U.S. 902 (1959); Note, "Title VII, Seniority Discrimination, and the Incumbent Negro," 80 *Harv. L. Rev.* 1260 (1967) .

64. See, e.g., Ford Motor Co. v. Huffman, 345 U.S. 330 (1953); Vaca
v. Sipes, 386 U.S. 171 (1967).

65. 345 U.S. 330 (1953).

66. Id. at 340–41.

67. Id. at 343.

68. See, e.g., Jennings v. Jennings, 91 N.E. 2d 899 (Ohio Ct. App. 1949).

69. 323 U.S. at 202.

70. See, e.g., Morey v. Doud, 354 U.S. 457, 463 (1957) ("we start with the established proposition that the 'prohibition of the Equal Protection Clause goes no further than the invidious discrimination.' ").

71. See, e.g., the Trailmobile litigation: Trailer Co., 51 N.L.R.B. 1106 (1943); Trailer Co., 53 N.L.R.B. 1248 (1943); Hess v. Trailer Co., 31 Ohio Op. 566 (C.P. 1944); Whirls v. Trailmobile Co., 64 F. Supp. 713 (S.D. Ohio 1945), aff'd, 154 F.2d 866 (6th Cir. 1946), rev'd, 331 U.S. 40 (1947); Britt v. Trailmobile Co., 179 F.2d 569 (6th Cir.), cert. denied, 340 U.S. 820 (1950). Humphrey v. Moore, 375 U.S. 335 (1964). See generally Mark L. Kahn, "Seniority Problems in Business Mergers," 8 *Ind. & Lab. Rel. Rev.* 361 (1955); Comment, "Seniority and Business Mergers: The Union's Duty of Fair Representation," 35 *U. Chi. L. Rev.* 342 (1968).

72. See, e.g., Lipset, Trow, and Coleman, supra note 10.

73. Lipset, *Political Man*, supra note 10.

74. Id. at 390, 392, 393.

75. Ford Motor Co. v. Huffman, supra note 64 at 338.

76. Humphrey v. Moore, 375 U.S. 335 (1964).

77. Vaca v. Sipes, 386 U.S. 171 (1967).

78. See especially Chapter 2 supra.

79. Compare Philip Selznick and Harold Vollmer, "Rule of Law in Industry: Seniority Rights," 1 *Ind. Rel.* 97 (1962). See generally Harold M. Vollmer, *Employee Rights and the Employment Relationship* (Berkeley and Los Angeles, University of California Press, 1960).

80. Compare Clyde W. Summers, "Individual Rights in Collective Agreements: A Preliminary Analysis, 9 *Buffalo L. Rev.* 239 (1960); Kurt L. Hanslowe, "Individual Rights in Collective Labor Relations," 45 *Cornell L. Q.* 25 (1959).

81. Compare Ferro v. Railway Express Agency, Inc., 296 F.2d 847 (2d Cir. 1961); Gainey v. Brotherhood of Railway and Steamship Clerks, 313 F.2d 318 (3d Cir. 1963).

82. Miranda Fuel Co., 140 N.L.R.B. 181 (1962), enforcement denied on other grounds, 326 F.2d 172 (2d Cir. 1963). See Truck Drivers Local Union 568 v. N.L.R.B., 65 L.R.R.M. 2309 (D.C. Cir. May 18, 1967). In addition to the articles cited in note 53 supra, see, e.g., Michael I. Sovern, "Race Discrimination and the National Labor Relations Act: The Brave New World of Miranda," 16 *N.Y.U. Conf. on Labor* 3 (1963); Alfred W. Blumrosen, "The Worker and Three Phases of Unionism: Administrative and Judicial Control of the Worker-Union Relationship," 61 *Mich. L. Rev.* 1435, 1504–23 (1963);

Note, "Unfair Representation as an Unfair Labor Practice," 63 *Mich. L. Rev.* 1081 (1965); Comment, "Racial Discrimination and the Duty of Fair Representation," 65 *Colum. L. Rev.* 273 (1965).

83. See brief for the Board in Local Union No. 12, United Rubber Workers v. N.L.R.B., 368 F.2d 12 (5th Cir. 1966) at 15–16. This case enforced the Board's order, 150 N.L.R.B. 312 (1964), holding that § 8(b)(1)(A) had been violated.

84. Local Union No. 12, United Rubber Workers (David Bruckner), 150 N.L.R.B. 312 (1964).

85. But cf. Cox, "The Duty of Fair Representation," supra note 53.

86. But cf. Archibald Cox and Derek C. Bok, *Cases and Materials on Labor Law* 330–31 (5th ed., Brooklyn, The Foundation Press, 1962).

87. Independent Metal Workers Union, Local No. 1 (Hughes Tool), supra note 51 at 1588 (footnotes omitted).

88. Id. at 1590.

89. International Assn. of Machinists v. Gonzales, 356 U.S. 617, 619 (1958).

90. See discussion of Calhoon v. Harvey, 379 U.S. 134 (1964), infra Chapter 5.

91. Cf. Sinclair Refining Co. v. Atkinson, 370 U.S. 195 (1962). See Harry H. Wellington and Lee A. Albert, "Statutory Interpretation and the Political Process: A Comment on Sinclair v. Atkinson," 72 *Yale L. J.* 1547 (1963).

92. See San Diego Building Trades Council v. Garmon, 359 U.S. 236 (1959).

93. See generally Harry H. Wellington, "Labor and the Federal System," 26 *U. Chi. L. Rev.* 542 (1959).

94. Cf. Smith v. Evening News Ass., 371 U.S. 195 (1962).

95. See ibid.; Humphrey v. Moore, 375 U.S. 335 (1964).

96. Vaca v. Sipes, 386 U.S. 171 (1967). The court also reasoned that were it to decide that courts were ousted from their "traditional supervisory jurisdiction [over fair representation], the individual employee injured by arbitrary or discriminatory union conduct could no longer be assured of impartial review of his complaint, since the Board's General Counsel has unreviewable discretion to refuse to institute an unfair labor practice complaint." Id. at 182. Yet pre-emption applies in other unfair labor practice situations where exactly the same possibility exists.

97. Humphrey v. Moore, 375 U.S. 335, 351–59 (1964) (Mr. Justice Brennan joined in this concurrence).

98. Id. at 352–54

99. Id. at 359.

100. This approach relies heavily upon the proviso to § 9(a), L.M.R.A. ("any individual employee . . . shall have the right at any time to present grievances to [his] employer and to have such grievances adjusted, without the intervention of the bargaining representative, as long as the adjustment is not inconsistent with the terms of a collective-bargaining contract."). Compare Clyde W. Summers, "Individual Rights in Collective Agreements and Arbitration," 37 *N.Y.U. L. Rev.* 362, 376–85 (1962), with Archibald Cox, "Rights Under a Labor Agreement," 69 *Harv. L. Rev.* 601, 621–24 (1956). For the situation under the Railway Labor Act, see Elgin Joliet & Eastern R.R. v. Burley, 325 U.S. 711 (1945), and Summers, id. at 385–88.

101. Summers, supra note 100.

102. See the decisions of the Wisconsin Supreme Court in Pattenge v. Wagner Iron Works, 275 Wis. 495, 82 N.W.2d 172 (1957), and Clark v. Hein-Werner Corp., 8 Wis. 2d 264, 99 N.W.2d 132 (1959), rehearing denied 8 Wis. 2d 277, 100 N.W.2d 317 (1960). Compare Donnelly v. United Fruit Co., 40 N.J. 61, 190 A.2d 825 (1963).

103. See Summers, supra note 100.

104. Compare W. Willard Wirtz, "Due Process of Arbitration," 11 *National Academy of Arbitrators Ann. Meeting Proceedings* 1 (1958), with Hays, *Labor Arbitration,* supra Chapter 3, note 77.

105. Vaca v. Sipes, 386 U.S. 171 (1967).

106. Id. at 185.

107. Ibid.

108. In *Miranda Fuel Co.,* supra note 82, the Board held the employer in violation of the statute since it had participated in the union's unfair labor practice.

109. Cf. Local 12, United Rubber Workers (David Bruckner), supra note 84.

110. See note 104 supra.

111. See Vaca v. Sipes, supra note 105, at 197–98.

112. The principle supporting finality in the good faith settlement of disputes is well established. See, e.g., dissenting opinion of Mr. Justice Frankfurter in D. A. Schulte, Inc. v. Gangi, 328 U.S. 108, 121–22 (1946).

113. Vaca v. Sipes, supra note 105, e.g., at 182.

114. Id. at 181.

CHAPTER 5

1. S. Rep. No. 187, 86th Cong., 1st Sess. 20 (1959).

2. Lipset, *Political Man,* supra Chapter 4, note 10, at p. 430.

3. Compare Paul Jacobs, *The State of the Unions* 137–51 (New York, Atheneum, 1963). See infra, Chapter 9.

4. See Chapter 4, note 10 supra. See generally Philip Taft, *Organized Labor in American History* (N.Y., Harper & Row, 1964); William M. Leiserson, *American Trade Union Democracy* (N.Y., Columbia University Press, 1959).

5. Infra, Chapter 9.

6. See, e.g., James v. Marinship Corp., 25 Cal. 2d 721, 155 P.2d 329 (1944); Directors Guild of America, Inc. v. Superior Court of Los Angeles County, 48 Cal. Rep. 710, 409 P.2d 934 (1966).

7. See Leo Bromwich, *Union Constitutions* (New York, Fund for the Republic, 1959); *A.F.L.-C.I.O. Codes of Ethical Practices* (Washington, D.C., A.F.L.-C.I.O., 1957).

8. The findings of the Committee are set forth in the following reports: S. Rep. No. 1417, 85th Cong., 2d Sess. (1958); S. Rep. No. 621, 86th Cong., 1st Sess. (1959); S. Rep. No. 1139, 86th Cong., 2d Sess. (1960).

9. See, e.g., Local 104 v. International Brotherhood of Boilermakers, 158 Wash. 480, 291 Pac. 328 (1930); Bell v. Sullivan, 183 Misc. 543, 49 N.Y.S.2d 388 (Sup. Ct., N.Y. 1944).

10. See, e.g., Dusing v. Nuzzo, 177 Misc. 35, 29 N.Y.S.2d 882 (1941) (election); Collins v. International Alliance of Theatrical Stage Employees, 119 N.J. Eq. 230, 182 Atl. 37 (1935); Armstrong v. Duffy, 90 Ohio App. 233; 103 N.E.2d 760 (1951) (discipline).

11. See, e.g., Furniture Workers Union, Local 1007 v. United Brotherhood of Carpenters & Joiners, 6 Wash. 2d 654, 108 P.2d 651 (1940); Ellis v. American Federation of Labor, 48 Cal. App.2d 440, 120 P.2d 79 (1941).

12. See Clyde W. Summers, "The Law of Union Discipline: What the Courts Do in Fact," 70 *Yale L. J.* 175 (1960).

13. For two comprehensive and detailed studies of the substantive and procedural law, see Clyde W. Summers, "Legal Limitations on Union Discipline," 64 *Harv. L. Rev.* 1049 (1951), and Summers, supra note 12.

14. Summers, supra note 12 at 199.

15. Polin v. Kaplan, 257 N.Y. 277, 281–82, 177 N.E. 833, 834 (1931).

16. Lab. Dep. Bull. No. 1350, *Disciplinary Powers and Procedures in Union Constitutions* 26 (Washington, D.C., Gov't Printing Office, 1963).

17. Id. at 4–6.

18. See, e.g., Reilly v. Hogan, 32 N.Y.S.2d 864 (Sup. Ct.), aff'd, 264 App. Div. 855, 36 N.Y.S.2d 423 (1942); Madden v. Atklus, 4 App.

Div. 2d 1, 162 N.Y.S.2d 576 (1957), aff'd, 4 N.Y.2d 283, 151 N.E.2d 73 (1958).

19. See Summers, supra note 12 at 200–06.

20. See, e.g., Gleeson v. Conrad, 81 N.Y.S.2d 368 (Sup. Ct. 1948) modified, 276 App. Div. 861, 93 N.Y.S.2d 667 (1949); Polin v. Kaplan, supra note 15.

21. "Contracts of adhesion" is a phrase that seems to have been introduced into our legal vocabulary by Edwin W. Patterson. See Patterson, "The Delivery of a Life-Insurance Policy," 33 *Harv. L. Rev.* 198, 222 (1919).

22. See Summers, supra note 12.

23. Madden v. Atkins, 4 N.Y.2d 283, 293; 151 N.E.2d 73, 78 (1958).

24. Compare Karl N. Llewellyn, *The Common Law Tradition* 362–71 (Boston, Little Brown, 1960).

25. In this sense, and without wanting to push the analogy too far, the individual might be thought of as a private attorney general. Cf. Associated Industries of New York State, Inc. v. Ickes, 134 F.2d 694 (2d Cir. 1943).

26. Railroad Co. v. Lockwood, 17 Wall (84 U.S.) 358 (1873).

27. The leading case is Henningsen v. Bloomfield Motors, Inc., 32 N.J. 358, 161 A.2d 69 (1960).

28. Cf. Jacob E. Decker & Sons v. Capps, 139 Tex. 609, 619, 164 S.W.2d 828, 832–33 (1942). Compare William L. Prosser, "The Assault upon the Citadel," 69 *Yale L. J.* 1099 (1960); Prosser, "The Fall of the Citadel," 50 *Minn. L. Rev.* 791 (1966); Friedrich Kessler, "Products Liability," 76 *Yale L. J.* 887 (1967).

29. The National Traffic Safety Agency, established by the National Traffic and Motor Vehicle Safety Act, 80 Stat. 718 (1966). But cf. Ralph Nader and Joseph A. Page, "Automobile Design and the Judicial Process," 55 *Calif. L. Rev.* 645 (1967).

30. The Labor-Management Reporting and Disclosure Act, 73 Stat. 519 (1959), 29 U.S.C. §§ 401 et seq. (1964) (cited hereafter by section and L.M.R.D.A.).

31. For general surveys of both parts of the statute, see, e.g., Benjamin Aaron, "The Labor-Management Reporting and Disclosure Act of 1959" (Pts. I & II), 73 *Harv. L. Rev.* 851, 1086 (1960); Russell A. Smith, "The Labor-Management Reporting and Disclosure Act of 1959," 46 *Va. L. Rev.* 195 (1960); Archibald Cox, "Internal Affairs of Unions under the Labor Reform Act of 1959," 58 *Mich. L. Rev.* 819 (1960).

32. Compare the majority and dissenting opinions in Yanity v. Benware, 376 F.2d 197 (2d Cir. 1967).

33. § 101 (a)(1), L.M.R.D.A.

34. § 101(a)(2), L.M.R.D.A.

35. The U.A.W. has tried to deal with the biased union tribunal problem by providing for public review. See generally Walter E. Oberer, "Voluntary Impartial Review of Labor: Some Reflections," 58 *Mich. L. Rev.* 55 (1959); Jerome H. Brooks, "Impartial Public Review of Internal Union Disputes: Experiment in Democratic Self-Discipline," 22 *Ohio St. L. J.* 64 (1961); David Y. Klein, "U.A.W. Public Review Board Report," 18 *Rutgers L. Rev.* 304 (1964).

36. § 101(a)(5), L.M.R.D.A.

37. The enforcement provision is § 102, L.M.R.D.A. The provision requiring exhaustion of union remedies is § 101(a)(4), L.M.R.D.A. See Detroy v. American Guild of Variety Artists, 286 F.2d 75 (2d Cir. 1961), cert. denied, 366 U.S. 929.

38. § 103, L.M.R.D.A. See generally Clyde W. Summers, "Pre-emption and the Labor Reform Act—Dual Rights and Remedies," 22 *Ohio St. L. J.* 119 (1961).

39. The four main provisions are: (a) § 301(a), L.M.R.D.A., which requires every labor organization having or assuming a trusteeship to report on that fact at stated intervals to the Secretary of Labor; (b) § 302, which sets out the purposes for which a trusteeship may be established; (c) § 303, which safeguards the election process and the treasury of the trusteed local; (d) § 304, which provides for two methods of enforcing sections 302 and 303: (i) by complaint to the Secretary of Labor, who may bring a civil action in a federal court, or (ii) by suit of a member of a local in a federal court. See generally, Note, "Landrum-Griffin and the Trusteeship Imbroglio," 71 *Yale L. J.* 1460 (1962).

40. § 401(a), L.M.R.D.A.

41. § 401(b), L.M.R.D.A.

42. § 401(c); 401(e), L.M.R.D.A.

43. § 401(e), L.M.R.D.A.

44. Ibid.

45. Ibid.

46. § 402(b), L.M.R.D.A.

47. § 402(c), L.M.R.D.A.

48. Salzhandler v. Caputo, 316 F.2d 445 (2d Cir.), cert. denied, 375 U.S. 946 (1963).

49. See Salzhandler v. Caputo, 199 F. Supp. 554, 555 (S.D.N.Y. 1961).

50. 316 F.2d at 118

51. Ibid.

52. Id. at 446.

53. 105 Cong. Rec. 6476, 86 Cong., 1st Sess. (1959).

54. 316 F.2d at 449–50.

55. See Note, "Free Speech, Fair Trial, and Factionalism in Union Discipline," 73 *Yale L. J.* 472 (1964).

56. See Summers, supra note 12, at 185–87.

57. For commentary on the decision see, e.g., Banton H. Hall, "Freedom of Speech and Union Discipline: The Implications of Salzhandler," 17 *N.Y.U. Conf. on Lab.* 349 (1964); Benjamin C. Sigal, "Freedom of Speech and Union Discipline: The "Right" of Defamation and Disloyalty," 17 *N.Y.U. Conf. on Lab.* 367 (1964).

58. New York Times Co. v. Sullivan, 376 U.S. 254, 270 (1964).

59. Ibid.

60. Id. at 279–80.

61. Calhoon v. Harvey, 379 U.S. 134 (1964).

62. Id. at 135.

63. Id. at 135–36.

64. Id. at 136.

65. Id. at 138–39.

66. Id. at 143 (Stewart, J., concurring).

67. Ibid.

68. Id. at 140.

69. See generally Note, "Union Elections under the LMRDA," 74 *Yale L. J.* 1282 (1965).

70. See text of S. 505, 86th Cong., 1st Sess. (1959), § 303 ("The duties imposed and the rights and remedies provided by this title shall be exclusive."). In its amended form, this became § 403.

71. See, e.g., statements of Clyde W. Summers, *Hearings on Union Financial and Administrative Practices and Procedures before the Subcommittee on Labor of the Committee on Labor and Public Welfare* 594, 613, 85th Cong., 2d Sess. (1958); ACLU, *A Labor Union "Bill of Rights"—Democracy in Labor Unions—The Kennedy-Ives Bill* (Sept. 1958). Cf. statement of Archibald Cox, *Hearings on S. 505 before the Subcommittee on Labor of the Senate Committee on Labor and Public Welfare,* 86 Cong., 1st Sess. 135 (1959).

72. See generally Summers, supra note 38.

73. See, e.g., Texas & Pacific R.R. v. Abilene Cotton Oil Co., 204 U.S. 426 (1907).

74. 379 U.S. at 144–45.

75. Note. "Election Remedies under the Labor-Management Reporting and Disclosure Act," 78 *Harv. L. Rev.* 1617, 1624 (1965).

76. Clyde W. Summers, "Judicial Regulation of Union Elections," 70 *Yale L. J.* 1222, 1248 (1961).

CHAPTER 6

1. Alexander Heard, *The Costs of Democracy* 208 (Chapel Hill, University of North Carolina Press, 1960) (Cited hereafter as Heard).

2. S. Rep. No. 395, 85th Cong., 1st Sess. 49 (1957).

3. From an address before the Economic Club of Detroit, October 15, 1956. Quoted in Neil W. Chamberlain, *Source Book on Labor* 372–73 (2d ed. New York, McGraw-Hill, 1964).

4. S. 3074 (1956), cited by Vivian Vale, "American Labour's Political Freedom: A British View," 13 *Political Studies* 281, 285 n. 2 (1965).

5. See generally Grant McConnell, *Private Power and American Democracy* 11–29 (New York, Alfred A. Knopf, 1966).

6. *The Federalist Papers* 77 (New York, Mentor Book, Clinton Rossiter, ed., 1961).

7. Perry Miller, *The Life of the Mind in America* 209 (1965).

8. The Case of Twenty Journeymen Tailors, People v. Faulkner, New York (1836), *Courier and Enquirer,* May 31, 1836, reproduced in 4 Commons and Gilmore 315, 322.

9. *The Federalist Papers,* supra note 6 at 78–84.

10. Elihu Root, *Addresses on Government and Citizenship* 143 (Bacon and Scott ed., 1916), quoted in United States v. United Automobile Workers, 352 U.S. 567, 571 (1957).

11. *Report of the Joint Committee of the Senate and Assembly of the State of New York Appointed to Investigate the Affairs of Life Insurance Companies* 397 (1906), quoted in United States v. United Automobile Workers, supra note 10 at 573. See Merlo J. Pusey, *Charles Evans Hughes, 1,* 140–68 (New York, Macmillan, 1951).

12. Samuel Eliot Morison and Henry Steele Commager, *The Growth of the American Republic, 2, 1865–1950,* 217 (New York, Oxford University Press, 1950). Compare Robert A. Dahl, "Business and Politics: A Critical Appraisal of Political Science," 53 *Amer. Pol. Sci. Rev.* 1 (1959).

13. On "Voluntarism," see generally *Labor and American Politics* 83–107, eds. Charles M. Rehmus and Doris B. McLaughlin (Ann Arbor, University of Michigan Press, 1967). Michael Rogin, "Voluntarism: The Political Functions of an Antipolitical Doctrine," 15 *Ind. & Lab. Rel. Rev.* 521 (1962).

14. Samuel Gompers, "Political Labor Party—Reconstruction—Social Insurance," 26 *American Federalist* 33, 43 (1919).

15. Reprinted in *Labor and American Politics,* supra note 13 at 94.

16. See Rogin, supra note 13 at 534–35.

17. A.F.L. *Proceedings 1902* at 182.

18. See Gompers, supra note 14 at 41. (If labor formed a political party, he argued: "Every sail" would be "trimmed to the getting of votes.")

19. Compare Avery Leiserson, "Organized Labor as a Pressure Group," 274 *Annals of the American Academy* 108 (March 1951).

20. 34 Stat. 864 (1907).

21. The history is traced in the opinion of the Court in United States v. United Automobile Workers, 352 U.S. 567, 575 et seq. (1957).

22. 43 Stat. 1070 (1925).

23. 54 Stat. 767 (1940), amending 53 Stat. 1147 (1939).

24. See Louise Overacker, "Labor's Political Contributions," 54 *Pol. Sci. Q.* 56, 58 (1939).

25. See Heard, at 169.

26. S. Rep. No. 151, 75th Cong., 1st Sess. 135 (1937). See Joseph E. Kallenbach, "The Taft-Hartley Act and Union Political Contributions and Expenditures," 33 *Minn. L. Rev.* 1 (1948).

27. The act's official title is the War Labor Disputes Act, 57 Stat. 163 (1943).

28. This history is traced in Kallenbach, supra note 26, at 6–9; Joseph Tanenhaus, "Organized Labor's Political Spending: The Law and its Consequences," 16 *J. of Politics* 441, 445–50 (1954).

29. See 12 L.R.R.M. 2544–45 (1943).

30. 60 Stat. 839 (1946); 2 U.S.C. §§ 261–70 (1964).

31. Final Report of the House Select Committee on Lobbying Activities, H. Rep. No. 3239, 81st Cong., 2d Sess. 4 (1951).

32. See United States v. Harriss, 347 U.S. 612 (1954).

33. 61 Stat. 136, 159 (1947), as amended, 18 U.S.C. § 610 (1964).

34. United States v. United Automobile Workers, 352 U.S. 567, 575 (1957).

35. United States v. Congress of Industrial Organizations, 335 U.S. 106, 134 (1948).

36. See, e.g., the Pennsylvania legislation, Title 25, §§ 3225, 3543, as amended, June 3, 1943, P.L. 851, § 1. See generally Kallenbach, supra note 26, at 9–11.

37. On the political action organizations of international unions, see generally Heard at 172–73.

38. But see John F. Lane, "Analysis of the Federal Law Governing Political Expenditures by Labor Unions," 9 *Labor L. J.* 725 (1958). On COPE, see generally Mary Goddard Zon, "Labor in Politics," 27 *Law & Contemporary Problems* 234 (1962).

39. United States v. Congress of Industrial Organizations, 335 U.S. 106, 134 (1948) (footnote omitted) (concurring opinion).

40. Id. at 112.

41. 335 U.S. 106 (1948).

42. Transcript of Record, at 5.

43. Ibid.

44. 335 U.S. at 123.

45. Ibid.

46. Ibid.

47. Id. at 121.

48. 352 U.S. 567 (1957).

49. Id. at 585.

50. Id. at 589.

51. Id. at 592.

52. Quoted in Lane, "Analysis of the Federal Law Governing Political Expenditures by Labor Unions," supra note 38 at 733–34 (1958).

53. 172 F. 2d 854 (2nd Cir. 1949).

54. United States v. Anchorage Central Labor Council, 193 F. Supp. 504 (D. Alaska 1961); United States v. Warehouse and Distribution Workers Union Local 688, 47 L.R.R.M. 2005 (E.D. Mo. 1960).

55. United States v. Construction and General Laborers Union No. 264, 101 F. Supp. 869 (W.D. Mo. 1951).

56. For an evaluation of the wisdom of § 304, see "Financing Presidential Campaigns," pp. 20–21 (*Report of Presidential Commission on Campaign Costs,* 1962) (The statute "reflects a proper congressional policy.").

57. Alexis de Tocqueville, *Democracy in America* 177, ed. J. P. Mayer and Max Lerner (New York, Harper and Row, 1966).

58. Robert A. Dahl, *A Preface to Democratic Theory* 145 (Chicago, University of Chicago Press, 1956).

59. David B. Truman, *The Governmental Process* 510 (New York, Alfred A. Knopf, 1955) (Emphasis in original). But compare, e.g., Sidney Verba, "Organizational Membership and Democratic Consensus," 27 *J. of Politics* 467 (1965).

60. Truman, *The Governmental Process,* supra note 59 at 512–13.

61. Id. at 512.

62. 25 *Cong. Q.* 1161 (July 7, 1967). Reported union political expenditures often run below the amounts reported by other organizations, such as the A.M.A. Many organizations decline to report. Ibid.

63. On the techniques of business in the political arena see Note, "Corporate Political Affairs Programs," 70 *Yale L. J.* 831 (1961).

64. Heard, at 170.

65. See Grant McConnell, *Private Power and American Democracy* 322 (New York, Alfred A. Knopf, 1966) ("Understandably, the smaller

craft unions can be expected to behave along the old lines of voluntarism. A craft union with a small membership cannot hope to act effectively in politics or be expected to forego the tactical advantages of concentrating its energies on the narrow economic interests of the craft."). The "Hotel and Restaurant Employees are inconspicuous in political campaigns, although like all major unions, they show concern in legislative matters touching their interests." Heard, at 172.

66. "Trends and Changes in Union Membership," 89 *Monthly Lab. Rev.* 510–13 (1966). See Irving Bernstein, "The Growth of American Unions, 1945–1960," 2 *Lab. History* 131 (1961).

67. Dahl, supra note 58 at 125.

68. Heard, at 208 (footnote omitted).

69. See Arthur Kornhauser, Harold L. Sheppard, and Albert J. Mayer, *When Labor Votes* (New York, University Books, 1956); Harold L. Sheppard and Nicholas A. Masters, "The Political Attitudes and Preferences of Union Members: The Case of the Detroit Auto Workers," 59 *American Pol. Sci. Rev.* 437 (1959).

70. E.g., Kornhauser, et al., supra note 69 at 31–32, found that 24% of the U.A.W. membership in Detroit who voted in the 1952 presidential election voted for Eisenhower. Sheppard and Masters, supra note 69 at 447, found that about 15% of the union membership was opposed to union political action, and about a third of the membership was "non-labor politically minded and generally politically indifferent." Compare the assessment of Ruth Alice Hudson and Hjalmar Rosen in their study of the political attitudes of members of a "large Midwestern union": "The rank and file is split right down the middle about whether or not the union should be active in politics at all. . . . Fifty-five percent of the union members say yes; while almost half are somewhat negative." "Union Political Action: The Member Speaks." 7 *Ind. & Lab. Rel. Rev.* 404, 408. (1954). Cf. Alton C. Bartlett, "How Rank and File Leaders View Union Political Action," 17 *Lab. L. J.* 483 (1966); Nicholas A. Masters, "The Organized Labor Bureaucracy as a Base of Support for the Democratic Party," 27 *Law & Contemp. Probs.* 252 (1962); Nicholas A. Masters, "The Politics of Union Endorsement of Candidates in the Detroit Area," 1 *Midwest J. Pol. Sci.* 136 (1957).

71. Another classic example, of a somewhat different sort, is described in Irving Bernstein, "John L. Lewis and the Voting Behavior of the C.I.O.," 5 *Public Opinion Quarterly* 233 (1941).

72. See, e.g., Sheppard and Masters, supra note 69. See generally on voting behavior and the factors that shape it, Angus Campbell, Philip E. Converse, Warren E. Miller, and Donald E. Stokes, *The American Voter* (New York, John Wiley, 1960); Bernard R. Berelson, Paul F.

Lazarsfeld, and William N. McPhee, *Voting* (Chicago, University of Chicago Press, 1954); V. O. Key, Jr., *The Responsible Electorate* (Cambridge, Mass., Belknap Press, 1966); Robert E. Lane, *Political Ideology* (Glencoe, The Free Press, 1962).

CHAPTER 7

1. See Chapter 4 supra.

2. See generally Clyde W. Summers, "The Law of Union Discipline: What the Courts Do in Fact," 70 *Yale L. J.* 175 (1960); Mitchell v. International Assoc. of Machinists, 16 Cal. Rptr. 813, 49 L.R.R.M. 2117 (Cal. Dist. Ct. App. 1961); Hurwitz v. Directors' Guild of America, Inc., 364 F.2d 67 (2d Cir.), cert. denied, 385 U.S. 971 (1966).

3. Compare Frank v. National Alliance of Bill Posters, 89 N.J.L. 380, 99 Atl. 134 (1916), with Directors' Guild of America, Inc. v. Superior Court of Los Angeles County, 48 Cal. Rptr. 710, 409 P.2d 934 (1966).

4. International Assoc. of Machinists v. Street, 367 U.S. 740 (1961).

5. Railway Labor Act, § 2 Eleventh, added by 64 Stat. 1238 (1951), 45 U.S.C. § 152 Eleventh (1964).

6. See, e.g., Benjamin Aaron, "Some Aspects of the Union's Duty of Fair Representation," 22 *Ohio St. L. J.* 39, 63 (1961) : "stripped of all its disguises, the *Street* case . . . emerges as simply another attack on the validity of the union shop; and the issues it raises are neither novel nor particularly significant."

7. The agreement is reproduced in the *Street* Record, at 205–17.

8. See supra Chapter 6. The Amicus brief for the A.F.L.-C.I.O. contains a good, short, and uncontroverted historical survey of the political and legislative activities of American labor from its colonial beginnings. See Brief for the A.F.L.-C.I.O. as Amicus Curiae, 14–28. "A look at the history of union political action supplies abundant proof that labor's interest in politics is as old as its interest in the closed shop or the union shop." Id. at 14.

9. Railway Employees' Dep't. v. Hanson, 351 U.S. 225 (1956).

10. Id. at 234.

11. Id. at 236.

12. Compare Public Utilities Comm'n v. Pollak, 343 U.S. 451 (1952).

13. See, e.g., Smith v. Allwright, 321 U.S. 649 (1944); Shelley v. Kraemer, 334 U.S. 1 (1948); Burton v. Wilmington Parking Authority, 365 U.S. 715 (1961); Evans v. Newton, 382 U.S. 296 (1966), Reitman v. Mulkey, 387 U.S. 369 (1967).

14. 351 U.S. at 231–32.

15. Compare Otten v. Baltimore & O. R.R., 205 F.2d 58 (2d Cir. 1953), aff'd sub. nom. Otten v. Staten Island Rapid Transit Ry, 229 F.2d 919 (2d Cir.), cert. denied, 351 U.S. 983 (1956).

16. Order of R.R. Telegraphers v. Railway Express Agency, Inc., 321 U.S. 342, 346 (1944).

17. Compare Clay P. Malick, "Toward a New Constitutional Status for Labor Unions: A Proposal," 21 *Rocky Mt. L. Rev.* 260 (1949); Arthur S. Miller, *Private Governments and the Constitution* (occasional paper for the Center for Study of Democratic Institutions, 1959); Joseph L. Rauh, Jr., "Civil Rights and Liberties and Labor Unions," 8 *Labor L. J.* 874 (1957).

18. 326 U.S. 501 (1946).

19. Compare Harold W. Horowitz, "The Misleading Search for 'State Action'—Under the Fourteenth Amendment," 30 *S. Cal. L. Rev.* 208 (1957); Louis Henkin, "Shelley v. Kraemer: Notes for a Revised Opinion," 110 *U. Pa. L. Rev.* 473 (1962); Charles L. Black, Jr., " 'State Action,' Equal Protection, and California's Proposition 14," 81 *Harv. L. Rev.* 69 (1967).

20. 351 U.S. at 235.

21. See supra Chapter 1.

22. See generally Charles L. Black, Jr., *The People and the Court* (New York, Macmillan, 1960).

23. 351 U.S. at 238.

24. §§ 8(b)(4), 8(e), and 8(b)(7), L.M.R.A.

25. Compare the discussion in Reitman v. Mulkey, 387 U.S. 369, at 375–81 (1967).

26. 367 U.S. at 749.

27. Id. at 804–05.

28. Id. at 749.

29. Id. at 768–69.

30. Id. at 750.

31. Ibid.

32. Id. at 770.

33. Id. at 763–64.

34. Id. at 767.

35. "Under [the Wagner Act] a proviso to section 8(3) permits voluntary agreements for compulsory union membership provided they are made with an unassisted labor organization representing a majority of the employees at the time the contract is made." S. Rep. No. 105, 80th Cong., 1st Sess. 5 (1947).

36. This was true at least where state law did not prohibit such contracts. "When the committees of the Congress in 1935 reported

the bill which became the present National Labor Relations Act, they made clear that the proviso in Section 8(3) was not intended to override state laws regulating the closed-shop." Ibid.

37. "Numerous examples were presented to the committee of the way union leaders have used closed-shop devices as a method of depriving employees of their jobs, and in some cases a means of securing a livelihood in their trade, or calling, for purely capricious reasons." Id. at 7.

38. "Until the beginning of the war only a relatively small minority of employees (less than 20 percent) were affected by contracts containing any compulsory features. According to the Secretary of Labor, however, within the last 5 years over 75 percent now contain some form of compulsion." Id. at 6.

39. See Chapter 4 supra.

40. See S. Rep. No. 105, 80th Cong., 1st Sess. (1947).

41. See, e.g., Hearings on S. 55 before the Senate Committee on Labor and Public Welfare, 80th Cong., 1st Sess. 796–808, 1004, 1425, 1687, 2145 (1947); Hearings on H.R. 8 before the House Committee on Education and Labor, 80th Cong., 1st Sess. 305 (1947).

42. See, e.g., S. Rep. No. 2262, 81st Cong., 2d Sess. (1950); H.R. Rep. No. 2811, 81st Cong., 2d Sess. (1950). But see 96 *Cong. Rec.* 17049–50 (1951).

43. S. Rep. No. 2262, 81st Cong., 2d Sess. 2–3 (1950).

44. The canon is easy to explain where, in its absence, a court could with equal plausibility, interpret a statute in either of two ways. "It is elementary when the constitutionality of a statute is assailed, if the statute be reasonably susceptible of two interpretations, by one of which it would be unconstitutional and by the other valid, it is our plain duty to adopt that construction which will save the statute from constitutional infirmity. *Knights Templars' Indemnity Co. v. Jarman,* 187 U.S. 197, 205. And unless this rule be considered as meaning that our duty is to first decide that a statute is unconstitutional and then proceed to hold that such ruling was unnecessary because the statute is susceptible of a meaning, which causes it not to be repugnant to the Constitution, the rule plainly must mean that where a statute is susceptible of two constructions, by one of which grave and doubtful constitutional questions arise and by the other of which such questions are avoided, our duty is to adopt the latter. *Harriman v. Interstate Com. Comm.,* 211 U.S. 407." U.S. ex rel Attorney General v. Delaware & Hudson Co., 213 U.S. 407–08 (1909).

45. See Railway Employees' Dep't v. Hanson, 351 U.S. 225, 231 (1956).

46. See Chapters 4 and 6 supra.

47. Kent v. Dulles, 357 U.S. 116 (1958).

48. "To repeat, we deal here with a constitutional right of the citizen, a right which we must assume Congress will be faithful to respect. We would be faced with important constitutional questions were we to hold that Congress . . . had given the Secretary authority to withhold passports to citizens because of their beliefs or associations. Congress has made no such provision in explicit terms; and absent one, the Secretary may not employ that standard to restrict the citizens' right of free movement." Id. at 130.

49. For an analogous case, see Greene v. McElroy, 360 U.S. 474 (1959).

50. In both Kent v. Dulles, 357 U.S. 166 (1958), and Greene v. McElroy, 360 U.S. 474 (1959), the Court was strongly influenced by a delegation problem closely related to the avoidance doctrine. "In many circumstances, where the Government's freedom to act is clear, and the Congress or the President has provided general standards of action and has acquiesced in administrative interpretation, delegation may be inferred. . . . But this case does not present that situation. We deal here with substantial restraints on employment opportunities of numerous persons imposed in a manner which is in conflict with our long-accepted notions of fair procedures. Before we are asked to judge whether, in the context of security clearance cases, a person may be deprived of the right to follow his chosen profession without full hearings where accusers may be confronted, it must be made clear that the President or Congress, within their respective constitutional powers, specifically has decided that the imposed procedures are necessary and warranted and has authorized their use. Such decisions . . . must be made explicitly not only to assure that individuals are not deprived of cherished rights under procedures not actually authorized, . . . but also because explicit action, especially in areas of doubtful constitutionality, requires careful and purposeful consideration by those responsible for enacting and implementing our laws. Without explicit action by lawmakers, decisions of great constitutional import and effect would be relegated by default to administrators who, under our system of government, are not endowed with authority to decide them." Greene v. McElroy, 360 U.S. 474, 506–07 (1959). See generally Alexander M. Bickel, *The Least Dangerous Branch* (Indianapolis, Bobbs-Merrill, 1962).

This delegation problem is present in *Street* in a somewhat different but closely related form. The union stands in the position of the administrator and makes "decisions of great constitutional import and effect." It might well be argued that power to make these decisions must be delegated to unions explicitly for the same reasons that power must be explicitly delegated to administrators.

51. Cf. Harlan, J., concurring in Greene v. McElroy, 360 U.S. at 509.

52. Brief for the United States in Machinists v. Street, at 18.

53. Mr. Justice Frankfurter dissenting, in Machinists v. Street, 367 U.S. at 806.

54. 367 U.S. at 768.

55. See 367 U.S. at 810 (Frankfurter, J., dissenting).

56. Brotherhood of Railway & S. S. Clerks v. Allen, 373 U.S. 113 (1963).

57. The court majority reproduced the governing English statute (The Trade Union Act of 1913, 2 & 3 Geo. V, c. 30) as an appendix to its opinion. Id. at 124. See generally Cyril Grunfeld, "Political Independence in British Trade Unions: Some Legal Aspects," 1 *British J. Ind. Rel.* 23 (1963); K. W. Wedderburn, *The Worker and the Law* 297–303 (Harmondsworth, Middlesex, England, Penguin Books, 1965).

58. 373 U.S. at 118 (emphasis in original).

CHAPTER 8

1. See, e.g., Albert Rees, *The Economics of Trade Unions* 96 (Chicago, University of Chicago Press, 1962). "In real terms, this redistribution can be thought of as arising in either or both o[f] two ways: first, the money wages of non-union workers may be held down by the reallocation of labor produced by unionism [see infra note 2]; second, the non-union workers may have to pay more for the products produced by union labor."

2. Id. at 69–94. "Most economists . . . would agree that unions, in so far as they have the power to raise relative wages, reduce employment in the union sector and increase it in the non-union sector. This is a worse allocation of labor than would exist without unions, in the sense that a shift of labor toward the union sector could increase the total output of the economy. In the union situation, the same individual might be able to earn $2.00 an hour in non-union employment and $2.20 in union employment, and he might be entirely willing to make the shift if jobs were available in the union sector. That this situation reduces the national output follows from viewing the wage as a measure of what the worker is worth to the employer and to the economy. The union employer is not willing to add another man at $2.20 because the man would not contribute that much to the value of production, but there would usually be some wage just below the union wage at which the worker would

be hired and at which he would still be willing to shift. The difference between this wage and the wage in the non-union sector after he has shifted is the measure of the loss in output from having him in the wrong place. In the absence of the union, as more workers shifted the wage differential would tend to disappear, along with the potential gain in output from further reallocation." Id. at 93.

"The view that unions make for a worse allocation of labor does not necessarily imply an unfavorable judgment of the total effect of unions. There are many other aspects of union activity . . . and an economy has other and perhaps even more important goals than the most efficient allocation of resources." Id. at 94.

3. See, United Mine Workers of America v. Pennington, 381 U.S. 657 (1965); Local Union No. 189, Amal. Meat Cut. v. Jewel Tea Co., 381 U.S. 676 (1965). See generally Ralph K. Winter, Jr., "Collective Bargaining and Competition; The Application of Antitrust Standards to Union Activities," 73 *Yale L. J.* 14 (1963).

4. See, e.g., *N. Y. Times*, Aug. 1, 1966 at 1, cols. 5 and 8.

5. Id. at 16, col. 7.

6. Address delivered before the National Academy of Arbitrators on Feb. 1, 1963, 52 L.R.R.M. 11, 12–13 (1963).

7. See, e.g., Irving Bernstein, "The Economic Impact of Strikes in Key Industries," in *Emergency Disputes and National Policy* 24–45 (Irving Bernstein, Harold L. Enarson, R. W. Fleming, eds.; N.Y., Harper, 1955) (cited hereafter as *Emergency Disputes*).

8. George H. Hildebrand, "An Economic Definition of the National Emergency Dispute," in *Emergency Disputes* 3, at 6–7.

9. Compare Neil W. Chamberlain, *Social Responsibility and Strikes* (N.Y., Harper, 1953); Neil W. Chamberlain and Jane M. Schilling, *The Impact of Strikes, Their Social and Economic Costs* (N.Y., Harper, 1954).

10. See, e.g., Local 761, Int. Union of Elec., Radio and Machine Workers v. N.L.R.B., 366 U.S. 667 (1961).

11. L.M.R.A. §§ 206-10.

12. United Steelworkers of America v. United States, 361 U.S. 39, 41 (1959).

13. Id. at 48.

14. The emergency provisions of L.M.R.A. were invoked 24 times between 1947 and 1965. Since the intensification of the Vietnam war, they have been used several times. There have been strikes after the 80-day period in seven cases. See *National Emergency Disputes Under the Labor-Management Relations (Taft-Hartley) Act, 1947–65* (U.S. Dept. of Labor, Bureau of Labor Statistics, Bull. No. 1482, March 1966).

15. See, e.g., Charles M. Rehmus, "Operation of the National Emergency Provisions of LMRA," 62 *Yale L. J.* 1047 (1953); Frank C. Pierson, "An Evaluation of the National Emergency Provisions," in *Emergency Disputes* at 129. Compare *Final Report of the Ad Hoc Committee to Study National Emergency Disputes* of the Section of Labor Rel. Law of the Amer. Bar Assoc., in Committee Reports 318, 322–23 (1966) (Cited hereafter as *Report of Ad Hoc Committee*).

16. These differences are explained in Elgin, J. & E. Ry. v. Burley, 325 U.S. 711, 722–28 (1945).

17. See Comment, "Enjoining Strikes and Maintaining the Status Quo in Railway Labor Disputes," 60 *Colum. L. Rev.* 381 (1960).

18. Order of R.R. Telegraphers v. Chicago and N.W. Ry., 362 U.S. 330 (1960).

19. Pan American World Airways v. Flight Engineers Int'l Ass'n, 306 F.2d 840, 846 (2d Cir. 1962).

20. See Limited Arbitration Legislated for Railroad Dispute, 53 L.R.R.M. 25–45 (1963); Extension of Rail Strike Deadline by Act of Congress, 64 L.R.R. 307 (1967); Passage of Rail "Mediation-With-Finality" Law, 65 L.R.R. 216 (1967).

21. *The Public Interest in National Labor Policy* 105 (N.Y., Committee for Economic Development, 1961). See *Report of Ad Hoc Committee* 318, 338–39. "The emergency procedures . . . of the Railway Labor Act have been [in]voked in an aggregate of 171 cases since 1926 in railroads and since 1936 in airlines. In the 20 year period beginning with 1947, the Railway Labor Act has been [in]voked on 127 occasions, and strikes have occurred on 34 of these occasions after the expiration of the 30 days following the report of the emergency board." John T. Dunlop, *Procedures for the Settlement of Emergency Disputes* 3 (Paper presented to Int. Conference on Automation, Full Employment and a Balanced Economy, Rome, July 29, 1967).

22. L.M.R.A. §§ 201–04.

23. *New York Times,* April 23, 1964, at 1, col. 1.

24. Id., Aug. 1, 1966, at 1, col. 8.

25. But see Dunlop, supra note 21 at 8.

26. *The Public Interest in National Labor Policy,* supra note 21 at 94.

27. Cf. Thomas C. Schelling, *The Strategy of Conflict* 111–15 (New York, Oxford University Press, 1963).

28. Sen. Rep. No. 496, 82 Cong., 1st Sess. 26 (1951) (Minority).

29. *Social Responsibility and Strikes,* supra note 9 at 272.

30. See, e.g., Arthur J. Goldberg and Jack Barbash, "Labor Looks at the National Emergency Provisions," in *Emergency Disputes* at 109.

31. See generally Harry H. Wellington and Lee A. Albert, "Statutory Interpretation and the Political Process: A Comment on Sinclair v. Atkinson," 72 *Yale L. J.* 1547 (1963).

32. See, e.g., United States v. United Mine Workers of America, 330 U.S. 258 (1947).

33. The definitive work is John L. Blackman, Jr., *Presidential Seizure in Labor Disputes* (Cambridge, Mass., Harvard University Press, 1967).

34. Archibald Cox, "Seizure in Emergency Disputes," in *Emergency Disputes* at 224, 230.

35. Ibid.

36. See, e.g., S. 1456, 90th Cong., 1st Sess. (1967) (Javits Bill).

37. Cox, supra note 34.

38. See generally *Hearings, American Bar Association Special Committee on National Strikes in the Transportation Industries* (May 5, 6, 19, 20, June 9, 10, 1967).

39. See Chapter 3 supra.

40. For other ways of viewing compulsory arbitration, see, e.g., R. W. Fleming, "The Search for a Formula," in *Emergency Disputes*, at 200, 207–17; Chamberlain, supra note 9 at 276–79.

41. Paul Jacobs, *The State of the Unions* 265–66 (New York, Atheneum, 1963).

42. See generally W. Willard Wirtz, "The 'Choice-of-Procedures' Approach to National Emergency Disputes," in *Emergency Disputes*, at 149.

43. Carl M. Stevens, "Is Compulsory Arbitration Compatible with Bargaining?," 5 *Ind. Rel.* 38 (1966).

44. See, e.g., *The Public Interest In National Labor Policy*, supra note 21 at 108–10.

45. See generally LeRoy Marceau and Richard A. Musgrave, "Strikes in Essential Industries: A Way Out," 27 *Harv. Bus. Rev.* 287 (1949); George W. Goble, "The Non-Stoppage Strike," 12 *Current Economic Comment* 3 (1950); Charles O. Gregory, "Injunctions, Seizure, and Compulsory Arbitration," 26 *Temple L. Q.* 397 (1953); David B. McCalmont, "The Semi-Strike," 15 *Ind. & Lab. Rel. Rev.* 191 (1962); Dunlop, supra note 21 at 7.

46. Chamberlain, supra note 9 at 279–81.

47. See, e.g., Fleming, supra note 40.

48. See generally, Wirtz, supra note 42; George P. Schultz, "The Massachusetts Choice-of-Procedures Approach to Emergency Disputes," 10 *Ind. & Lab. Rel. Rev.* 359 (1957); Archibald Cox, *Law and the National Labor Policy* 55–58 (Los Angeles, Inst. of Ind. Rel., Univ. of Calif., 1960).

49. Wirtz, supra note 42 at 152–56.

50. Id. at 158–59.

51. 1964 contract between Upholsterers' Int. Union and the Dunbar Furniture Co. of Berne, Indiana. See *Wall Street Journal,* May 20, 1964, at 1, col. 1.

CHAPTER 9

1. *New York Times,* July 31, 1966, § 4, at 1, col. 1.

2. See, e.g., Andrew Shonfield, *Modern Capitalism* (London, Oxford University Press, 1965); "A Special Issue on Incomes Policy," 2 *British J. Ind. Rel.* 309–59 (1964).

3. See *Economic Report of the President,* together with *The Annual Report of the Council of Economic Advisers* 8 (1960) [cited hereafter as *Report* (with date)].

4. 60 Stat. 23 (1946), as amended, 15 U.S.C. §§ 1021–23 (1964). On the relationship between wages and unemployment see, e.g., A. W. Phillips, "The Relation between Unemployment and the Rate of Change of Money Wage Rates in the United Kingdom, 1861–1957," 25 *Economica* 283 (1958); Paul A. Samuelson and Robert M. Solow, "Analytical Aspects of Anti-Inflation Policy," 50 *Amer. Econ. Rev.* 177 (1960 Supp.)

5. Compare *Report* IV-V (1960) with *Report* 16–17 (1962), and *Report* 12–13 (1967).

6. See generally Neil W. Chamberlain, *The Labor Sector,* 666–700 (New York, McGraw-Hill, 1965).

7. See generally *Factors Affecting the United States Balance of Payments: Compilation of Studies Prepared for the Joint Economic Committee,* 87th Cong., 2d Sess. (1962); Symposium: "Industrial Relations and World Trade," 1 *Ind. Rel.* 1–63 (1962).

8. James Tobin, "Check the Boom?" *The New Republic* 9, 11 (Sept. 3, 1966).

9. Id. at 11–12.

10. See Rees, *The Economics of Trade Unions* 48–68 (1962).

11. The economic literature in and around this subject is vast and the points of view therein displayed refreshingly diverse. See, e.g., *Wages, Prices, Profits and Productivity* (American Assembly, Columbia University 1959); *Study of Employment, Growth and Price Levels* (Joint Econ. Committee, 86th Cong. 2d Sess. 1959). See particularly, *The Problems of Rising Prices* (O.E.E.C. 1961); Otto Eckstein and Gary Fromm, "Steel and Post War Inflation," Study Paper No. 2, *Study of Employment, Growth and Price Levels* (Joint Econ. Committee,

86th Cong., 2d Sess. 1959). On the monopoly power of unions, compare Edward H. Chamberlain, "Labor Union Power and the Public Interest," in *The Public Stake in Union Power* 3–20 (ed. Philip D. Bradley, Charlottesville, Univeritsy of Virginia Press, 1959); Gottfried Haberler, "Wage Policy, Employment, and Economic Stability," in *The Impact of the Union* 34–62, (ed. David McCord Wright, New York, Kelley and Millman, 1956); F. A. Hayek, "Unions, Inflation and Profits," in *The Public Stake in Union Power* 46–62 supra.; Charles Edward Lindblom, *Unions and Capitalism* 138 et seq. (New Haven, Yale University Press, 1949); Fritz Machlup, *The Political Economy of Monopoly* 417 et seq. (Baltimore, Johns Hopkins Press, 1952), with *The Public Interest in National Economic Policy* 119 (New York, Committee for Economic Development, 1961); James S. Duesenberry, "Underlying Factors in the Post War Inflation," in *Wages, Profits and Productivity* 61–89 (The American Assembly, Columbia University, 1959); Milton Friedman, "Some Comments on the Significance of Labor Unions for Economic Policy," in *The Impact of the Union* 204–34, supra.

12. "When demand outruns the growth of productive resources, prices and wages will rise even in the most highly competitive markets. (Indeed, they may rise faster and farther than where large firms and long-term labor contracts give some degree of stability.) That kind of 'demand-pull' inflation can be held in check by fiscal and monetary policies which keep demand in line with productive capabilities. If labor markets are efficient, control of demand-pull inflation will not require restraints on demand that would lead to a high unemployment rate. . . . But businesses and unions can push prices up even when resources are not fully utilized. That kind of 'cost-push' inflation, too, can be controlled by lowering demand, but only at the cost of an unacceptable degree of economic slack. Frequent recessions, chronically high unemployment, idle capacity, and a low rate of investment may purchase price stability—but the cost is too high." *Report* 119 (1967).

13. See Milton Friedman, "What Price Guideposts?" in *Guidelines, Informal Controls, and the Market Place* 17–39, (ed. George P. Schultz and Robert Z. Aliber, University of Chicago Press, 1966) (cited hereafter as *Guidelines*.)

14. *Report* 185 (1962).

15. *Guidelines* 64 (emphasis in original).

16. *Report* 8 (1960).

17. "Since this arithmetic is frequently not understood, it will be useful to give an example. If a worker in a particular firm is paid $2 an hour—$80 a week—and contributes to the production of 200

units a week, output per man-hour is 5 units (200 units divided by 40 hours) and unit labor cost is $.40 ($80 divided by 200 units). If, for whatever reason, output rises by 3 percent, to 206 units a week—with no extra labor time required—output per man-hour is also up 3 percent, to 5.15 units (206 units divided by 40 hours). If the wage rate also rises by 3 percent, to $2.06 an hour ($82.40 a week), unit labor costs will remain at $.40 ($82.40 divided by 206 units). If the price of the product is unchanged, the margin between price and unit labor cost—availbale to pay for others' contributions to production—will be the same. But with 3 percent more units sold, the total amount available to pay others, including owners, will also rise by 3 percent." *Report* 120–21 (1967).

18. The Council of Economic Advisers itself has made this clear. See *Report* 186–88 (1962). See Chamberlain, supra note 6 at 690–92.

19. *Report* 186–88 (1962).

20. *Report* 92 (1966).

21. *Report* 188–90 (1962).

22. The development is recounted with admirable candor in the 1967 *Report* at 123.

23. *Report* 128 (1967).

24. Id. at 128–29.

25. See *New York Times*, April 11, 1962, at 1, col. 5.

26. News Conference, April 11, 1962, reported in *New York Times*, April 12, 1962, at 20, col. 1.

27. See *New York Times*, April 12, 1962, at 1, cols. 1 and 2; Id. April 13, 1962, at 1, col. 8; Id., April 14, 1962, at 10, col. 4.

28. Id., April 14, 1962, at 1, col. 8.

29. See generally Grant McConnell, *Steel and the Presidency, 1962* (New York, Norton, 1963).

30. The aluminum story may be found in *New York Times*, Oct. 30, 1965, at 45, col. 1; id., Nov. 1, 1965, at 1, col. 1; id., Nov. 2, 1965, at 1, col. 6; id., Nov. 6, 1965, at 1, col. 8; id., Nov. 10, 1965, at 9, col. 8; id., November 11, 1965, at 1, col. 1. The copper story is reported at id., Nov. 17, 1965 at 65, col. 1; id., Nov. 18, 1965, at 1, col. 1; id., Nov. 21, 1965, § 3, at 1, col. 8.

31. See Philip B. Kurland, "Guidelines and the Constitution: Some Random Observations on Presidential Power to Control Prices and Wages," in *Guidelines* 209–41; Note, "Wage-Price Guidelines: Informal Government Regulation of Labor and Industry," 80 *Harv. L. Rev.* 623, 635–46 (1967).

32. See Note, supra note 31 at 630–35; John T. Dunlop, "Guideposts, Wages, and Collective Bargaining," in *Guidelines* 81, 85–92.

33. *Report* 123–24 (1967).

34. Dunlop, supra note 32 at 83, 84. But cf. John Sheahan, *The Wage-Price Guideposts* 79–95 (Washington, The Brookings Institution, 1967).

35. Compare the majority statement of an Organization for European Economic Co-operation Study Group: "The second idea for avoiding a wages policy is that the bargaining strength of labour should be reduced so that labour could not gain excessive wage increases; i.e. bargaining strength is a kind of monopolistic power (which it is) and the answer is to restore competition. While this is a view that has appeal from an economic standpoint because the benefits of competition are constantly to be seen in the economy, we cannot support it. This is not only because restoring sufficient competition in the labour market seems almost a technical impossibility in a contemporary industrial economy, but because it has implications for the whole organisation and functioning of the economy, the consequences of which cannot be foreseen." William Fellner, Milton Gilbert, Bert Hansen, Richard Kahn, Friedrich Lutz, Pieter de Wolff, *The Problem of Rising Prices* 57 (O.E.E.C., 1961). The quotation appears in a portion of the work to which Professors Fellner and Lutz expressed reservations. Id. at 63–65.

36. See Benjamin Aaron, "Governmental Restraints on Featherbedding," 5 *Stan. L. Rev.* 680 (1953).

37. See supra, Chapter 2.

38. Compare Fellner, Gilbert, et. al., *The Problem of Rising Prices,* 55–65 (O.E.E.C., 1961); Address of Labor Secretary Arthur J. Goldberg before the Executives' Club in Chicago, February 23, 1962.

39. L.M.R.A. § 9.

40. L.M.R.A. § 8(b) (4)(c).

41. L.M.R.A. § 8(b)(4) (A) and (B). See generally Howard Lesnick, "The Gravamen of the Secondary Boycott," 62 *Colum. L. Rev.* 1363 (1962).

42. L.M.R.A. § 8(b)(7). See generally Bernard D. Meltzer, "Organizational Picketing and the NLRB; Five on a Seesaw," 30 *U. of Chi. L. Rev.* 78 (1962).

43. L.M.R.A., Title II.

44. See, e.g., N.L.R.B. v. Mackey Radio and Tel. Co., 304 U.S. 333 (1938); N.L.R.B. v. Erie Resistor Corp., 373 U.S. 221 (1963); N.L.R.B. v. Brown, 380 U.S. 278 (1965); American Shipbuilding Co. v. N.L.R.B., 380 U.S. 300 (1965).

45. See Inland Steel Co. v. N.L.R.B., 170 F. 2d 247 (7 Cir. 1948).

46. N.L.R.B. v. Truitt Mfg. Co., 351 U.S. 149 (1956).

47. See generally Philip Ross, *The Government as a Source of Union Power: The Role of Public Policy in Collective Bargaining*

(Providence, Brown University Press, 1965). See Chapter 2, note 8 supra.

48. Gardner Ackley, "The Contribution of Guidelines," in *Guidelines* 67 at 72–73.

49. See E. H. Phelps Brown, "Guidelines for Growth and for Incomes in the United Kingdom: Some Possible Lessons for the United States," in *Guidelines* 143–63.

50. See Harold L. Enarson, "The Politics of an Emergency Dispute: Steel, 1952," in *Emergency Disputes and National Policy* 46 (1955). See generally Edward Robert Livernash, *Collective Bargaining in the Basic Steel Industry: A Study of the Public Interest and the Role of Government* 231–307 (U.S. Dept. Lab., 1961).

51. See Alan K. McAdams, *Power and Politics in Labor Legislation* (New York, Columbia University Press, 1964).

Index

industry units, 322; limitations
on economic power of, 322;
opposition to bargaining reforms, 333; opposition to legislation, 333; fair representation
left to court decisions, 360;
effect on wage and employment levels, 374–75. *See also*
Union hiring halls
*United Automobile Workers,
U.S. v.*, "voluntary" use of
union dues, 229–31
United Mine Workers, Smith-
Connally Act as response to,
222
United States Steel Corp.: price
rises, 316; unlimited power of,
340, 341
United Steelworkers of America,
political spending, 215
Unlawful employment practices,
under Civil Rights Act, 153

Vaca v. Sipes: protection of individual during contract time,
174, 178–79; union duty to
process individual grievance,
181–82; union responsibility
for monetary harm to individual, 182
Veterans Preference Act, 157
Vietnam war: economic growth
related to, 300; effect of ending on economy, 305; use of
L.M.R.A. emergency powers, 375
Violence, by journeymen, 17
Voluntarism: as dominant pre-
New Deal labor theory, 219 ff.;
political expenditures despite,
222; preservation by nonstoppage strike, 293

Wage and price controls: alternatives to guideposts, 319–20;

antitrust aspect of, 320;
O.E.E.C. study group report on,
381; wartime models, 319–20
Wage and price guideposts:
breached by airline strike, 298;
particular industries, 311;
proposed, 311; implementation
of standard, 315–16; quasi-
legal obligations, 316; success
not clear, 318; not integrated
with bargaining, 319; restrictive influence of, 319; collective bargaining standard, 325;
duty to bargain vs. duty to
comply, 325; Council of Economic Advisers' formulation,
325–26; educational role, 326
Wage push, effect on prices, 303
Wages: differentials as fair, 156;
minimum wage legislation,
247; increase without jeopardy
to price stability, 306–07; increase tied to productivity
rates, 306–07; fairness of aggregate increases, 310; noninflationary increases, 311–12;
guidepost modifications of,
312–13; rate increases in un-
deremployed industry, 313; related to bargaining position,
313; overall productivity
guide, 314; fairness to public
considered, 314; guideposts,
314–15; restraint defined, 315;
standard for higher increases,
315
Wagner Act: earliest version of
Labor-Management Relations
Act, 39; as source of collective bargaining law, 42; example of democratic union
government, 189; closed shop
under, 255–56; political dis-